Verbal Complexes

Verbal Complexes

Hilda Koopman and
Anna Szabolcsi

The MIT Press
Cambridge, Massachusetts
London, England

This book was set in Times New Roman on '3B2' by Asco Typesetters, Hong Kong, and was printed and bound in the United States of America.

Library of Congress Cataloging-in-Publication Data

Koopman, Hilda Judith.
  Verbal complexes / Hilda Koopman and Anna Szabolcsi.
    p.   cm. — (Current studies in linguistics series ; 34)
  Includes bibliographical references.
  ISBN 0-262-11253-1 (alk. paper) — ISBN 0-262-61154-6 (pbk. : alk. paper)
    1. Languages, Modern—Verb phrase. 2. Hungarian language—Verb phrase. 3. Dutch language—Verb phrase. 4. German language—Verb phrase. I. Szabolcsi, Anna, 1953–
II. Title. III. Series.
PB145.K66   2000
415—dc21   00-030388

Contents

Contents

Acknowledgments

This book grew out of Anna Szabolcsi's spring 1996 seminar on Hungarian at UCLA. The analysis of Hungarian as it appears here is the joint work of the two authors; the analysis of Dutch and German is Hilda Koopman's work.

An important source of inspiration for the present approach was the winter 1996 minicourse given at UCLA by Richard Kayne, whose ideas converged with work on remnant XP-movement by members of the local syntax community: Michael Nkemnji for Nweh, Tonia Androutsopoulou for split DPs in Greek, Roland Hinterhölzl for German and Dutch restructuring, Matt Pearson for Malagasy VOS structures, and others. With the rise of remnant movement, the idea that various phenomena traditionally attributed to head movement are best understood as XP-movement was pursued by Dominique Sportiche for the distribution of English verbs, by Peter Hallman for Germanic verb-second, and more recently by Felicia Lee for San Lucas Quiaviní Zapotec.

Marcel den Dikken and Ed Stabler read several versions of the manuscript and made many important comments; we did our best to follow their advice. We thank Dominique Sportiche for constructive comments. Among the many other people with whom we had a chance to discuss our work, at UCLA and elsewhere, we are especially grateful to Tonia Androutsopoulou, Reineke Bok-Bennema, Michael Brody, Manuel Español-Echevarria, Donka Farkas, Bob Frank, Peter Hallman, Henk Harkema, Roland Hinterhölzl, Teun Hoekstra, Julia Horvath, Richard Kayne, István Kenesei, Katalin É. Kiss, Jamal Ouhalla, Martin Prinzhorn, Henk van Riemsdijk, Andrew Simpson, Tim Stowell, and Temmi Szalai. The usual disclaimers apply.

Earlier versions of the proposals made here were presented at the Conference on Linguistic Theory in Eastern European Languages (CLITE, Szeged, April 1998) and in talks at the Hungarian Academy of Sciences (August 1996), University of California, Santa Cruz (June 1998), Utrecht University OTS (October 1998, January 1999), and Georgetown University (February 1999); and at several seminars at

UCLA. The current form of these proposals was presented in a series of lectures at the Universities of Venice (April–May 1999) and Vienna (June 1999), at conferences in Siena and Florence, and at NELS 30 (October 1999). We thank the audiences at these presentations for helpful criticism and suggestions.

Chapter 1
Introduction

1.1 The Phenomenon

The syntax of complex verb formation (also known as verb raising, verb projection raising, or the "third" construction) constitutes one the most difficult areas of syntax. It involves different types of complementation, restructuring phenomena, and the formation of strings of adjacent verbs in particular orders. To linguists working on the West Germanic languages (Dutch, West Flemish, German, etc.), this topic is extremely familiar, since it occupies a prominent position on the research agenda, in many respects comparable to that of clitics in Romance languages. Outside West Germanic it has received little attention, partly because the phenomenon is less visible (though it ties in with restructuring phenomena familiar from Romance languages), and partly because its properties have so far escaped real understanding. In this book we try to gain new insights into the properties of verbal complex formation and into the structure of the theory of Universal Grammar by presenting a simple analysis for a complex set of data in Hungarian, which in this respect bears uncanny similarities to West Germanic. We extend the analysis to Dutch and to a lesser extent to German, and we show how crosslinguistic variation is captured in the theory we adopt.

A small sample of the Hungarian data follows. The patterns are highlighted by numerical schemas, where *fogok* = 1, *akarni* = 2, *kezdeni* = 3, *menni* = 4, and *haza* = 5.

(1)   Nem fogok   akarni   kezdeni haza menni.   1 2 3 5 4
       not   will-1sg want-inf begin-inf home go-inf
       'I will not want to begin to go home.'

(2) a. Nem fogok   akarni   haza menni kezdeni.   1 2 5 4 3
        not   will-1sg want-inf home go-inf begin-inf
    b. Nem fogok   haza menni kezdeni akarni.   1 5 4 3 2
        not   will-1sg home go-inf begin-inf want-inf

(3)   Haza fogok   akarni   kezdeni   menni.   5 1 2 3 4
       home will-1sg want-inf begin-inf go-inf
       'I will want to begin to go home.'

The order of the infinitives in (1) is similar to the English or Dutch order (4). In
addition, the inverted orders (2a) and (2b), which are reminiscent of German (5)–(6),
are also available.

(4) omdat   ik Marie zal moeten   beginnen op te bellen   1 2 3 5 4
      because I Marie will must-inf start-inf up to call-inf
      'because I will have to start to call up Marie'

(5) weil   Peter Maria anrufen   können will   3 2 1
      because Peter Maria up-call-inf can-inf want
      'because Peter wants to be able to call up Maria'

(6) weil   ich die Maria habe anrufen   können müssen   1 5 4 3 2
      because I   the Maria have up-call-inf can-inf must-inf
      'because I had to be able to call up Maria'

Finally, in contexts like (3) the particle *haza* associated with the lowest infinitive
procliticizes to the finite verb. The resulting string is also familiar from Dutch (7).

(7) omdat   ik Marie op zal willen   beginnen te bellen   5 1 2 3 4
      because I Marie up will want-inf start-inf to call-inf
      'because I will want to start to call up Marie'

Such patterns have typically been analyzed as constituting three different phenomena. The English order is not thought to involve any kind of complex verb formation; the German order is thought to involve head movement; and prefix climbing
is analyzed as XP-movement. Not only are the latter two handled differently, but the
identity of the participating verbs is overlooked. We are going to present a highly
uniform and mechanical analysis, using a restrictive set of theoretical assumptions, to
be discussed in section 1.2.

Two features of the analysis are of more general interest. First, we analyze complex
verb formation exclusively in terms of XP-movement. This eliminates one major
motivation for the existence of head movement in grammar. Importantly, this sim-
plification is not achieved by excluding inversion phenomena from the scope of syntactic rules and relegating them to the unknown territories of PF. Instead, we show
that on the XP-movement analysis complex verb formation obeys standard syntactic
constraints.

Second, we make do with unusually restrictive assumptions about syntax. We show
that a comprehensive account of the data is possible using nothing but overt movement (strong features). It is not necessary to appeal either to covert movement (LF

movement or feature movement) or to economy/optimality considerations to account for the fact that inversion appears to be optional in some constructions and either obligatory or excluded in others.

1.2 Theoretical Assumptions

In some respects the particular theoretical assumptions underlying this book continue the direction in which research was headed in the late 1980s. In other respects they exploit some basic results of research in the 1990s—in particular, extensive use of heavy pied-piping and remnant movement.

An important line of research in the 1980s led to the conclusion that syntactic representations are large structures, much larger than previously thought on the basis of the actual lexical material in a particular sentence. Syntactic structures themselves became quite simple, binary-branching structures, obeying the X-bar schema, with both lexical heads and functional heads projecting.[1] The specifier-head configuration emerged as "the" syntactic licensing configuration: particular constituents (DPs, *wh*-phrases, etc.) must appear in a specifier-head relation with a designated head, and they get into this configuration by movement, either overt or covert. The Case module of the Government-Binding Theory (Rouveret and Vergnaud 1980, Chomsky 1981) thus became a particular instance of a more general theory of specifier-head licensing.[2] Continuing this line of research, we assume a quite general theory of licensing: there are many types of constituents that need to appear in the specifier of some designated projection. For convenience, we call these projections *L(anding)Ps*. In particular, we are forced to account for the different distribution of complement clauses (CPs) and small clause complements in this way.[3] CPs are licensed in the specifier of *LP(cp)* (= the landing site for CP). Small clauses are licensed in a position slightly higher than VP, for which we adopt Zwart's (1993) and Koster's (1994) label *PredP*.[4]

Thus, we continue the trend begun in the 1980s: there is actually more movement than previously thought, but movement itself is highly constrained and takes place for licensing purposes only.[5] In particular, movement can take place for morphological reasons, for semantic reasons, or to make a projection interpretable. We adopt the following principle from Koopman 1996:

(8) *Principle of Projection Activation* (PPA)
    A projection is interpretable iff it has lexical material at some stage in the derivation.

The PPA prohibits representations in which neither the specifier nor the head position is associated with lexical material at any stage of the derivation. Another well-formedness condition assumed in Koopman 1996 is as follows:

(9) *Generalized "Doubly Filled Comp Filter"* (modified Linear Correspondence Axiom)
    No projection has both an overt specifier and an overt head at the end of the derivation.

The modified LCA also implies the following in the domain of head movement:

(10) An overt head cannot adjoin to an overt head.

Our analyses will abide by this principle, although it will play a very limited role in forcing particular analytical choices.

Analytical work in the 1990s (Nkemnji 1992, 1995, Sportiche 1993, Koopman 1993, 1996) and work inspired by Kayne (1994) has changed our understanding of empirical phenomena. In particular, it has become clear that languages make use of heavy pied-piping (movement of large chunks of structure) and remnant movement (movement of a constituent containing the trace of previously extracted material; see Den Besten and Webelhuth 1990), with the concomitant assumption that movement always takes place to the left (Kayne 1994). We fully exploit large structures in conjunction with these types of processes. As a result, we are able to present an analysis that relies on overt movement of lexical material only, that is local, and that works mechanically identically in all contexts. Different distributional properties follow naturally from whether subextraction or pied-piping takes place in a particular context. (The choice between these is not free but is determined by a type of filter that specifies the maximum size of a structure in a particular position at the end of the derivation. We refer to this type of filter as a *complexity filter*.) Our analysis does not need to appeal to economy conditions; in particular, there is no need to assume Procrastinate for the type of data that we are considering.

What becomes the focus of theoretical inquiry, then, are conditions on subextraction, pied-piping, and remnant movement. The preliminary assumptions that we make in this book are as follows (see a detailed discussion in section 4.2):

(11) *Extraction*
    Only (full) specifiers and (full) complements on their own projection line are extractable.

(12) *Pied-piping*
    A category XP can pied-pipe YP iff XP is in the specifier of YP or X adjoins to Y.

(13) *Remnant movement*
    A category XP containing the trace of an extracted element can move to a position that c-commands the extracted element.

We assume that head movement is available in Universal Grammar, although it is constrained by the modified LCA and by strict locality, as in Koopman's (1994, 1995b) theory.

(14) *Head movement*

Head movement is strictly local. Feature checking involves two steps: adjunction and receptor binding.

We argue that the formation of verbal complexes is best analyzed as XP-movement. Furthermore, in the spirit of Sportiche (1997), Hallman (1998), and Lee (1999), we assume that it is at least possible to form morphological words by XP-movement as well. Thus, although head movement is retained, it is eventually restricted to an ancillary role, to aid pied-piping by a complement and to derive the right word order in certain restricted cases (as in Kayne 1998b).

Chapter 2
Background Information on Hungarian

2.1   Functional Projections in Hungarian

We assume that Hungarian sentences contain at least the functional projections given in (1). Szabolcsi (1996, 1997) argues in detail that this much structure is necessary to account for data that do not involve particles and infinitives at all. In chapter 4 this structure will be enriched.

(1)

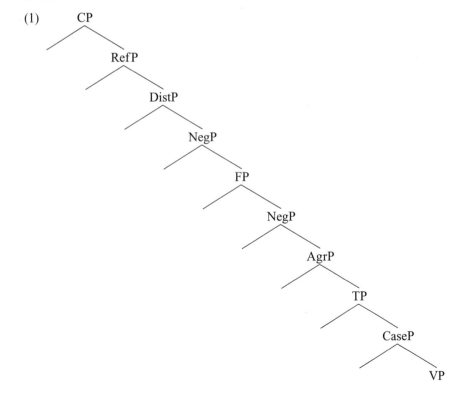

For present purposes it suffices to indicate what kind of role each projection plays, without reviewing the detailed argument (for which, see the above-mentioned papers).

2.1.1   The Ā-(Nonargument) Projections RefP, DistP, and FP

Hungarian marks the scope of many operators by overtly moving them into designated positions; the linear order of these positions is fixed (É. Kiss 1987, 1991). In (1) Ref(erential)P is the position of names, definites, and wide scope indefinites; Dist(ributive)P is the position of universals and a set of other operators. Szabolcsi's (1997) analysis of these positions as RefP and DistP is inspired by Beghelli and Stowell 1997. The assumption that sentences contain the functional projection F(ocus)P comes from Brody 1990. FP is the position for emphatic or contrastive focus as well as modified numeral QPs. For example (traces omitted):

(2) [$_{RefP}$ Két fiúval   [$_{DistP}$ minden problémáról   [$_{FP}$ egy lány [$_{AgrP}$ beszélt ...]]]].
      two boy-with   every   problem-about   a   girl   talked
      'There are two boys x such that for every problem y, it was a girl who talked about y with x.'

The verb can also be focused, a construction that Brody (1995) analyzes as head adjunction to F, and Puskás (1997) as XP-movement.

2.1.2   NegP

A focused XP and the verb can be negated independently or even simultaneously. When two negations occur, they do not cancel each other out. Small capital letters indicate focus.

(3) Nem MARIVAL   nem beszéltem.
      not   Mari-with   not   talked-1sg
      'It was not Mari that I did not talk with (i.e., it was someone else that I did not talk with).'

Since the two negations share a variety of syntactic properties and since it is semantically unproblematic to treat both as sentential negation, it is natural to postulate two NegPs, with the *nem* head of the higher one selecting for FP and the *nem* head of the lower one selecting for AgrP. For further details on the two NegPs, see appendix B, section B.1.3.

2.1.3   The A(rgument) Positions

Following Koopman (1996), the structure in (1) distinguishes AgrPs and CasePs. The assumption is that only pro resides in the specifier of AgrP ([Spec, AgrP]); overt noun phrases land in [Spec, CaseP]. Following Stowell (1993), TP has a phonetically empty operator in its specifier.

Hungarian is known as a "nonconfigurational" language in the sense that it does not exhibit the usual simple diagnostics of a hierarchical argument order, for example, subject/object asymmetries in crossover and superiority. We remain agnostic on how this should be accounted for.

2.2   How High is the Finite Verb?

The finite V must pick up its own morphological features. This puts it at least as high as Agr$_S$. Does it move higher than AgrP? The XPs in [Spec, RefP] and [Spec, DistP] need not be adjacent to the verb; thus, their presence does not trigger any further verb movement. On the other hand, the XP in [Spec, FP] can only be overtly separated from the finite verb stem by the lower negation, as in (3), and/or the emphatic particle *is* 'indeed, lit. too', as in (4). Following Szalai (1996), we assume that emphatic *is* heads a functional projection of its own.

(4) Megígértem, hogy MARIVAL   beszélek, és   MARIVAL   is   beszéltem.
     promised-1sg that   Mari-with talk-1sg and Mari-with too talked-1sg
     'I promised that it would be Mari that I would talk with, and it was Mari that I talked with, too (= indeed).'

Horvath (1986) has argued that V assigns a [focus] feature to the focused XP. Brody (1990, 1995) uses this idea to account for the position of V, assuming that V adjoins to F, in whose specifier the focused XP is located. There are two problems with this analysis.

First, Kenesei (1994) argues, with reference to phrases that occupy [Spec, FP] but only have a subconstituent focused (in terms of both accent and contrastive interpretation), that the [focus] feature cannot arise through assignment to [Spec, FP]. It must be due to lexical assignment or random assignment in syntax. Consequently, the motivation for V-to-F movement vanishes. For details, see appendix B, section B.1.2.

Second, the fact that the finite verb can be separated from the focused phrase by *nem* and/or *is* is problematic for V-to-F movement. Either head movement cannot be local, or V needs to incorporate these particles and carry them along in the manner of inflectional affixes. Both assumptions are undesirable from the perspective of a local theory of head movement. See appendix B, section B.1.4.

The structure in (1) predicts the correct position of the finite verb without the assumption of a special head movement step. When the verb appears in the AgrP projection (either via head movement or via some kind of XP-movement), nothing but the Neg head *nem* and/or the Is head *is* can separate it from the material in [Spec,

FP], because (1) AgrP has at most a pro specifier, (2) NegP and IsP have no filled specifiers, and (3) there is no other intervening projection. We show that this analysis easily accounts for the position of separable prefixes in finite clauses, although not for the optional inversion of the prefix in infinitival clauses with focus, noted in Brody 1995.

(5) a. Nem lenne   helyes ÉJFÉLKOR   haza menni.
       not would-be right midnight-at home go-inf
       'It would not be right to go home at midnight.'
    b. Nem lenne   helyes ÉJFÉLKOR   menni haza.
       not would-be right midnight-at go-inf home
       'It would not be right to go home at midnight.'

Brody analyzes this as an optional variant of V-to-F movement. The phenomenon is not as unconditional as Brody's analysis would suggest, however. It depends on the phonological weight of the prefix or other material that plays the same role. As reviewed in appendix B, section B.1.5, with monosyllabic prefixes inversion is close to ungrammatical. With a longer prefix, inversion is fairly optional. When an infinitival sequence of one more level of embedding plays the same role, inversion is practically obligatory. Marcel den Dikken (personal communication) has suggested that this might indicate that we are dealing with a PF phenomenon. This is the assumption we will adopt; we do not attempt to incorporate this phenomenon into our syntax.

If the verb does not move beyond AgrP, the independently motivated analysis of Hungarian fully conforms to Koopman's (1996) Generalized Doubly Filled Comp Filter (modified LCA).

(6) No projection has both an overt specifier and an overt head at the end of the
    derivation.

RefP and DistP have overt specifiers and therefore do not have overt heads. If FP has an overt specifier, its head is empty. It can have an overt head only if the verb itself is focused; but then the specifier is empty. Agr and T heads are overt but have no overt specifiers.

2.3   Separable Prefixes in Neutral and Nonneutral Sentences

Hungarian verbs have separable prefixes. In so-called neutral sentences, which contain at most filled RefPs or DistPs but, crucially, no FP or NegP, the prefix attaches to the finite verb. (In Hungarian orthography the procliticized prefix and the verb are spelled as one word. We often write them as two words to make the examples and their glosses more transparent.)

(7) a. Mari be ment.   (*Mari* is in RefP)
    Mari in went-3sg
    'Mari went in.'

   b. Mindenki be ment.   (*mindenki* is in DistP)
    everyone in went-3sg
    'Everyone went in.'

   c. Be mentem.
    in went-1sg
    'I went in.'

In nonneutral sentences (i.e., ones that contain FP and/or NegP), the prefix is stranded postverbally (typically, but not necessarily, adjacent to the finite verb).

(8) a. (Csak) MARI ment   be.   (*Mari* is in FP)
    only   Mari went-3sg in
    'Only Mari went in.'

   b. Nem mentem be.   (*nem* is in NegP)
    not   went-1sg in
    'I didn't go in.'

The question most relevant from the perspective of this book is what position the prefix *be* occupies in the two types. The simplest assumption might be that it occupies the same position in both (7) and (8). This position might be either part of a complex head *bement(em)* or the specifier of an as yet unknown pre-AgrP projection. (8) might then be derived from (7) by a verb movement step, triggered by the presence of FP or NegP.

(9) focus/negation ment$_i$ be t$_i$

Apart from the fact that it is not obvious where and how V might be moving (see section 2.2), we have independent evidence that this analysis is not general enough. When the sentence contains a series of subject control verbs that we will call *auxiliaries*, the prefix of the lowest infinitive procliticizes to the finite verb in neutral sentences.

(10) Be fogok   akarni   menni.
    in will-1sg want-inf go-inf
    'I will want to go in.'

The analysis in (9) would suggest that the negated version of (10) is (11a). But (11a) is unacceptable, as observed by Kenesei (1989). (11b) and (11c) are the correct orders.

(11) a. *Nem fogok$_i$ be t$_i$ akarni   menni.
    not   will-1sg in   want-inf go-inf
    'I will not want to go in.'

    b. Nem fogok akarni be menni.
          not   will-1sg want-inf in go-inf
          'I will not want to go in.'
    c. Nem fogok be menni akarni.
          not   will-1sg in go-inf want-inf
          'I will not want to go in.'

The moral is twofold. First, the prefix does not occupy the same position in neutral and nonneutral sentences. To use the pretheoretical labels that we will adopt here, it "climbs" to one kind of position in neutral sentences, and it "inverts" into another kind of position in nonneutral ones. The analyses of climbing and inversion need to be unified in theoretical terms, but the landing sites cannot be equated in descriptive terms. Second, simple examples like (7) and (8) are deceptive, because they do not contain enough material to diagnose the positions of the lexical items. Thus, throughout this book we will examine longer infinitival sequences. The analyses of the simple examples follow as a by-product.

2.4   The Organization of the Discussion of Hungarian

In this book we examine the two kinds of verbal complex formation exemplified in (10) and (11): climbing and inversion. At first sight, climbing looks like XP-movement and inversion like head movement. We argue in detail that a head movement analysis of inversion is untenable; we instead develop an XP-movement analysis, which then extends to climbing with minor modifications.

We introduce the data piecemeal, each piece appearing when it plays a role in the argument. In appendix B we pull together the examples that occur in the text, and we add more for clarification. Thus, readers can enjoy the kind of logical presentation familiar from papers on better-known languages but can also develop their own grasp of the facts by consulting appendix B.

In chapter 3 we focus on why inversion cannot be analyzed as head movement. First we present the basic data involving prefixes that suggest a head movement analysis. Then we observe other facts indicating that an XP-movement variety of inversion must also be available, which makes the head movement analysis at best redundant. Finally, we show that because a grammar that allows both XP-movement and head movement to create inverted orders makes some incorrect predictions, it is important to eliminate the (redundant) head movement option. In sum, the argument is that even if head movement is available in Universal Grammar, the phenomenon we are investigating is best analyzed as XP-movement.

In chapter 4 we develop the XP-movement analysis of inversion, considering the full range of expressions that invert. The analysis relies heavily on pied-piping and remnant movement. An important feature is that it accounts for the alternative orders without reference to covert movement (feature movement or LF movement) and without invoking economy considerations. We demonstrate that the proposal not only accounts for the existing strings but also excludes the ungrammatical ones on principled grounds.

In chapter 5 we discuss independent evidence for the constituent structure (often, also the categories) that we assign to the intermediate steps created by recursive inversion. This evidence comes from the fact that some, but not other, strings created by those intermediate steps can undergo overt long-distance movement (focusing) or participate in scrambling. Then we turn to climbing (the phenomenon observed in neutral sentences). We show that the very same mechanisms that needed to be postulated in chapter 4 are present here, with the addition of some facts that are directly related to the absence of FP or NegP. Thus, the analyses of nonneutral and neutral sentences are as unified as, say, those of declarative and interrogative clauses. Finally, with all the pieces of the analysis in place, we address how nonauxiliaries block inversion and climbing.

In chapter 6 we focus on our proposal that the complements of auxiliaries are always CPs. We discuss data pertaining to subjunctive complements, operator projections, object agreement, and verbal co-occurrence restrictions and argue that they either directly support our analysis or are at least compatible with it.

Chapter 3
Inversion: Why XP-Movement?

3.1 The Basic Patterns

The basic phenomenon of inversion can be demonstrated using a verb with a so-called separable prefix, embedded under a sequence of "auxiliaries." The pretheoretical term *auxiliary* is due to Kálmán et al. (1989), who first identified these classes; it refers to a member of a closed class of subject control verbs that do not carry main accent in neutral sentences.

(1) *Auxiliaries*
fog 'will', lehet 'may', szokott 'tend', szokás 'be customary', tetszik 'lit. please', szabad 'be permitted', szeretne 'would like', kell 'must', akar 'want', talál 'happen to', bír 'be able', tud 'be able to/know how to', kezd 'begin', kíván 'wish', mer 'dare', óhajt 'desire', próbál 'try', szándékozik 'intend'

The verbs in (1) contrast with those in (2), for instance. The behavior of the latter, an open class of subject control verbs that carry main accent in neutral sentences, will be analyzed after the proposal for auxiliaries is developed.[1]

(2) *Nonauxiliary infinitival-complement-taking verbs*
elfelejt 'away-forget = forget', elkezd 'away-begin = begin', megpróbál 'perf-try = try', fél 'is afraid', habozik 'hesitate', szégyell 'is ashamed', utál 'hate', szeret 'like', imád 'love', siet 'hasten', and so on

Let us assume that the underlying order of the auxiliary sequence in Hungarian is essentially the same as the English surface order. To focus on the patterns, we will notate verbs and prefixes with numbers.

(3) fogok   (kezdeni) (akarni) menni be
    will-1sg begin-inf want-inf go-inf in
    1   2   3   4   5

We are interested in the surface orders emerging from (3) in sentences in which the matrix is nonneutral (i.e., contains NegP and/or FP), but the infinitival clauses themselves do not contain operators with a potential blocking effect.

The only acceptable surface orders are the ones in (4) through (6). Note that strings like (5b) and (6b,c) are also grammatical if intonation indicates that *haza-menni* and *hazamenni akarni*, respectively, are focused inside the infinitival clause. We assume that under focusing they have somewhat different structures, as a result of which this possibility is irrelevant. Unless otherwise specified, we are interested in the nonfocused versions throughout the book.

(4)   [Nem] fogok   be menni.   1 5 4
        [not]   will-1sg in go-inf
        'I will [not] go in.'

(5) a. [Nem] fogok   akarni   be menni.   1 3 5 4
        [not]   will-1sg want-inf in go-inf
        'I will [not] want to go in.'

   b. [Nem] fogok   be menni akarni.   1 5 4 3
        [not]   will-1sg in go-inf want-inf
        'I will [not] want to go in.'

(6) a. [Nem] fogok   kezdeni   akarni   be menni.   1 2 3 5 4
        [not]   will-1sg begin-inf want-inf in go-inf
        'I will [not] begin to want to go in.'

   b. [Nem] fogok   kezdeni   be menni akarni.   1 2 5 4 3
        [not]   will-1sg begin-inf in go-inf want-inf
        'I will [not] begin to want to go in.'

   c. [Nem] fogok   be menni akarni   kezdeni.   1 5 4 3 2
        [not]   will-1sg in go-inf want-inf begin-inf
        'I will [not] begin to want to go in.'

All these orders are equally acceptable. The length of the string does not affect its acceptability in terms of grammaticality, although a longer sequence of auxiliaries may be more difficult to contextualize.

The insightful observation that the surface orders are partial mirror images of the one in (3) is due to Kenesei (1989). He assumes that the underlying order is something like (6c), and orders like (6a), which comes closest to (3), are formed by a series of rightward movements.

On the assumption that movement always takes place to the left, the following informal algorithm can be said to produce the above patterns. *Be* inverts with *menni*, *bemenni* with *akarni*, *bemenni akarni* with *kezdeni*, and *bemenni akarni kezdeni* with *fogok*. The last step is invisible, because finite *fogok* moves on to Case, T, and Agr.

The first inversion step (*be* with *menni*) is obligatory; the rest are optional, as (6a,b) show.

(7)   __ fogok   __ kezdeni __ akarni   __ menni   be

We will mnemonically call the orders involving inversion *inverted orders* and the others *English orders*.

As mentioned above, all the remaining orders are unacceptable. They fall into four types. First, a prefix fails to invert.

(8) *Nem fogok   menni *be*.   *V_{inf}PF
      not   will-1sg go-inf in

Second, a prefix inverts with a verb that is not its governing verb.

(9) *Nem fogok   kezdeni *be*$_i$ akarni   menni t$_i$.   *1 2 5 3 4
      not   will-1sg begin-inf in want-inf go-inf

Third, a segment with an internal English order inverts.

(10) *Nem fogok   [*akarni   be menni*]$_i$ kezdeni   t$_i$.   *1 3 5 4 2
       not   will-1sg want-inf in go-inf   begin-inf

Fourth, a verb inverts without taking its prefix or complement along.

(11) *Nem fogok   *akarni*$_i$ kezdeni   t$_i$ be menni.   *1 3 2 5 4
       not   will-1sg want-inf begin-inf   in go-inf

These are the core facts that a theory of inversion needs to account for.

Shortly, in section 3.4, we introduce another set of expressions whose behavior is significantly similar to that of prefixes; the collective label to be used is *VM*. The above generalizations are upheld when *prefix* is replaced by *VM*.

3.2   Head Movement or XP-Movement: The Structure of the Argument

The question we address in the rest of this chapter is whether inversion is to be attributed to head movement. In section 3.3 we observe that the head movement analysis is initially plausible for the above data, which involve prefixes. In section 3.4 we show, however, that parallel data involving XP-inversion make a pure head movement analysis of inversion insufficient. In section 3.5 we show that even prefixes are capable of moving unboundedly, probably as XPs, in other contexts (climbing); thus, reserving a head movement analysis for their inversion is redundant. In section 3.6 we show that the same conclusion holds for the intermediate steps of recursive inversion: inverted infinitival structures undergo unbounded movement (focusing), indicating that they also have XP status. Finally, in section 3.7 we show that head movement cannot be allowed in inversion, even redundantly.

If the head movement analysis of inversion is insufficient and redundant and makes incorrect predictions, then it is necessary to adopt a pure XP-movement analysis. We develop the details of this analysis in chapter 4.

3.3 The Plausibility of the Head Movement Analysis

Previous literature on Hungarian contains no comprehensive analysis of the data considered in this book.[2] On the other hand, the patterns described above are familiar (with some crosslinguistic variation) from German and Dutch and have traditionally been analyzed in terms of head movement and, more recently, XP-movement.[3]

Some striking properties of the Hungarian inversion data lend initial plausibility to the same analysis; if so, sequences like *bemenni* (5 4) and *bemenni akarni* (5 4 3) are complex heads. The relevant suggestive properties are as follows.

Prefixes, the expressions that obligatorily invert, consist of bare head material. The interpretations of the units they form with the selecting verbs range from the more or less transparent to the entirely opaque; compare *bemenni* 'to go in' with *berúgni* 'to get drunk, lit. to kick in'. These units are input to derivational morphology.

(12) a. be men-és
          in go-deverbal (with a productive derivational suffix)
      b. be men-et
          in go-deverbal (with an unproductive derivational suffix)

This can be taken as direct evidence that these units form words; that is, they either come from the lexicon as such or are products of head movement.[4]

The larger units formed by optional inversion are likewise limited to containing head material: dependents must be left behind.

(13) a. Nem fogom [szét szedni akarni] a rádiót.
          not will-1sg apart take-inf want-inf the radio-acc
          'I will not want to take apart the radio.'
      b. *Nem fogom [szét szedni a rádiót akarni].
          not will-1sg apart take-inf the radio-acc want-inf

Matrix material can be scrambled with infinitival material on the English order, but it cannot break units formed by inversion. All the examples in (14) mean 'Mari will not begin to want to go in'.

(14) a. Nem fog (Mari) kezdeni (Mari) akarni (Mari) be (*Mari) menni.
          not will (Mari) begin-inf (Mari) want-inf (Mari) in (*Mari) go-inf
                    1   2   3   5   4

b. Nem fog (Mari) kezdeni (Mari) *be* (**Mari*) *menni* (**Mari*) *akarni.*
   not will (Mari) begin-inf (Mari) in (*Mari) go-inf (*Mari) want-inf
        1   2   5   4   3

c. Nem fog (Mari) *be* (**Mari*) *menni* (**Mari*) *akarni* (**Mari*) *kezdeni.*
   not will (Mari) in (*Mari) go-inf (*Mari) want-inf (*Mari) begin-inf
        1   5   4   3   2

Finally, as shown in section 3.2, inversion proceeds in small steps, which is also
suggestive of head movement.

In this book we do not develop the details of a head movement analysis; instead,
we proceed directly to the problems that it encounters.

3.4 The Insufficiency of a Pure Head Movement Analysis

Even if inversion data involving prefixes are amenable to a head movement analysis,
there are other inversion data that cannot possibly be. Separable prefixes are not
the only kind of expression that participates in the first, obligatory inversion step.
Examples of all of the types follow; each type represents an open class and is pervasive in the language.[5] In (15) we exemplify expressions that obligatorily invert with
their selecting verb (in infinitival clauses that are complements of auxiliaries in nonneutral sentences).

(15) *Expressions that obligatorily invert with their selecting verb*
   1. Separable prefixes
      a. be menni
         in go-inf
         'to go in'
      b. be rúgni
         in kick-inf
         'to get drunk'
   2. Directional or locative PPs containing a full DP
      c. a   szobába   menni
         the room-into go-inf
         'to go into the room'
      d. a   szobában maradni
         the room-in   stay-inf
         'to stay in the room'
   3. Predicative APs or NPs, typically Case-suffixed
      e. ostobának bizonyulni
         stupid-dat prove-inf
         'to turn out to be stupid'

f. elnökké   választani
    president-translative elect-inf
    'to elect [someone] president'
4. Determinerless arguments, Case-marked
g. újságot   olvasni
    newspaper-acc read-inf
    'to engage in newspaper reading'

For completeness, we add expressions that optionally invert with their selecting verb
(in infinitival clauses that are complements of auxiliaries in nonneutral sentences).

(16) *Expressions that optionally invert with their selecting verb*
5. VM-less infinitival verbs
h. úszni   akarni
    swim-inf want-inf
    'to want to swim'

All these expressions have been dubbed *verbal modifiers* (VM) in recent Hungarian
descriptive literature. For ease of pretheoretical reference, we adopt this cover term.

The significance of the new data is that the VMs in class 2 are obviously not bare
heads: they contain DPs, complete with an overt definite article.

On the assumption that Case is checked or picked up in some specifier position, the
presence of Case suffixes in classes 3 and 4 also suggests that these VMs are phrasal.

Furthermore, these predicative expressions may have complex internal structure.

(17) a. a világ   legostobább emberének   bizonyulni
         the world-nom stupidest   man-poss-dat prove-inf
         'to prove to be the stupidest man in the world'
     b. a társaság   elnökévé   választani
         the association-nom president-poss-translative elect-inf
         'to elect [someone] president of the association'

The conclusion is that although prefix inversion may be analyzed as head movement, the inversion of "big VMs" necessitates a parallel XP-movement analysis.

In fact, a dual analysis may have its merits. Although bare (prefixal) VMs and big
VMs are alike in that they invert obligatorily, they differ with regard to whether they
allow the containing unit to invert.

(18) a. [[VM + V_{inf}] V_{inf}], where VM comes from class 1 or 5
     b. *[[VM + V_{inf}] V_{inf}], where VM comes from class 2, 3, or 4

For illustration, compare (5a,b), with a VM of class 1, and (19a,b), with a VM of
class 2.

(5) a.   [Nem] fogok   akarni   *be menni.*
      [not]   will-1sg want-inf in go-inf
      'I will [not] want to go in.'
  b.   [Nem] fogok   *be menni* akarni.
      [not]   will-1sg in go-inf want-inf
      'I will [not] want to go in.'

(19) a.   [Nem] fogok   akarni   *a   szobában maradni.*
      [not]   will-1sg want-inf the room-in   stay-inf
      'I will [not] want to stay in the room.'
  b.   *[Nem] fogok   *a   szobában maradni* akarni.
      [not]   will-1sg the room-in   stay-inf   want-inf
      'I will [not] want to stay in the room.'

On the standard assumption that only heads adjoin to heads, the big VM is not in an adjoined position when it precedes its selecting infinitive, but occupies a designated specifier position. If the next inversion step is only possible through head movement, we have an explanation for why big VMs bleed it.

If this suggestion is correct, then infinitival verbs themselves must count as heads, despite their infinitival morphology (viz., the suffix *-ni*), because infinitival Vs as VMs feed the inversion of the complex that contains them. On the other hand, predicative nominals count as "big VMs" regardless of how complex their internal structure is: they never feed inversion.

(20) a.   *[Nem] fogok   ostobának bizonyulni   akarni.
      [not]   will-1sg stupid-dat prove-inf   want-inf
      'I will [not] want to prove stupid.'
  b.   *[Nem] fogok   a   világ   legostobább emberének   bizonyulni akarni.
      [not]   will-1sg the world-nom stupidest   man-poss-dat   prove-inf   want-inf
      'I will [not] want to prove to be the stupidest man in the world.'

3.5   The Redundancy of Head Movement: Evidence from VM-Climbing

In this section we show that even those VMs whose inversion can be attributed to head movement are capable of moving as XPs in another context.

As mentioned in section 2.3, neutral sentences (whose tensed clause has no NegP or FP) have a distinctive order. A description is given in (21). The term *auxiliary* refers to the same class (1) that was relevant for inversion. (In fact, Kálmán et al. (1989) established the classification solely on the basis of climbing data in neutral sentences.)

(21) *VM-climbing in neutral sentences*

    a. In neutral sentences all types of VMs must precede either their selecting verb, if this verb is finite, or a finite auxiliary.

    b. Only auxiliaries can intervene between the surface position and the source position of the VM.

    c. Auxiliaries must appear in the English order.

    d. If the climbing VM has dependents of its own, they must be left behind.

The relevant examples involving prefix climbing were as follows ((7c) and (10) of section 2.3):

(22) Be mentem.   2 1
     in went-1sg
     'I went in.'

(23) Be fogok   akarni   menni.   4 1 2 3
     in will-1sg want-inf go-inf
     'I will want to go in.'

As (21a) states, these data are replicated by all VMs. For example:[6]

(24) A szobában fogok   akarni   maradni.   4 1 2 3
     the room-in   will-1sg want-inf stay-inf
     'I will want to stay in the room.'

(25) Úszni   fogok   akarni.   3 1 2
     swim-inf will-1sg want-inf
     'I will want to swim.'

The significance of the climbing facts is as follows. Climbing is a defining property of the entire class of VMs, phrasal or not. Since phrasal VMs can only occupy XP positions, their landing site must be an XP position preceding the finite verb or auxiliary. Phrasal VMs therefore do not form complex heads with their finite host. The resulting structure is comparable to English *DP's*, with DP in a specifier position and *'s* in a head position. The prosodic phenomenon of procliticization simply does not translate into syntactic head constituency. Now note that all VMs have identical climbing properties; no bifurcation even remotely comparable to the one summarized in (18) exists. It is therefore reasonable to assume that they all are headed for the same XP position—including the bare ones.[7]

How "unbounded" is VM-climbing? One suggestion, inspired by Farkas and Sadock 1989, might be that the auxiliary sequence intervening between the surface and the source positions is reanalyzed as one complex head. But this is unlikely: the sequence can be broken by scrambled matrix material.[8] It is true that scrambling in (26) is not as impeccable as in English orders in nonneutral sentences (see (14)), but no speaker of Hungarian we have consulted has judged the examples ungrammatical. Their degraded character is probably due to the fact that neutral sentences have a generally more rigid order and observe stricter restrictions related to "communicative dynamism."

(26) (?)(Mari) be fog (Mari) kezdeni (Mari) akarni (Mari) menni (Mari).
  (Mari) in will (Mari) begin-inf (Mari) want-inf (Mari) go-inf (Mari)
  'Mari will begin to want to go in.'

Consequently, the climbing of the VM counts as "unbounded" movement.

If the landing site of VM-climbing is invariably an XP position, we understand why VM-climbing can skip over several infinitives. This is an expected property of phrasal movement, not head movement.[9]

É. Kiss (1994, 59) similarly assumes that climbing is XP-movement and presents powerful corroborating evidence. She observes that a handful of predicates like *kell* 'must' may take a subjunctive complement and nevertheless allow climbing.

(27) Szét kell, hogy szedjem a rádiót.
  apart must that take-subj-1sg the radio-acc
  'I must take apart the radio.'

É. Kiss argues that it would be unimaginable for *szét* 'apart' to move out of the *hogy* 'that' clause by head movement; even though *szét* contains only bare head material, it must be climbing as an XP. (We may add that not only particles but indeed all VMs climb into the *kell*-clause in the same way.)

The moral of these data is that all VMs, bare and big alike, can constitute XPs on their own and are capable of moving as such. Thus, if the existence of undoubtedly phrasal VMs calls for an XP-movement analysis of inversion, that analysis will extend to inversion involving bare VMs. Having both a head and a phrasal analysis for inversion is by and large redundant.

What do we make, then, of the observations that were suggestive of head movement?

The fact that prefixed verbs can be input to derivational morphology turns out to be irrelevant: the same holds for all VM+V combinations. See a detailed description in Szabolcsi 1994.

The fact that only head material participates in inversion also fails to diagnose head movement. Consider the moral of the following climbing example:

(28) Mutogatni fogja akarni a játékot a gyerekeknek. (neutral sentence)
  show-inf will-3sg want-inf the toy-acc the children-to
  '(He/She) will want to show the toy to the children.'

We have just established that the VM that climbs (here: *mutogatni* 'show-inf') must be an XP. But although this is an XP, it cannot include any of the internal arguments of 'show'. As illustrated in (29), these therefore must have been separated from the constituent that undergoes XP-movement, prior to the movement of what remains in XP.

(29)

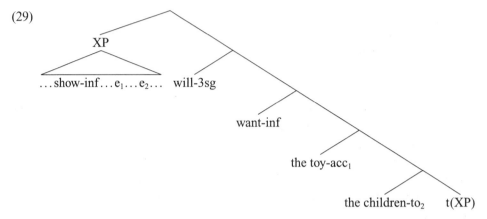

The derivation of this sentence involves what Den Besten and Webelhuth (1990) have dubbed *remnant movement*. The clausal architecture must therefore be such that it contains whatever landing sites are necessary to host the dependents of V, including DPs, PPs, APs, and CPs. But then the same landing sites will also serve as hosts for the dependents of an inverting infinitival verb.

Remnant movement will play a crucial role throughout our analysis.

The only data in the analysis for which we have made use of inversion as head movement pertain to the contrast in (18). If these can be accounted for solely with XP-movement, then preserving head movement for bare VMs has no compelling support.

3.6   The Redundancy of Head Movement: Evidence from Focusing

Independent evidence pointing to the same conclusion is provided by the contrastive focusing of various portions of the auxiliary sequence. As mentioned at the outset, Hungarian has a surface syntactic position into which contrastively focused expressions are obligatorily moved. Since the normal inhabitants of this position are arbitrarily large DPs or PPs, it is certainly an XP position. We labeled it [Spec, FP]. Contrastive focusing, like *wh*-movement, is "unbounded."

As noted by Kenesei (1989), all VMs and all inverted sequences can be contrastively focused. The longer the focused string, the more special context it requires, but as (30a–d) show, there seems to be no purely grammatical limit. On the other hand, as (30e) shows, no string with an internal English order can be focused.

(30) a. BE fogok   kezdeni akarni   menni.   [FP 5] 1 2 3 4
         in will-1sg begin-inf want-inf go-inf
         'I will begin to want to go in[side], and not out, away, etc.'

    b. BEMENNI fogok kezdeni akarni.   [FP 5 4] 1 2 3
        'It is to go in that I will begin to want (I will not begin to want to cry,
        etc.).'

    c. BEMENNI AKARNI fogok kezdeni.   [FP 5 4 3] 1 2
        'It is to want to go in that I will begin (I will not begin to cry, etc.).'

    d. BEMENNI AKARNI KEZDENI fogok.   [FP 5 4 3 2] 1
        'It is to begin to want to go in that I will [do] (I will not cry, etc.).'

    e. *AKARNI BEMENNI fogok kezdeni.   *[FP 3 5 4] 1 2

The significance of (30b–d) is this. These focused strings are inverted structures
containing prefixes. We have shown that if head movement is involved in inversion at
all, it creates precisely such strings. On the head movement analysis, these strings are
complex heads. But (30b–d) demonstrate that each of them also has a life as an XP.
This completes the argument concerning the redundancy of invoking head movement
in inversion.

3.7   The Fallacy of the Head Movement Analysis

Redundancy might not be an absolute argument against an analysis that makes use
of both head and phrasal movement (although it seems like quite a strong argument
to us). We will show that if head movement is allowed in the formation of such
complexes at all, incorrect predictions result.

   In this section we review problems that arise when one actually wants to implement a head movement analysis. Since any implementation requires specific
assumptions, the problems are more technical in nature than the ones reviewed in
previous sections.

   Suppose that bare VMs undergo head movement and left-adjoin to the infinitive to
form a complex word (V) with it, as in (31).

(31)
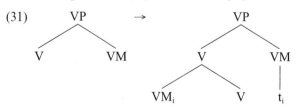

The newly formed complex V could optionally invert with a selecting auxiliary. (VM
is 4.)

(32) ... V2 [VM V3] → ... [VM V3]$_i$ V2 t$_i$

This analysis raises three major problems. The first two problems relate to the fact that an infinitive cannot invert with the selecting auxiliary, leaving its own VM behind. (See the fourth disallowed type of inversion, exemplified by (11).) This is true irrespective of how big the VM is.

(33) ... V2 [[$_{XP}$ VM] V3] → *V3$_i$ V2 [[$_{XP}$ VM] t$_i$]

(34) ... V2 [[$_X$ VM] V3] → *V3$_i$ V2 [[$_X$ VM] t$_i$]

Problem 1: How is (33) blocked? (33) involves an unambiguously phrasal VM (e.g., *a szobában* 'in the room'). As shown above, phrasal VMs must move to a specifier position to the left of the selecting infinitival. If head movement is indeed involved in complex verb formation, it is totally mysterious what blocks inversion in (33). There is simply nothing wrong with head movement across an intervening XP (e.g., I-to-C movement in *What book do you like?*, verb-second, etc.). Nor does there seem to be any obvious phonological reason that inversion is blocked, either. We could argue that inversion in (33) is blocked because it would leave the VM without phonological support to its right. However, this is observationally false: a VM does not need phonological support to its right. As tensed clauses reveal, a verbal trace suffices.

(35) Nem maradok$_i$ [$_{XP}$ a   szobában t$_i$].
     not   stay-1sg   the room-in
     'I am not staying in the room.'

Problem 2: How is (34) blocked? (34) involves a bare VM. Unlike the one in (33), the derivation in (34) is excorporation of the infinitive out of the complex head it forms with the bare VM.[10] Now consider the following fuller set of relevant data. Although excorporation of V out of the VM+V unit is required in tensed sentences (see (36a), the analogue of (35) with a bare VM), it is impossible in the case of inversion serving complex verb formation (36b,c); the entire VM+V unit must pied-pipe (36d).

(36) a. nem mentem be   V1$_i$ [$_V$ VM t$_i$]
         not went-1sg in
     b. *menni akarni be   *V3$_i$ V2   [$_V$ VM t$_i$]
         go-inf want-inf in
     c. *akarni menni be   *V2 ...V3$_i$ [$_V$ VM t$_i$]
         want-inf go-inf in
     d. be menni akarni   [$_V$ VM V3]$_i$ V2   t$_i$
         in go-inf want-inf

Pattern (36c) is otherwise not unheard of. Infinitival clauses, just like tensed clauses, contain an FP that can host a contrastively focused DP, for instance. In this case the infinitival V optionally excorporates and moves next to the focused phrase.

(37) Nem akartam   ÉPPEN MOST menni$_i$ [haza t$_i$].
     not   wanted-1sg right now go-inf   home
          V1   V2   VM
     'I did not want to go home right now (I wanted to go home either earlier or
     later).'

The head movement analysis of these data leads to a paradox. Suppose that we say
something along the following lines. In tensed clauses the verb must excorporate
from the complex head, because there is no other way for it to check inflectional
morphology: [+tense] is strong. In infinitives [−tense] is weak, and the infinitive
therefore procrastinates.[11] Notice now that the derivation of both (36b) and (36c)
would involve a movement of V3 to [−tense] as an intermediate step. We might say
that it is the prohibition against V moving to the weak [−tense] before Spell-Out that
rules out (36b,c).

But this prohibition is untenable. Consider the grammatical (38). Since *úszni*
'swim-inf' has infinitival morphology, the derivation must involve moving it to
[−tense] first, as (39) illustrates.

(38) Nem fogok   úszni   akarni.
     not   will-1sg swim-inf want-inf
     'I will not want to swim.'

(39)

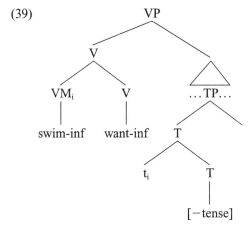

The need for *akarni* 'want-inf' to form a complex with its infinitival VM "overrides"
the weakness of [−tense], so to speak. This means, in turn, that blocking this intermediate step cannot be used to account for the ungrammaticality of (36b,c).[12] Then,
if verb movement is involved in complex verb formation at all, and if excorporation
of an infinitive is in principle possible (see (37)), why must the entire VM+V$_{inf}$ complex pied-pipe in (36)? We conclude that this paradox is the artifact of allowing head
movement to create inversion.

Problem 3: How do complex heads check inflectional features? This problem pertains to how the grammatical examples are actually obtained. If the head movement mechanics proposed in Koopman 1994, 1995b are adopted, a complex head should never be able to pick up inflectional morphology.

On Koopman's proposal, the feature-checking type of head movement consists of two steps, as shown in (40). First, the lexical head adjoins to the inflectional head. Second, receptor binding takes place: the inflectional head itself moves onto the lexical head to bind the pertinent receptor of the lexical head. Both movement steps require that the moved element c-command its trace. This entails that a complex head as such cannot check a morphological feature.

(40)

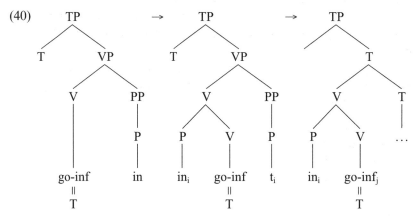

In the resulting structure, T cannot move to bind the =T receptor of the complex head because, owing to the branching V node, that head is too low and the trace of T-movement would not be c-commanded. This predicts, as Koopman points out, that the head of the verbal complex must excorporate before feature checking.[13] In the present example only *menni* 'go-inf' can usefully move to T; *be+menni* 'in-go-inf' cannot.

This entails, however, that although the order *bemenni* 'in-go-inf' came about, it cannot survive the checking of the infinitival feature, and orders like *bemenni akarni* 'in-go-inf want-inf' or *bemenni akarni kezdeni* 'in-go-inf want-inf begin-inf' do not even have a chance to come about.[14]

More generally, Koopman's technology of receptor binding entails that complex heads consisting of more than two components may come about only if no inflectional heads intervene. Thus, verbal complexes should not have tense and their components should not assign case. But both assumptions seem untenable. Infinitives have their own morphology: Hungarian is an agglutinating language in which the sole function of the suffix *-ni* is to mark infinitives. In addition, transitive infinitives assign accusative case just as transitive finite verbs do. So at least the T and the Case heads present a problem.

As Hans Bennis (personal communication) points out, analogous problems arise under somewhat different assumptions concerning the mechanics of feature checking. Thus, problem 3 is not an artifact of Koopman's specific assumptions.

We conclude that a head movement analysis simply cannot be made to work within the assumptions about phrase structure that we have adopted, even for the cases in which it initially seems plausible—that is, in which the Head Movement Constraint is satisfied. Given these arguments, there seems to be no other option than to pursue a phrasal analysis for all instances of complex verb formation.

We believe that the above arguments essentially carry over to the head movement (-like) elements of the proposals in Brody 1997, 2000, and É. Kiss 1998a,b (see note 2).

Chapter 4
The XP-Movement Analysis

4.1 The Basic Idea of the XP-Movement Analysis

We now develop the phrasal analysis of inversion, first for sentences containing focus/negation, then for VM-climbing in neutral sentences. In chapter 3 we argued that head movement is not involved in the derivation of the verbal complex at all. This leaves no other option than to develop the XP analysis. (The first to propose an XP analysis for similar phenomena was Hinterhölzl (1997a).)[1] We have already established the following:

(1) *XP-movement*
   The VMs and verbs that move are XPs; they land in designated specifier positions. The illusion that heads are moving is due to the fact that nonhead material, if there is any, is removed from the XP.

More technically:

(2) *Remnant movement*
   What looks like head movement in complex verb formation is remnant movement.

   Let us begin with the lexical requirements that drive complex verb formation. The first is a simple one: the VMs that obligatorily invert with the selecting verb (PPs, APs, NPs; see (15) in chapter 3) must raise to a designated specifier position close to V. We assume that there is a projection labeled VP+ right above VP. VP+ is the constituent dedicated to complex verb formation: VM moves to [Spec, VP+]. (As we will show later, a second projection, PredP, is also involved in the complex verb formation process.)

(3) a. VM moves to [Spec, VP+] above the selecting V.

Second, a specific subset of verbs that were dubbed "auxiliaries" and are called "restructuring" verbs in the literature on other languages have the lexical property that they must combine with a constituent that is slightly larger than VP and contains the infinitive and the VM of the infinitive, if it has one. This constituent is nothing but VP+, and the site of combination is the specifier of the VP+ associated with the auxiliary. (We might say that auxiliaries need a VP+ as their VM.)

(3) b. "Auxiliaries" require a VP+ in their [Spec, VP+].

We will refer to (3b) as the auxiliary's need to have a carrier of the [vp+] feature in its specifier. Presumably, (3b) is not an arbitrary but a universal property of this class of verbs (see also Bošković 1997, chap. 5), we hope ultimately reducible to a semantic property. We remain uncommitted as to exactly what it is (but see Szabolcsi 1986, 1987 for one suggestion).[2] (3a,b) yield derived structures of the type shown in (4a,b).

(4) a.   b.

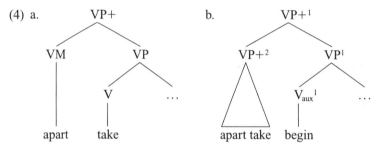

Both subcases of (3) involve feature checking, and we assume, generally, that each feature can be used only once. This ensures the locality of each step in the derivations. There is no ambiguity regarding what category moves: one that has a pertinent unchecked feature does, and there is always only one such category.

So far we have not touched upon the following two analytically and theoretically interesting issues.

The first issue pertains to the optionality of inversion. What happens in clauses with an auxiliary that do not exhibit inversion? If inversion is driven by some lexical property, it cannot be just optional. Is the relevant property satisfied covertly, by LF movement or feature movement? We show that it is possible to account for the full range of the data using nothing but overt movement (strong features).

(5) *Overt movement*
    Auxiliaries always form a complex predicate with VP+ overtly. Inversion sometimes looks optional, because another overt leftward movement makes it invisible.

The real parameter that underlies the contrast between inverted and English orders pertains to pied-piping.

(6) *Pied-piping*
   The VP+ that forms a complex predicate with an auxiliary may pied-pipe either
   just morphological projections or as much as CP.

The pied-piping of CP results in an English order because of the way it interacts with
independently motivated leftward movements (see below).

   The second issue pertains to the coexistence of neutral and nonneutral sentences.
We have seen that the same auxiliaries allow inversion and VM-climbing. Therefore,
the checking of whatever relevant feature auxiliaries have must be a proper part of
the derivation of climbing structures. We develop an analysis that is unified in that it
obeys this requirement. In other words, the auxiliary overtly forms a complex predicate with VP+ in neutral sentences as well as in nonneutral sentences. The reason why
only the lowest VM appears to climb is that VP leaves VP+, as a result of which only
the VM in the specifier is carried up.

(7) *VP+/VP splitting*
   VP may either stay inside VP+ or split out of VP+ (before VP+ undergoes its
   first move).

Thus, disregarding tensed clauses for the moment, there are three constituents
whose movement is at stake: VP_{inf}, $VP+_{inf}$, and CP. The infinitival clauses of the
three Hungarian constructions under discussion are distinguished by the following
parameters:

(8) a. | | VP+/VP splitting |
| --- | --- |
| Nonneutral sentences | no |
| Neutral sentences (climbing) | yes |

b. | | VP+ pied-pipes CP |
| --- | --- |
| English orders in nonneutral sentences | yes |
| Inverted orders in nonneutral sentences | no |

   The same two parameters play a central role in determining crosslinguistic variation, to be discussed in chapters 7 and 8. Dutch and German auxiliaries are subject to
the complex verb formation requirement just as Hungarian ones are. Some of the
striking ordering differences are determined by the extent to which each language
forces or allows VP+ splitting and CP pied-piping. VP regularly splits out of VP+ in
Dutch infinitives, but in German infinitives it does not, except for marked cases
involving infinitives that exhibit the IPP (*infinitivus pro participium*) effect (see chapter
7). A VP+ with a prefixal VM pied-pipes the infinitival CP in Dutch, but not in
German.

   In other words, crosslinguistic differences (just like cross-construction differences
in a single language) do not derive from whether movement takes place overtly or
covertly. They derive from what size phrases overt movement carries up.

Let us now make the above ideas more concrete in terms of actual structures. Many details will be glossed over at this point. We offer full derivations in sections 4.3, 4.5, 4.6, and 5.2.4.

The basic idea of the analysis is to exploit methods Universal Grammar allows to resolve the tension that arises between lexical requirements of auxiliaries and general structural requirements. We assume that any infinitival VP+ is automatically embedded within a larger structure: the infinitival CP. The assumption that "restructuring" is compatible with the complement's being a CP is supported by the fact that VMs climb out of subjunctive clauses with overt complementizers (recall (27) in chapter 3); we will take up this issue in section 6.1. Which order comes about—English or inverted—depends on how movement gets VP+ into the position where it can satisfy the auxiliary that selects this CP.

VP+ picks up its infinitival morphology, which we gloss over in this section, and moves to [Spec, CP]. This movement serves to assure the selecting verb (whether it is an auxiliary or not) that the CP complement is infinitival.

(9) The infinitival status of the clause selected by the auxiliary is checked in CP.[3]

(10)   CP

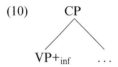

If the selecting verb is an auxiliary, VP+ needs to move to the auxiliary's VP+ to form a complex predicate. To do so, VP+ may extract from CP or it may pied-pipe CP. In (11) it extracts.

(11)   VP+^{1}

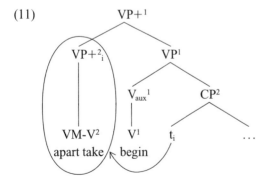

We assume that CP has its own licensing position, to be called $LP(cp)$. As shown in (12), the next two steps move CP^2 to LP(cp) and, as above, VP+^{1} to [Spec, CP^1]. These steps do not affect the internal order of VM-V^2-V^1.

(12)

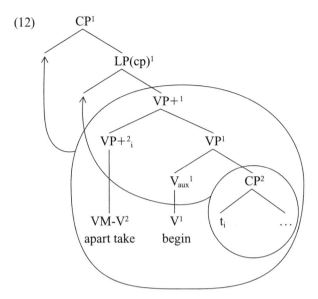

Once the remnant VP+^{1} reaches [Spec, CP^1], nothing can break VM-V^2-V^1 up: the inverted order is cemented.

What happens if VP+^{2}, instead of extracting from CP, pied-pipes CP? The result is shown in (13).

(13)

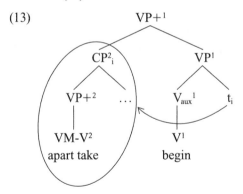

The pied-piping of CP makes a dramatic difference, because CP must extract to its own licensing position, LP(cp). The subsequent step, the movement of VP+^{1} to [Spec, CP^1] shown in (14), now moves a remnant that dominates nothing but V^1.

(14)

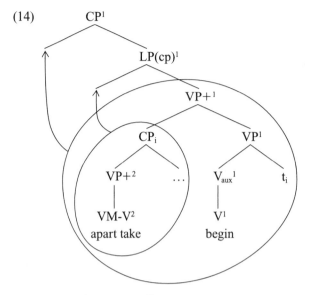

The result, V^1 ... VM-V^2, is none other than the English order.

Let us now turn to neutral sentences. As discussed earlier, auxiliaries must form a complex with their complement's VP+ in neutral sentences just as they do in non-neutral ones. The reason why only the lowest VM appears to climb to the tensed level is that, in every clause, VP splits out of VP+. Specifically, in neutral sentences the infinitival VP alone moves to [Spec, CP] to assure the selecting verb of the infinitival character of the complement, and the remnant VP+ that dominates nothing but the material in its specifier forms a complex with the selecting auxiliary. See (15).

(15)

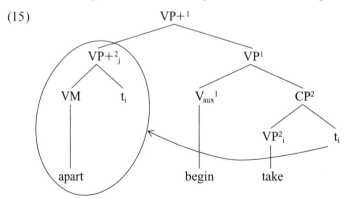

From here on, the same steps repeat themselves: CP^2 moves to $LP(cp)^1$, VP^1 to CP^1, the remnant $VP+^1$ to the next auxiliary, and so on.

In the sections to follow we discuss the general assumptions and spell out the derivations of nonneutral sentences in detail. We will reserve discussion of neutral sentences until chapter 5.

The extensive use of remnant movement might give the impression that these derivations are unusually complex. Addressing this question, Stabler (1999) shows that, in a computationally well defined sense, the proposal sketched above is in fact extremely simple. (The 1998 version of the proposal that Stabler examined differs from the present one in certain minor respects, which do not affect complexity.)

4.2   General Assumptions

Research on functional categories in the last decades has shown syntactic structures to be large, and simple in design. Large structures go against the basic intuition, shared by many linguists, that silent structure is very costly and should be avoided—that it is less costly to shift complexity to other components of the grammar, like the morphology, the lexicon, or the rule component (manipulation of features).

We do not share this intuition. Larger structures have proven useful in providing space for careful empirical accounts of numerous phenomena: the internal structure of VP, the syntax of DP, the syntax of verbs, wh-in-situ, the distribution of quantifier types, the fine structure of CP, the syntax of tense, the distribution of adverbials and aspectual categories. These accounts may be among the main achievements of the 1980s and 1990s. We propose to accept, rather than fight, larger structures and to turn them to our advantage—that is, to more fully exploit the possibilities that they offer.

Large structures lead to complexity: one must determine what movements take place overtly or covertly, exactly where particular constituents are spelled out, how various movements interact, and so on. Reducing complexity by trimming structures forces one to shift the complications elsewhere and often results in an unfortunate reduction of the empirical coverage (i.e., shifting phenomena that no longer fit into the periphery). We propose, instead, to reduce complexity by simplifying structural design and movement, and by postulating strict conditions on which parts of the structure are movable (which potentially subsume the island conditions and the Empty Category Principle (ECP)).

Large structures allow the basic building blocks of syntax to be simplified to a unique structural design, which we take to be the basic unidirectional [specifier [head complement]] configuration, as in Kayne 1994. We depart from much current work in the Minimalist Program by excluding multiple specifiers and adjunctions.

In short, we assume large universal structures that are built up from a unique, ever-repeating design (see specifics below). Syntactic structure is projected from features, and each feature projects, whether it is overtly realized in a particular language or not.

In order to be interpretable, a projection must contain phonologically realized material at some stage of the derivation (the Principle of Projection Activation of Koopman 1996). This is achieved by overt movement. Languages use limited means (i.e., overt material) to license big universal structures. This implies massive overt movement. In fact, along with the assumption that all movement is feature driven, as in Chomsky 1993, 1995, it implies that all features are "strong."

(16) All movement is overt (and affects a phonologically realized constituent).

This is the same assumption that Kayne (1998b) explores in other domains of data.

The fact that all movement is overt also simplifies derivations by eliminating the need for economy principles like Procrastinate.

Under these assumptions, crosslinguistic variation cannot be attributed to differences in the hierarchical order of projections (Cinque 1999, Koopman 1996, Sportiche 1998) or to whether a movement is overt (pied-pipes lexical material) or covert (consists merely of feature movement). Variation must be due to the movement of constituents of different sizes, as is suggested by Hallman (1997), Koopman (1996, 2000), and Sportiche (1998).

Regarding movable constituents, we assume that the *complement of X, or the specifier of the *complement of X, may move to [Spec, XP]. *Complement is the transitive closure of the complement relation. In other words, only full specifiers and full complements on their own projection line can extract; parts of specifiers cannot. (That is, in (17) AP, BP, and CP may extract to [Spec, XP], but DP and EP may not.)

(17) *Extraction*

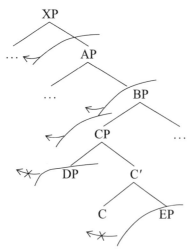

Remnant movement, introduced by Den Besten and Webelhuth (1987, 1990) and illustrated for Dutch in (18), will play a major role in our derivations.

(18) [[e$_i$ gelezen]$_j$ heeft Hans dat boek$_i$ niet e$_j$]
        read   has Hans that book not

The critical fact showing that Hungarian makes use of remnant movement is that when the lowest infinitive has no VM, it climbs like a VM. This verb must leave all its dependents behind. All orders of (19) in which *mutogatni* 'show-inf' climbs together with 'the toy-acc' and/or 'the children-to' are ungrammatical.

(19) Mutogatni fogja   akarni a játékot a gyerekeknek.   (neutral)
        show-inf   will-3sg want-inf the toy-acc the children-to
        '(He/She) will want to show the toy to the children.'

This example not only establishes the availability of remnant movement but also indicates that remnant movement must be the norm. Recall that climbing is unquestionably XP-movement. Therefore, the reason why *mutogatni* 'show-inf' is separated from its dependents probably does not lie with climbing per se. We are led to assume that both arguments and adjuncts have their own licensing positions (to be notated as LP(xp)) and move into them as soon as possible. Part of this assumption is familiar from the literature: DPs receive Case in designated specifier positions, and CPs are often recognized as having a particular distribution.[4] Since PP, AP, and AdvP need to be left behind just as DP and CP do (unless they happen to be VMs), we generalize movement to LP(xp) to all dependents. As a result, remnant movement becomes the norm. Müller (1998) presents a careful study of the empirical properties and theoretical availability of remnant movement. For the purposes of this book we essentially adopt Müller's assumptions.[5,6]

In chapter 3 we argued that even if head movement is available in Universal Grammar, the Hungarian facts we are concerned with are best characterized as XP-movement. This is the only serious commitment that we are making. Nevertheless, in order to spell derivations out in full detail, we cannot avoid taking a stand on whether inflectional morphology is picked up using head movement or XP-movement. We opt for XP-movement, for the sake of uniformity and because, as we show in section 5.2, there is at least one case where the XP-movement solution works much more smoothly. Since we have independent evidence for remnant movement (see (19)), it is quite natural to adopt Sportiche's (1997) and Hallman's (1998) assumption that there is no separate morphological component or morphological structure: words do not correspond to syntactic atoms or heads; rather, they correspond to syntactic constituents. In executing this idea, we presuppose the validity of the Generalized Doubly Filled Comp Filter, which Koopman (1996) derives as a corollary of her modification of Kayne's (1994) Linear Correspondence Axiom (LCA).[7]

(20) *Generalized Doubly Filled Comp Filter*
No projection may have both an overt specifier and an overt head at the end
of the derivation.

This entails that feature checking cannot be generally executed in the classical
specifier-head configuration: more structure is needed to cater to the possibility that
both terms are overt and the specifier does not move on. We assume that the constituent in which a verb picks up the inflectional morpheme Morph has the kind of structure shown in (21), where YP is a remnant whose rightmost overt element is the verb.
αP itself may be MorphP+, a position specifically designated to realize the relation
between YP and Morph, or any projection that happens to be right above MorphP.[8]

(21) *Morphology*

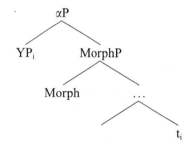

Since Morph is the actual suffix, not just a head checking some feature, YP must not
extract from αP, lest it get separated from its suffix. This, however, need not be
stipulated. Either there is no higher head that attracts YP, or if there is one, YP is
already buried in specifiers by the time that head is merged and thus cannot extract
on its own anyway. Consider, for instance, the case where αP is InfP+ and YP is
VP+. It is true that if the selector is an auxiliary, it will attract VP+. C is merged
earlier, however, and it attracts InfP+. By the time the auxiliary is merged, VP+ is
buried inside the specifier of a specifier and cannot extract. (The same holds if αP is
ModP+, where Mod is the suffix *-hat/-het* 'may' as in *szétszedhetni* 'apart-take-may-
inf = to be allowed to take apart'.)

Given that remnant movement and the notion of words as syntactic constituents
complement each other so nicely, it is interesting to ask whether remnant movement
is restricted to cases where the removal of dependents may be related to the head's
need to pick up inflectional morphology. The answer is no. We argue that VM-
climbing involves the climbing of a remnant VP+ that has its VP removed (see (15)
and section 5.2). As the discussion of nonneutral sentences will show, the same VP
can perfectly well acquire its infinitival morphology while contained in VP+. Thus,
VP+/VP splitting and the subsequent movement of the remnant VP+ are not trig-

gered by morphology. (Additionally, we will make regular use of remnant movement in cases motivated by uniformity, not by a particular descriptive argument.)

Even if morphology is taken care of by phrasal movement, we find it useful to retain head movement for at least two ancillary purposes: the treatment of certain cases of pied-piping (see below), and one possible treatment of VM-less verbs (see section 4.7). Both cases are such that they conform to the Generalized Doubly Filled Comp Filter (modified LCA).[9]

(22) *Corollary of the modified LCA*
In the following structure at most one of ZP, Y, and X may be overt:

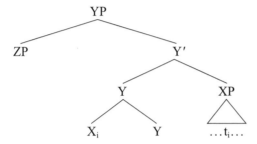

Note that we are not claiming that all head movements that are allowed by this corollary are actually exploited by Universal Grammar.

Pied-piping plays a crucial role in our account of English orders. We assume that the category that moves "inherits" the feature that needs checking through the head projection. Either the feature originates in specifier position and the head inherits it through (possibly multiple applications of) specifier-head agreement, or the head inherits it through head movement (or a combination of the two obtains). We illustrate both cases below.

(23) *Pied-piping via specifier-head agreement* (i.e., the *whose friend's brother* case)
XP inherits a feature from its *specifier (where "*specifier" is the transitive closure of the specifier relation).

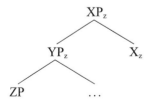

ZP agrees with Y; features of the head Y are features of YP.
YP agrees with X; features of X are features of XP.

Although this covers the *whose friend's brother* type of pied-piping, it does not cover the *about whom* type. For the latter case, which involves the inheritance of the complement's [wh] feature by PP, Koopman (1997) has proposed invoking head movement. Specifically, suppose *whom* is in the specifier of some YP, whose head Y receives the [wh] feature from *whom* via agreement. Y may now adjoin to the head of the extended projection of PP, thereby endowing PP with the [wh] feature, even though it comes from the complement.[10,11]

(24) *Head movement (and specifier-head agreement)* (i.e., the *about whom* case)

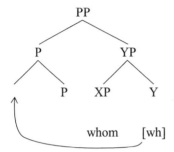

Finally, we assume that derivations obey the strict cycle (i.e., Chomsky's (1993) Extension Condition): as soon as a head is merged, movement into its specifier must take place.[12] This entails, for instance, that although the actual position of CP is clearly above InfP, the derivation in (25a), where first CP moves to LP(cp) and next the remnant VP+ moves to InfP+, is not possible. But the derivation in (25b) is also unavailable, since CP cannot extract when it is part of a specifier.

(25) a.   * LP(cp)   b.   * LP(cp)

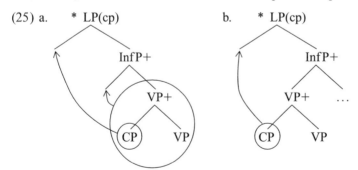

The only way to achieve the desired result is shown in (26).

(26)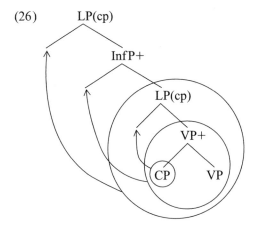

Given this, we will adopt the following tentative convention. This convention certainly needs refinement, given that there are other larger chunks of structure that may move together; we leave the proper general formulation open for further research.

(27) *Movement*
    a. By default, move only one category at a time.
    b. Exemption: Sequences of categories that may move together are (i) $\langle$YP+, YP$\rangle$, where YP+ is a projection motivated by the modified LCA, (ii) sequences involving operator projections like RefP, DistP, FP, and the projection hosting the verb (see note 11).

Furthermore, in addition to the licensing positions motivated by Case and other feature-checking reasons, we need a series of "stacking positions" above all XPs that are not exempted from the "move one category at a time" convention. To avoid a proliferation of labels, these stacking positions will also be called LP(xp). Thus:

(28) Where ZP is a category subject to the default "move one category at a time" (27a), a minimal building block has the following shape:

    LP(xp)*

      ZP

When $\langle a_1, \ldots, a_n \rangle$ is a sequence exempted in (27b), the members of the sequence should not normally be separated by LP(xp)*; the exception is where a_k is the trace of the category in [Spec, a_{k-1}]. (For example, if VP is to move to [Spec, VP+], VP+ and VP may need to be separated by LP(xp)* in the previous step, in order to strip V of its arguments; likewise, if AgrP+ is to move to FP to focus the verb.) This result may be ensured in various ways. One is to restrict the occurrence of LP(xp)* to the desired cases, in so many words. Another is to say that XPs always can be stacked between the members of exempt sequences, but their presence will typically cause the derivation to crash. See some discussion in section 4.7.

The positions LP(xp)* are not extrinsically ordered; rather, movement into them is constrained by the convention that it must replicate the already existing linear order of the pertinent XPs. That is, movement into LP(xp) cannot be used to reorder a string (although it may be a preparatory step for some reordering that is due to the subsequent landing sites of those XPs). If only complement movement is involved, this result immediately follows from the cycle, but if specifier movement is allowed, and it is, the convention needs to be stated separately.

The assumption of stacking positions is clearly against the minimalist spirit: it is difficult to see what feature might be checked in them. They are more reminiscent of adjunction to VP in the barriers framework. However, since it is possible to employ them in a completely mindless, mechanical fashion, we choose to live with them as a provisional solution that we hope will give way to a more insightful one. It is important to point out that none of our core empirical results are contingent on the assumption of stacking positions and the "move one category at a time" ruling. These merely serve to make analyses compatible with the strict cycle.

In this strictly cyclic system, there are two ways to reorder a string: one is to declare certain sequences of categories exempt from the "move one category at a time" ruling (as in (27)), and the other is to invoke specifier movement.[13] To illustrate the role of specifier movement, suppose we wish to reverse the linear order of VP and UP in (29) using XP and YP as landing sites. This is possible only if VP specifier-extracts to YP. Movement of the two complements (UP or the remnant ZP dominating VP) cannot have the desired effect.

(29)

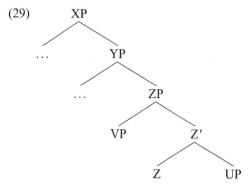

Thus, specifier extraction is a (potential) reordering device. We assume that specifier extraction is constrained so that it can only be triggered by feature checking. In other words, it cannot be used to move a phrase to a stacking position, except when this phrase is on its way to check a feature in a projection not yet merged.

The assumptions above, together with a few further assumptions to be introduced as we develop the detailed analyses, are pulled together as a reference guide in appendix A.

4.3 Inverted Order: A Preliminary Sample Derivation

To illustrate how some of these assumptions work, consider the derivation of the following sentence:

(30) Nem akartam   szét   szedni kezdeni a   rádiót.
      not   wanted-1sg apart take-inf begin-inf the radio-acc
      'I did not want to begin to take apart the radio.'

To simplify the derivation, we will ignore the PRO and pro subjects and abbreviate the DP 'the radio' as 'radio'.

We will slightly modify the inverted derivation in the next section, where we introduce PredP, but this will not reduce the usefulness of going through the exercise below.

V is merged with its VM (the PP *szét* 'apart') and its complement DP, and a complex verb VP+ is formed with the VM in its specifier.[14] This stage of the derivation is shown in (31).

(31)

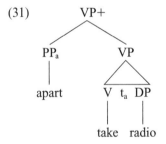

As shown in (32), DP moves out to its licensing position: we may assume that this first move is motivated by Case, but this assumption plays no role in the mechanics.

(32)

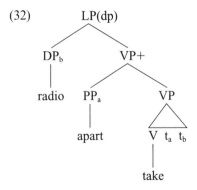

The infinitival feature is merged, projecting InfP and InfP+. VP+ moves to InfP+ to pick up its infinitival morphology (the suffix *-ni*). In view of (27), VP+ and VP are categories that can move together. This stage of the derivation is shown in (33).

(33)

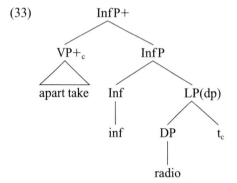

In this sample derivation we are assuming that there is no verbal functional projection above InfP+. If there were one, movement into it would proceed by the same kinds of steps as movement into InfP+.

InfP+ moves to CP to let the selecting auxiliary know that its complement is infinitival. See (35). InfP+ and InfP move together, but LP(dp) needs to be removed to a stacking position first, as in (34).

(34)

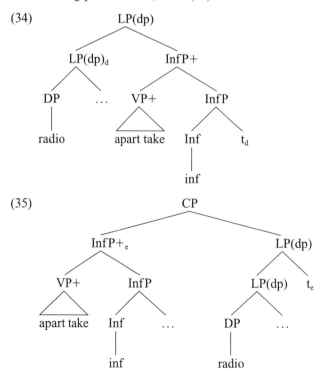

(35)

At this point we might merge the auxiliary directly with CP, or push LP(dp) up to a stacking position first. In this case the choice will not make a difference in order. But given the convention of moving one category at a time, we must choose the second route, as in (36)–(37).

(36)

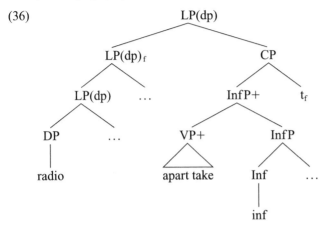

(37)

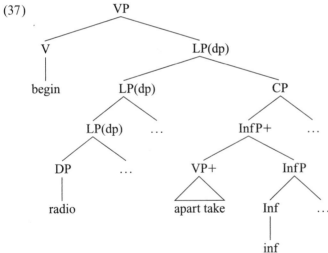

The auxiliary 'begin' needs to form a complex predicate with VP+. VP+ pied-pipes InfP+ to [Spec, VP+], to satisfy the auxiliary. InfP+ specifier-extracts from CP. At this stage the derivation looks like (38).

(38)

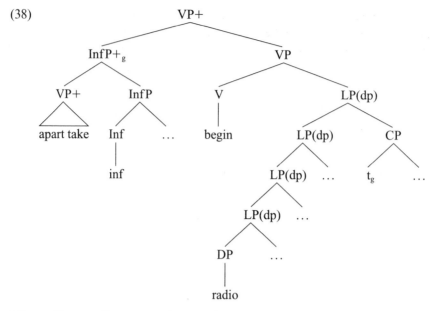

CP would normally move to its own licensing position, LP(cp). But this CP does not dominate overt material and therefore is not capable of activating LP(cp) in the spirit of the Principle of Projection Activation. Therefore, we make the following assumption:

(39) An XP from which all phonetically overt material has been removed does not need to be licensed.

This assumption does not affect the fact that a DP that dominates not a trace but pro, a lexical item that is simply phonetically null, needs to be licensed.

It would be convenient to delete such unlicensed categories, but that would involve deleting the traces they dominate. Thus, we assume that they can be carried along by subsequent movements, as an admissible exception to moving one category at a time.

In addition to the above principle, we will use an abbreviatory convention.

(40) To avoid complex structure where it is irrelevant, (a) will sometimes be written as (b).

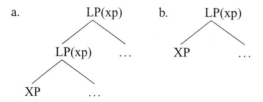

Note that this is merely a notational convention regarding how we spell out derivations: the traces dominated by the suppressed LP(xp) are not deleted.

Let us return to the derivation, whose last step was (38). LP(dp) with the empty CP is pushed up. The remnant VP+ moves to InfP+ to pick up infinitival morphology, as shown in (41).

(41)

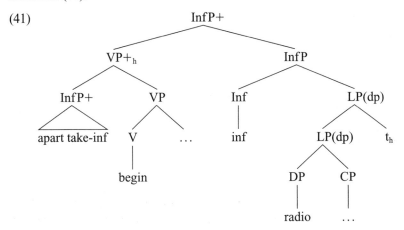

Again, LP(dp) is pushed up to a stacking position, as shown in (42).

(42)

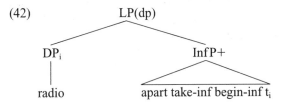

Now InfP+ needs to move to CP to check the infinitival nature of the clause. Notice that our structure contains two InfP+s: the one dominating 'apart take-inf begin-inf' and the one dominating just 'apart take-inf'. Is there any ambiguity regarding which of the two moves? There is none. The crucial reason is that each feature can be used only once. The smaller InfP+ has already used up its relevant feature within its own CP; at this point only the larger InfP+ has an active feature. In general, the fact that each feature can be used only once ensures the locality of each movement step, over and above whether one or more potentially extractable category is available. (In the present case the smaller InfP+ is part of a specifier and is thus not extractable on its own.) The result of InfP+-to-CP movement is shown in (43).

(43)

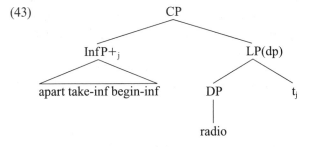

In now familiar steps, LP(dp) is pushed up and the auxiliary 'want' is merged with CP. InfP+ specifier-extracts to satisfy the auxiliary, resulting in the structure shown in (44).

(44)

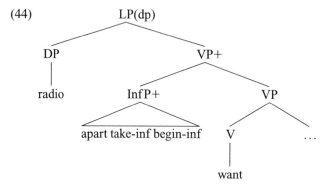

Next, the tense projection is merged. VP splits out of VP+ and moves to TP+ to pick up the past tense morpheme. We assume, with Stowell (1993), that the head of TP determines the relative order of utterance time (its specifier) and event time (its complement). Stowell assumes that the complement of TP is ZP (the event time phrase), rather than directly a verbal projection; we ignore this to simplify the diagram in (45), and we also suppress the operator in [Spec, TP].

(45)

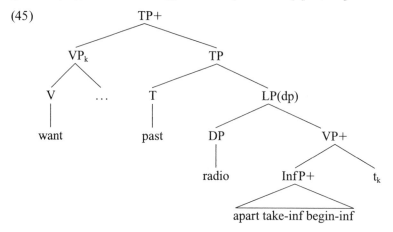

It may seem arbitrary that (in nonneutral sentences such as the one we are deriving) VP+ moves to InfP+ but VP moves to TP+. It turns out, however, that whether VP splits out of VP+ cannot be predicted on the basis of theoretical considerations: it seems like a microparameter responsible for much crosslinguistic and cross-constructional variation. The Hungarian situation is very similar to the German one, where VP generally stays in VP+ in infinitives but leaves VP+ in tensed clauses. In

matrix tensed clauses this is obvious from the fact that the separable particle is left
behind. In tensed complement clauses the possibility of across-the-board extraction
of the verb suggests the same (unless the particles are directly disjoined).

(46) dass die Sonne auf oder unter geht
      that the sun   up or   under goes
      'that the sun rises or sets'

See chapter 8 for further discussion.

   The tensed verb (dominated by the sequence $\langle$TP+, TP$\rangle$) still needs to pick up its
person-number agreement morphology in AgrP+. However, if we perform just this
step, with the preparatory movement of the LP(xp)s (shown in (47)), we get a linear
order (shown in (48)) that is grammatical but not ideal.

(47)

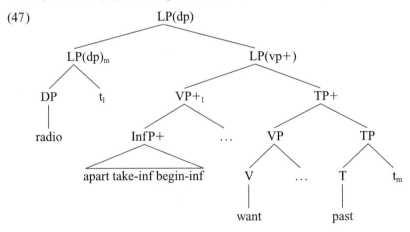

(48)

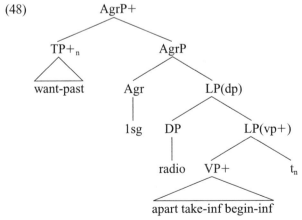

After negation is merged, this last step will yield the somewhat marked order (49),
instead of the unmarked, natural order (50).

(49) ?Nem akartam   a   rádiót   szét   szedni   kezdeni.
      not   wanted-1sg the radio-acc apart take-inf begin-inf

(50) Nem akartam   szét   szedni   kezdeni   a   rádiót.
      not   wanted-1sg apart take-inf begin-inf the radio-acc

The order where VP+ immediately follows the tensed verb is generally preferable to the one where it is separated from the tensed verb by one of its dependents, although the heavier VP+ is, the more separable it is. In other words, although (49) is not perfect, given its heavy VP+ *szétszedni kezdeni* it is much better than (51) with the very light VP+ *szét*.

(51) ??Nem szedtem   a   rádiót   szét.
       not   took-1sg the radio-acc apart
       'I didn't take apart the radio.'

(52)   Nem szedtem szét   a   rádiót.
       not   took-1sg apart the radio-acc
       'I didn't take apart the radio.'

If only light VMs preferred the position immediately following the tensed verb, the phenomenon might be relegated to Phonetic Form (PF). However, since even (49) is not perfect, it is desirable to cater to the preferred order in syntax. This can be achieved if we assume that tensed clauses contain, optionally perhaps, an as yet unknown landing site for VP+, right below AgrP. In the next section we will show that there is indeed a designated landing site for VP+, to be called PredP (adapted from Koster 1994 and Zwart 1994, 1997), that plays a crucial role in other constructions. Therefore, let us replace the step shown in (48) with the one shown in (53).

(53)

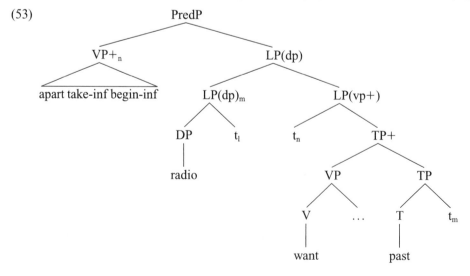

Now we can merge AgrP, move TP+ to AgrP+, and merge negation. The resulting final structure is shown in (54).

(54)

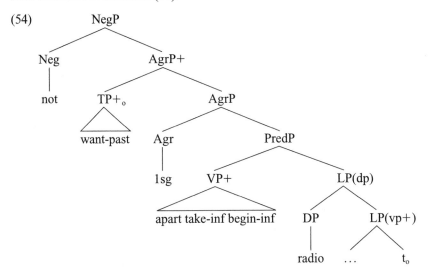

4.4   PredP, the Trigger of English Orders

For simplicity of exposition, in section 4.1 we identified the difference between inverted and English orders as follows. If VP+ extracts from [Spec, CP] and moves to satisfy the auxiliary selecting CP, an inverted order comes about. If VP+ pied-pipes CP to the auxiliary's VP+, an English order comes about. The reason is that VP+ stays in the auxiliary's VP+ and they move further together, whereas CP moves out of the auxiliary's VP+, so that when the remnant VP+ moves on, it dominates nothing but the auxiliary.

In this section we examine these matters in more detail. The basic insight will remain the same, but we need to refine the statement of what categories are involved (the VP+ versus CP distinction will not suffice), and we need to consider more complex cases.

The question we are addressing is this:

(55) What determines whether VP+ extracts on its own or pied-pipes a larger structure?

In the examples discussed in section 4.1, the choice is free: *szétszedni* 'apart-take-inf' may either invert with the selecting auxiliary *kezdeni* 'want-inf' (*szétszedni kezdeni*) or enter into an English order with it (*kezdeni szétszedni*). Thus, with the qualification that it is really InfP+, and not VP+, that is extracting in these cases, we register the following:

(56) In the following configuration, VP+ may pied-pipe either InfP+ or CP to the next VP+:

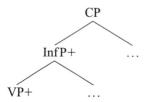

This follows from our theory of extraction. VP+ cannot extract on its own, because it is part of a specifier. The [vp+] feature of VP+, with which it can satisfy an auxiliary, percolates, via specifier-head agreement, to InfP+ and CP. Structurally, both the extraction of InfP+, a full specifier, and that of CP, the complement of a higher head, are legitimate.

There are, however, other examples in which an English order is forced. These examples fall into two main categories. (The data were introduced in chapter 3.) First, "big VMs" invert with their selecting verb just like particles do, but they bleed the inversion of the host with its own selector. (57) (= (18b) in chapter 3) summarizes the generalization; (58b) gives one example.

(57) *[[VM + V_{inf}] V_{inf}], where VM comes from class 2, 3, or 4.

(58) a. Nem fogok   akarni   *a   szobában maradni.*
         not   will-1sg want-inf the room-in   stay-inf
         'I will not want to stay in the room.'
     b. *Nem fogok   *a   szobában maradni* akarni.
         not   will-1sg the room-in   stay-inf   want-inf
         'I will not want to stay in the room.'

To account for the fact that big VMs are glued to their selectors just as small VMs are, we will assume that their Case (often quirky) is checked in VP+. To account for the unacceptability of (58b), it is straightforward to assume that (1) *a szobában maradni* 'the room-in stay-inf' does not extract from CP qua InfP+, but pied-pipes CP to the VP+ of *akarni* 'want-inf', and (2) CP subsequently leaves that VP+. The question is what forces pied-piping in this case.

Second, a verb must not invert with the next auxiliary up without taking along its VM or, generally, the specifier of its VP+.

(59) *Nem fogok   *akarni*$_i$ kezdeni t_i be menni.   *1 3 2 5 4
       not   will-1sg want-inf begin-inf   in go-inf

Why does this datum bear on CP pied-piping? (59) would result if the CP comple-

ment of *kezdeni* 'begin-inf' were as in (60) and the InfP+ *akarni* 'want-inf' extracted
to the VP+ above *kezdeni*.

(60)

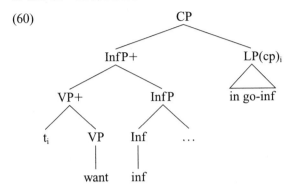

Again, the question is what prevents InfP+ extraction in this case.

In chapter 3 we also noted that an English order within the infinitival CP bleeds
inversion in the next clause up.

(61) *Nem fogok   [*akarni   be menni*]ᵢ kezdeni tᵢ.   *1 3 5 4 2
        not   will-1sg want-inf in go-inf   begin-inf

However, this case is excluded whether or not VP+ pied-pipes CP. It is useful to
consider why. The italicized segment of (61) would be the CP in (60). The first thing
to note is that extracting the specifier of such a CP yields (59), not (61). The second is
that if the whole CP were pied-piped to VP+, it would not stay there; instead, it
would move to get licensed in LP(cp), yielding the correct English order. Thus, our
core assumptions exclude this second way of obtaining (61), too. But third, in view of
our convention of moving one category at a time, even this second, innocuous analysis is unavailable: for CP to move, its complement LP(cp) must be pushed up first.
Effectively, then, a string like *akarni bemenni* 'want-inf in-go-inf' will not even transit
through the specifier of VP+.

To summarize, the exclusion of (58) and (59) requires that InfP+ pied-pipe CP—
or, to be more precise, a category that does not remain in VP+ once it satisfies
the auxiliary. At this point CP is the only candidate, but soon there will also be
another.

What may force the pied-piping of such a category, in view of the general assumptions above? There is only one purely structural circumstance that may do so: the fact
that InfP+ is buried too deeply in the specifier of CP to extract. Recall the assumption that parts of specifiers do not extract. Suppose now that there is a further projection between InfP+ and CP, so that the resulting specifier of CP looks like (62).

(62)

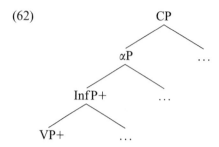

The feature of VP+ that the auxiliary selecting CP needs is inherited by InfP+, αP, and CP, through repeated applications of specifier-head agreement. This configuration does not allow the extraction of InfP+: it is part of a specifier. But the extraction of αP and CP is allowed. Let us first examine what αP might intervene between InfP+ and CP.

We approach the problem from a descriptive point of view, investigating what structural difference might be associated with bare VMs and big VMs. Dutch offers a relevant piece of data. One bare head VM in Dutch is *schoon* 'clean', which participates in the verbal complex *schoonmaken* 'clean-make'. Its modified version *erg schoon* 'very clean' is a phrasal VM. Surface order makes it clear that a bare VM may occur either inside or outside the verbal complex, but a phrasal VM must occur outside.

(63) a. omdat Jan het huis   heeft willen   *schoon*maken
         because Jan the house has   want-inf clean-make-inf
         'because Jan wanted to make the house clean'
     b. omdat Jan het huis *schoon* heeft willen   maken
         because Jan the house clean   has   want-inf make-inf
         (same)

(64) a. *omdat Jan het huis   heeft willen   *erg schoon*maken
         because Jan the house has   want-inf very clean-make-inf
         'because Jan wanted to make the house very clean'
     b. omdat Jan het huis *erg schoon* heeft willen   maken
         because Jan the house very clean   has   want-inf make-inf
         (same)

Koster (1994) and Zwart (1994, 1997) propose that big VMs (small clause predicates) move to a higher position that they call *PredP*.[15] (Although the ordering contrast between big and small VMs described above is well known, their proposal is not developed to account for it.)

How might adopting the PredP insight help us? Suppose that InfP+ is optionally dominated by PredP; that is, suppose that αP is PredP. If PredP is present above

InfP+, and InfP+ cannot extract from PredP right away (before PredP moves to CP), then VP+ must pied-pipe not only InfP+ but also either PredP or CP to the VP+ of the selecting auxiliary.

At the present stage of our work, we have a good understanding of the mechanics of the movement processes involved in deriving the various orders, but not of what causes the differing behavior of the classes of inverting and noninverting infinitives. Thus, for the time being we stipulate the membership of each class, and we stipulate when PredP is projected and/or whether the specifier of PredP can extract. The difference between "inverting infinitives" and "noninverting infinitives" can be characterized in either of the ways illustrated in (65) and (66) (likewise for other units that will be shown below to pattern with either one or the other).[16]

(65)   PredP

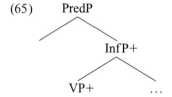

When the specifier of VP+ is a small VM or InfP+ (i.e., an inverted sequence), PredP is optionally projected above InfP+. Otherwise, PredP is obligatorily projected.

The idea in (65) is that *PredP* is a cover term for a variety of restructuring predicates. PredP occurs above VP+s with big VMs, VP+s with clausal specifiers, VP+s with nonauxiliaries, in tensed clauses, and so on, for possibly very different reasons. PredP attracts VP+ in much the same way auxiliaries do. VP+ pied-pipes InfP+ to PredP. The specifier of PredP can never extract. This approach seems correct but will not be developed here; it is explored in Koopman, in progress.[17]

The second option, (66), according to which PredP is always present, gives a mechanically simpler picture that can also be tied to language-internal and cross-linguistic variation. In what follows we will explore (66).

(66) PredP is always projected. VP+ is licensed in PredP. VP+ pied-pipes InfP+ to PredP.

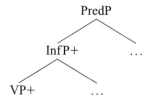

When the specifier of VP+ is a small VM or an inverted sequence, InfP+ optionally extracts from PredP. Otherwise, InfP+ cannot extract from PredP.

Assuming (66), we have the four possibilities shown in (67), depending on whether we choose specifier extraction or pied-piping. Whether "InfP+ to CP" movement is possible or not depends on which class the VP+ of InfP+ belongs to.

(67) a. InfP+ to CP to VP+: inversion
        Available to VP+s with small VMs, etc.

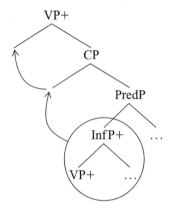

   b. PredP to CP+ to VP+: ?

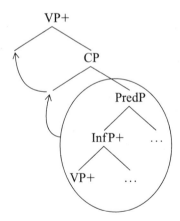

   c. InfP+ to CP, CP to VP+: English
      Available to VP+s with small VMs, etc.

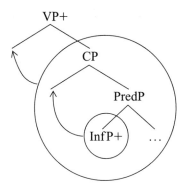

d. PredP to CP, CP to VP+: English
   Available to all VP+s

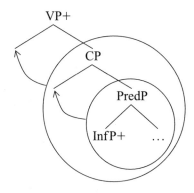

Of the four cases, (67b) seems problematic. Unless a further stipulation prevents it, PredP can extract from CP and move to the next VP+, just as CP itself can. Notice, however, a crucial difference between PredP and CP. Because CP has a licensing position outside VP+, creation of the grammatical English order is ensured by the removal of CP from VP+. However, PredP does not have a comparable licensing position; as a result, it stays inside VP+ and, despite all our efforts, produces the ungrammatical order in (59), repeated here.

(59) *Nem fogok *akarni*ᵢ kezdeni tᵢ be menni.   *1 3 2 5 4
     not   will-1sg want-inf begin-inf   in go-inf

The brute force remedy might be to stipulate either that PredP cannot extract from CP or that PredP is simply not the right category to satisfy the auxiliary, as a result of which the problematic derivation cannot arise.

We have a good empirical argument against this. In section 5.1, where we discuss the focusing of various segments, we will suggest that, besides the traditionally recognized focusable categories DP, PP, and so on, the category PredP (but not CP, for instance) can be focused in the tensed clause. But how can PredP reach the tensed clause? Consider (68).

(68)
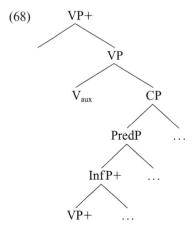

If PredP extracts from CP and immediately starts heading toward the tensed focus position, no category with VP+ in its specifier is left that might satisfy the auxiliary selecting CP. On the other hand, if VP+ pied-pipes CP to VP+, with PredP inside that CP, PredP can never extract (it becomes part of a specifier). There is only one way out: PredP must extract from CP and go to VP+ to satisfy the auxiliary—and then go on to the focus position. This leads to the conclusion that PredP can perfectly well form a complex with an auxiliary and indeed, sometimes it must. What it apparently cannot do is to stay in VP+.

To accommodate these facts, we may adopt either of two strategies. We may assume that PredP, just like CP, has an obligatory licensing position outside VP+. This amounts to saying that in the general case, whether InfP+ pied-pipes PredP or CP makes no difference (although it does make a difference when PredP needs to move further to FP). Or we may impose a limit on the complexity of the phrase that may stay in [Spec, VP+]. That is, InfP+, PredP, and CP may equally well satisfy the auxiliary, but nothing more complex than InfP+ may stay in [Spec, VP+]. The larger categories may show up in [Spec, VP+] only if they have an independent reason to specifier-extract later. CP always has such a reason. PredP has one only if it has a [focus] feature; if it does not, the derivation crashes.

The first option seems like a reckless extension of feature checking. It is true that the second option appeals to an arbitrary limitation on admissible structural complexity, but it is intuitively consonant with the observation that the categories that surface in [Spec, VP+] need to be "small and simple" in various, crosslinguistically different ways. Thus, the generalization is this:

(69) *Hungarian Complexity Filter* (to be revised in (70) in chapter 5)
VP+ may pied-pipe any *β*P to the auxiliary in the next clause, but *β*P must
move on if it is more complex than InfP+.

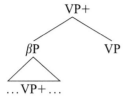

4.5 Inverted Order: Updating the Derivation with PredP

The introduction of PredP changes very little in the derivation of the inverted order
as reviewed above. (70) repeats (33).

(70)

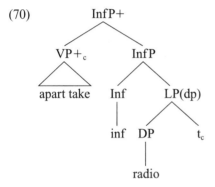

In the modified derivation InfP+ does not directly move to CP, because VP+ needs
to first make a stop to check a feature in PredP. Since C will need InfP+, VP+ must
pied-pipe InfP+ to PredP. Because the VM is small, InfP+ can specifier-extract from
PredP to CP. LP(dp) needs to be removed to a stacking position, as before. This is
shown in (71)–(73).

(71)

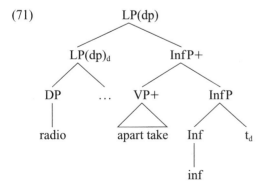

(72)

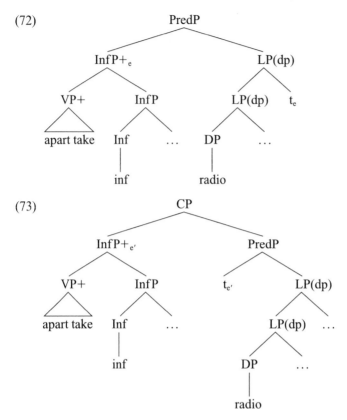

(73)

Now InfP+ extracts from CP+ to VP+, as before. In the subsequent cycles InfP+ can extract from [Spec, PredP] again, because it dominates an inverted order (its VP+ has InfP+, not a trace of CP, in its specifier).

4.6   English Order: A Sample Derivation

The following sample derivation illustrates the English order.

(74) Nem akartam   kezdeni szét szedni a   rádiót.
     not wanted-1sg begin-inf apart take-inf the radio-acc
     'I didn't want to begin to take apart the radio.'

The first steps of this derivation are identical to the first steps of the one reviewed above. V is merged with its VM (the PP *szét* 'apart') and its complement DP, and a complex verb VP+ is formed with the VM in its specifier, as shown in (75).

(75)

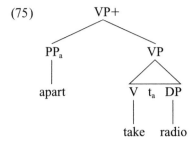

DP moves out to its licensing position, as shown in (76). We may assume that this first move is motivated by Case, but this assumption plays no role in the mechanics.

(76)

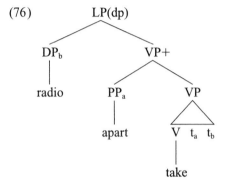

The infinitival feature is merged, projecting InfP and InfP+. As shown in (77), VP+ moves to InfP+ to pick up its infinitival morphology (the suffix -*ni*). In view of (27), VP+ and VP are categories that can move together.

(77)

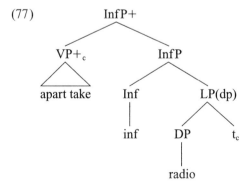

We assume that VP+ needs to check a feature in [Spec, PredP]. Since CP will need InfP+, VP+ pied-pipes InfP+ to PredP, as shown in (79). InfP+ and InfP can move together. As a preparatory step, shown in (78), LP(dp) is pushed to a stacking position.

(78)

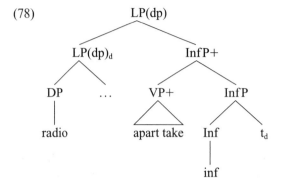

(79)

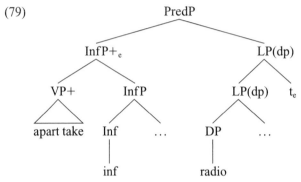

Now InfP+ needs to get to CP to check the infinitival status of the complement clause. The derivations for the inverted and the English orders diverge at this point. 'Apart' is a small VM, so the InfP+ hosting VP+ has two options: either it extracts from PredP, as above, or it pied-pipes PredP. We are now choosing the second option, shown in (81) (with the preparatory step of pushing LP(dp) to a stacking position; see (80)). After this single divergent step, the derivation for the English order proceeds as in the inverted case.

(80)

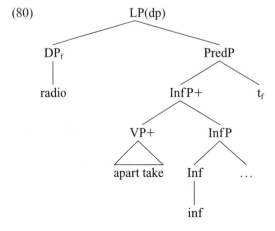

(81)

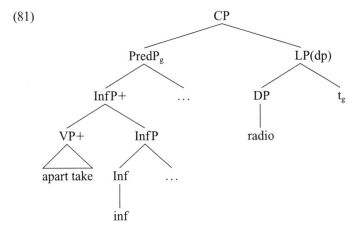

Once the auxiliary 'begin' is merged, it requires VP+ to form a complex with it. Since the InfP+ containing VP+ cannot extract (it is a specifier of a specifier), it must pied-pipe either PredP or CP. To achieve a converging derivation, we will choose CP; see (83)–(84). Again, LP(dp) is pushed up as a preparatory step; See (82).

(82)

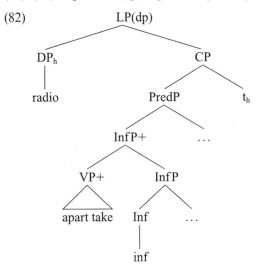

(83)

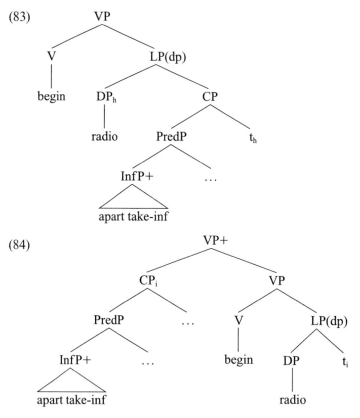

(84)

Now CP needs to move out to LP(cp), as shown in (86); recall that this is a licensing step, not a stacking one. But given our convention that the order of LP(xp)s must mimic the already given order of their inhabitants, and given that CP precedes DP, LP(dp) needs to be pushed up before LP(cp) is merged, as shown in (85).

(85)

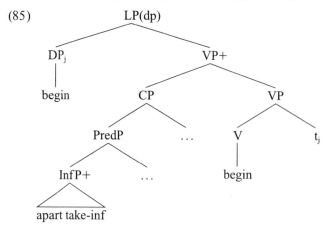

(86)

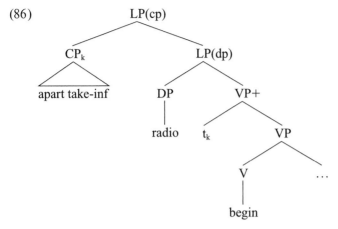

VP+ picks up its infinitival morphology in InfP+; this step is shown in (87).

(87)

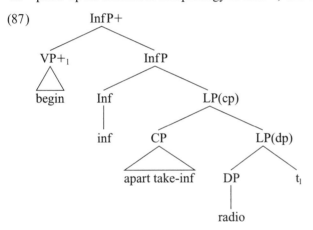

Now PredP is projected and VP+ moves to PredP to check a feature, pied-piping InfP+ as shown in (89). The two LP(xp)s are pushed up first, as shown in (88).

(88)

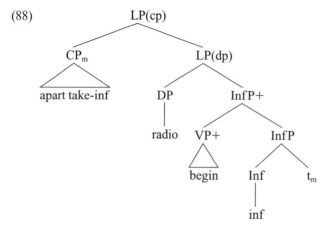

(89)

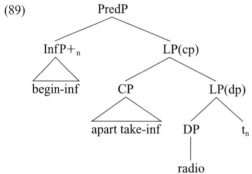

In now familiar steps, whose result is shown in (90), InfP+ moves to CP to signal the infinitival character of the complement. Because the specifier of its VP+ was CP, not InfP+, it must pied-pipe PredP (English orders bleed inversion). The two LP(xp)s are pushed up first.

(90)

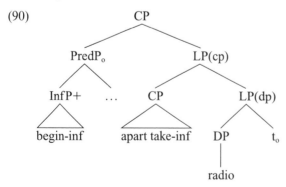

Next, as (91) illustrates, the matrix verb 'want' is merged, and InfP+ pied-pipes CP to the VP+ of 'want'. The two LP(xp)s are pushed up.

(91)
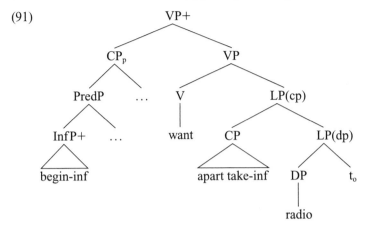

The CP dominating 'begin-inf' extracts to get licensed in LP(cp), but again, to preserve the existing order, LP(cp) and LP(dp) are pushed up first. The resulting structure is shown in (92).

(92)
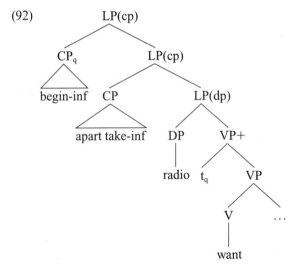

Now 'want' needs to pick up its past tense morpheme. We noted that Hungarian, just like German, has VP+/VP splitting in tensed clauses; that is, only VP moves to TP+. It is not obvious, however, that VP+/VP splitting should apply in an unqualified manner. In the present constellation, the specifier of VP+ has already been removed; see (93). If just VP moves to TP+, VP+ is left empty, and if it then moves to PredP, it cannot activate PredP with overt material.

(93)

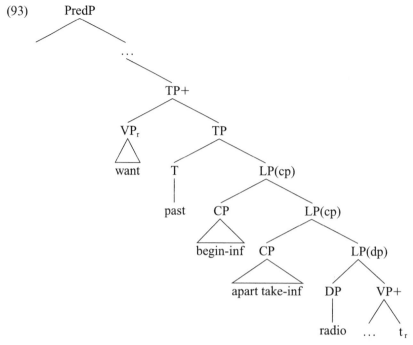

We see three ways to resolve this conflict. One possibility is to say that a vacated VP+ does not need to check any feature in PredP and, conversely, PredP need not be projected in this case. This is similar to the reasoning we used in connection with exempting a vacated CP from moving to LP(cp). But we may want to maintain that PredP is present in all clauses, especially if we think of PredP as a restructuring predicate, as suggested in Koopman, in progress. This leaves us with two ways out.

We may qualify VP+/VP splitting as follows:

(94) *Nonvacuous VP+/VP splitting*
In Hungarian VP+/VP splitting applies only when [Spec, VP+] is filled (with material distinct from VP) at the relevant stage of the derivation. Otherwise, VP stays inside VP+ and VP+ moves.

The distinctness qualification becomes relevant when the specifier of VP+ is nothing but VP (see section 4.7), and it will be shown to have important empirical consequences in section 5.2, where neutral sentences are discussed.

If we adopt this modification, the derivation will take the following course, beginning with (95).

(95)

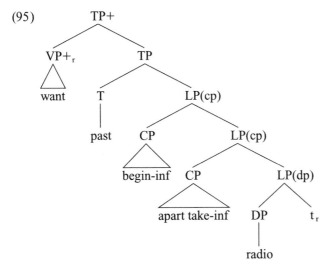

As shown in (96), the stacking positions are pushed up, and VP+ pied-pipes TP+ to PredP.

(96)

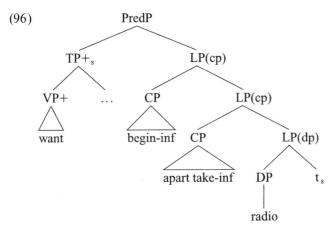

Finally, as shown in (97), TP+ extracts to, or pied-pipes PredP to, AgrP+, and NegP is merged.

(97)

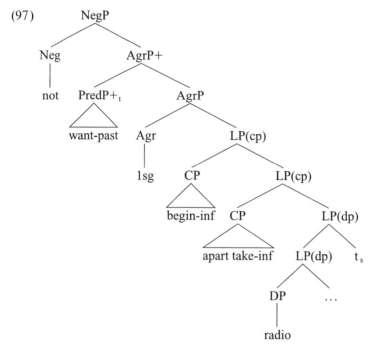

The third possibility is to say that in (91) CP is not pied-piped to VP+ but, instead, PredP extracts to VP+ on its own. Since PredP does not leave VP+, VP+ is not emptied of phonetic material, the higher PredP can be activated, and all is well. Well, not all: the Hungarian Complexity Filter disallows keeping PredP in VP+. But if we had an independent reason to revise the Hungarian Complexity Filter in such a way that it allows keeping complex material in VP+ just in case VP splits out, the problem vanishes. We will indeed propose such a revision in chapter 5, (70).

This entails that there are two ways of keeping PredP and activating it in the above context: by requiring VP+/VP splitting to be nonvacuous (94) or by revising the Hungarian Complexity Filter for the cases where VP+/VP splitting occurs ((70) in chapter 5). Informally, the two revisions amount to the following:

(98) Keep some phonetic material inside VP+ (= (94)).

(99) If VP splits out, the specifier of VP+ may be complex (= (70) in chapter 5).

As far as Hungarian is concerned, both requirements have independent support in the one other domain where VP+/VP splitting occurs, namely, in neutral sentences; therefore, we keep them both. In our view, the fact that the tensed portions of nonneutral English orders can be derived in two slightly different ways is not a problem.

4.7   VP+ Is Present in All Clauses

All the examples so far have involved verbs that have a VM (*szétszed* 'apart-take') or form a complex with the VP+ of their complement (i.e., auxiliaries). In these cases a designated category moves to [Spec, VP+]. What happens in the absence of such a designated category? Taxonomically, the following cases need to be considered:

(100) Plain VM-less verbs (e.g., *dolgoz-* 'work')

(101) Nonauxiliary infinitival-complement-taking verbs (e.g., *utál* 'hate')

The discussion below will focus on VM-less verbs embedded under some auxiliary (to be referred to as *the lowest infinitive*), but the conclusion to be reached in this section carries over to the same verbs in tensed clauses and to nonauxiliary infinitival complement takers.

The simple generalization is this:

(102) When the lowest infinitive has no VM, it behaves like a VM itself.

This can be made more precise as follows. In nonneutral sentences the VM-less lowest infinitive (here, *dolgozni* 'work-inf') may invert with its selector or occur in the English order.

(103) Nem fogok   akarni   kezdeni dolgozni.   (English)
       not   will-1sg want-inf begin-inf work-inf
       'I will not want to begin to work.'

(104) Nem fogok   akarni   dolgozni kezdeni.   (one inversion)
       not   will-1sg want-inf work-inf begin-inf
       'I will not want to begin to work.'

Inversion in (104) also feeds inversion in the next clause.

(105) Nem fogok   dolgozni kezdeni   akarni.   (two inversions)
       not   will-1sg work-inf begin-inf want-inf
       'I will not want to begin to work.'

In other words, in nonneutral sentences *dolgozni* 'work-inf' exhibits the same behavior as *szétszedni* 'apart-take-inf'. This is quite natural, but note that in accounting for the behavior of *szétszed*, we capitalized on the fact that it was dominated by VP+, with its VM in the specifier, as in (106).

(106)

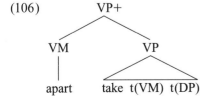

It is the presence of VP+ that enables *szétszed(ni)* to satisfy the selecting auxiliary (the auxiliary must form a complex with VP+). If *dolgozni* can do the same, it must also be dominated by VP+.

Neutral sentences corroborate this conclusion quite spectacularly. When the lowest infinitive has no VM, it climbs like a VM itself, with the same obligatory force. Compare:

(107) *Szét* fogom akarni   szedni   (a   rádiót).
   apart will-1sg want-inf take-inf (the radio-acc)
   'I will want to take apart the radio.'

(108) *Dolgozni* fogok   akarni.
   work-inf will-1sg want-inf
   'I will want to work.'

In (15) we anticipated the analysis of VM-climbing, to be fleshed out in section 5.2. The gist of the analysis is that VM does not climb on its own. Instead, VP+ forms a complex with the auxiliary, as in inverted sequences, but only after its VP is removed to InfP+ and CP (a case of VP+/VP splitting). Thus, only the VM is left inside VP+, as shown in (109).

(109)

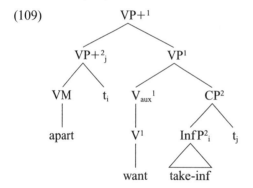

Given that in neutral sentences *dolgozni* 'work-inf' has the same distribution as *szét* 'apart', we must conclude that the derivation is essentially as follows. *Dolgozni* is dominated by VP+. VP+ moves to InfP+ to pick up its infinitival morphology. InfP+ moves to CP to assure the selector of the infinitival nature of the clause, and then it specifier-extracts from CP to form a complex with *akar* 'want'. The result is shown in (110).

(110)

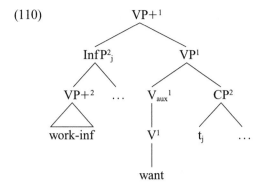

From here on, the derivations of the two neutral sentences proceed in the same way, with VP+/VP splitting at every level. This accounts for the fact that although the neutral and the nonneutral inverted derivations with *dolgozni* are identical up to the point just reviewed, they diverge immediately when VP^1 splits out of $VP+^1$. Relevant here is the observation that the parallelism supports the conclusion that *dolgoz-* 'work' is dominated by VP+.

We thus conclude that VP+ is universally present, whether or not the verb in VP has a VM. The Principle of Projection Activation requires, then, that either the head or the specifier of VP+ contain overt material at some point in the derivation. Thus, *dolgoz-* must raise to VP+ either by V-adjunction to V+ (111a) or by VP-movement to [Spec, VP+] (111b).

(111) a.   VP+   or   b.   VP+

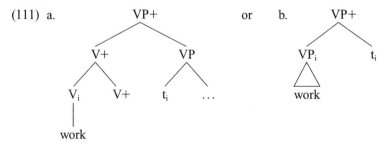

Note that the head movement analysis is legitimate, because VP+ has no overt specifier or head. The question is to what extent both analyses are compatible with the strict cycle when the verb has a dependent, as in (112).

(112) dolgozni a   cikken
      work-inf the paper-on
      'to work on the paper'

Dolgoz- 'work' moves to VP+ without its dependent. For the head movement analysis, this is entirely unproblematic. The VP-movement analysis presupposes that there are licensing or stacking positions for the verb's dependents between VP and VP+, as in (113). This is unproblematic for VM-less verbs.

(113)

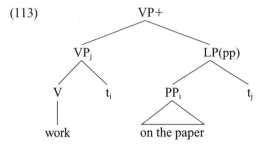

Does the same assumption cause trouble when the verb has a VM that moves to VP+? It may, if a dependent of V actually moves to LP(xp) between VP+ and VP, as shown in (114).

(114) ∗

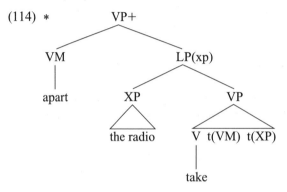

But this use of LP(xp) is never necessary. A V with a VM does not need to get rid of the dependent XP inside VP+; it can always wait for XP to move out after VP+ is merged and VM moves, the situation illustrated in (115).

(115)

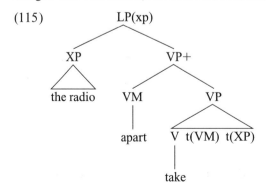

The illegitimate use of LP(xp) can be excluded in various ways. The most natural one is to say that it disrupts the relation between [Spec, VP+] and the head of VP. More mechanically, according to the "move one category at a time" convention, ⟨VP+, VP⟩ can move together but ⟨VP+, LP(xp)⟩ or ⟨VP+, LP(xp), VP⟩ cannot, and as a result (115) cannot do any harm even if it comes about. Alternatively, if this requirement were to be relaxed, movement to a stacking position could be made a last resort operation, to prevent idle movements that can only cause harm.

Given these considerations, we will opt for the VP-movement analysis (111b) for simplicity.

As mentioned at the outset, the conclusions we reached carry over to all verbs that lack a VM, that is, to *dolgoz-* 'work' in tensed clauses, as in (116a), and to non-auxiliary infinitival complement takers like *utál* 'hate', as in (116b).

(116) a.

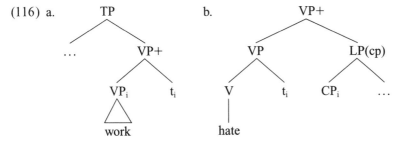

We note that the behavior of *dolgoz-* 'work' and *utál* 'hate' is otherwise not fully identical, an issue to be taken up in section 5.3; but the dissimilarity pertains to structure above VP+ and does not affect our present conclusion.

Chapter 5
Evidence from Related Constructions

5.1   Evidence for Constituent Structure: Scrambling and Focusing

The global structures of inverted and English orders compare as follows. In the structure of an inverted sequence, the VP+s are nested, as in (1).

(1)

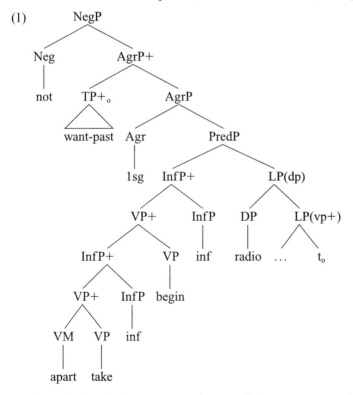

On the other hand, the structure of an English sequence contains a set of independent CPs, as shown in (2).

(2)

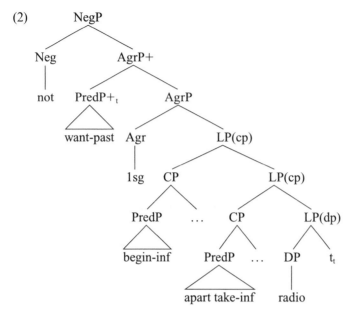

In this section we consider how scrambling and focusing provide supporting evidence for these structures.

5.1.1   Scrambling

First, recall the scrambling data introduced in chapter 3. Note that, in this context, *scrambling* means that matrix material can intervene between the individual infinitives in the English order but it cannot break units formed by inversion. (The relative order of the infinitives themselves is inviolable.) All the examples in (3) mean 'Mari will not begin to want to go in'.

(3) a. Nem fog (Mari) kezdeni   (Mari) akarni   (Mari) *be (*Mari) menni.*
        not   will (Mari) begin-inf (Mari) want-inf (Mari) in (*Mari) go-inf
              1   2   3   5   4
    b. Nem fog (Mari) kezdeni   (Mari) *be (*Mari) menni (*Mari) akarni.*
        not   will (Mari) begin-inf (Mari) in (*Mari) go-inf (*Mari) want-inf
              1   2   5   4   3
    c. Nem fog (Mari) *be (*Mari) menni (*Mari) akarni   (*Mari) kezdeni.*
        not   will (Mari) in (*Mari) go-inf (*Mari) want-inf (*Mari) begin-inf
              1   5   4   3   2

In this book we do not attempt to develop a theory of scrambling—we do not consider how scrambling is to be handled by a grammar where all movement is triggered by feature checking. We note, however, that the structures in (1) and (2) provide excellent input to any such theory. Because inverted sequences have a nested structure, we do not expect matrix material to be able to penetrate them. On the other hand, because English sequences contain a set of independent CPs, it is in principle possible for extraneous material to intervene between those CPs, as long as their relative order is preserved, in accordance with our convention.

Note, incidentally, that although the starred data are straightforwardly accounted for under a head movement theory of inversion, the acceptable scrambling data would be extremely difficult to account for. If the formation of verbal complexes is feature driven, then, when it does not happen overtly, it must take place in some covert manner. If LF movement creates verbal complexes when the surface order is English, it is entirely mysterious how extraneous material can intervene between the components. The only alternative is to check the relevant features in some syntactically quite unconstrained, and thus uninteresting, manner.

5.1.2 Focus

Let us now turn to contrastive focusing. In chapter 3 we reviewed data concerning the contrastive focusing of inverted sequences. At that point these data served to argue that every intermediate step of recursive inversion has XP status.

First, recall the observation ((30) in chapter 3, repeated here as (4)) that all inverted sequences containing a bare VM can be contrastively focused (4b–d), whereas no string with an internal English order can (4e).

(4) b.   BE MENNI fogok   kezdeni akarni. $[_{FP}$ 5 4] 1 2 3
         in go-inf will-1sg begin-inf want-inf
         'It is to go in that I will begin to want (I will not begin to want to cry, etc.).'

     c.   BE MENNI AKARNI fogok   kezdeni. $[_{FP}$ 5 4 3] 1 2
         in go-inf want-inf will-1sg begin-inf
         'It is to want to go in that I will begin (I will not begin to cry, etc.).'

     d.   BE MENNI AKARNI   KEZDENI fogok. $[_{FP}$ 5 4 3 2] 1
         in go-inf want-inf begin-inf will-1sg
         'It is to begin to want to go in that I will [do] (I will not cry, etc.).'

     e. *AKARNI   BE MENNI fogok   kezdeni.   *$[_{FP}$ 3 5 4] 1 2
         want-inf in go-inf will-1sg begin-inf

Add now that big VM + V sequences can also be focused.

(5) Csak A   VÁROSBAN MARADNI nem akartam   semmiképp.
    only the city-in   stay-inf   not wanted-1sg in any case
    'The only thing I did not want in any case was to stay in the city.'

The fact that *a városban maradni* 'the city-in stay-inf' can be focused indicates that a unit at least as big as PredP can occur in focus. The reason is that when VP+ contains a big VM, it inescapably pied-pipes PredP. (4d), where the whole inverted sequence is focused, points to the same conclusion: we see from (1) that the whole inverted sequence is under PredP in the tensed clause. Can InfP+ with VP+ in its specifier also be focused? The data in (4b) provide decisive evidence that it cannot. The auxiliaries intervening between FP and the source position of the focused phrase are invariably in the English order. (4b), repeated here, can only be interpreted as 'begin to want (to go in)' and never as 'want to begin (to go in)'. The latter interpretation would obtain if the pre-extraction structure were 1 5 4 3 2.

(4) b. BE MENNI fogok   kezdeni   akarni.
       in go-inf will-1sg begin-inf want-inf
       'It is to go in that I will begin to want (I will not begin to want to cry, etc.).'
       *'It is to go in that I will want to begin (I will not want to begin to cry, etc.).'

This indicates that *bemenni* 'in-go-inf' is focused qua PredP. Recall that English orders are due to pied-piping, and pied-piping is forced by the presence of PredP. (When the VM is small or the order in InfP+ is inverted, the pied-piping of PredP, and hence the switch to the English order, is optional.)

The fact that these PredPs are in turn dominated by CP raises the question whether it is perhaps CP that is focused. The following fact argues against this. We have seen that an infinitival clause may contain operator projections like FP, DistP, and RefP. If it does, the whole infinitival clause is pied-piped to VP+ of the selecting auxiliary and triggers the English order above it.[1]

(6) a. Nem fogok   akarni   [CP (mindig) csak Marival   beszélni].
         not will-1sg want-inf   always only Mari-with talk-inf
         'I will not want for it to be the case that I always talk only with Mari.'
    b. *Nem fogok   [InfP+ beszélni] akarni   (mindig) csak Marival.
         not will-1sg   talk-inf want-inf always only Mari-with
    c. *Nem fogok   [CP (mindig) csak Marival   beszélni] akarni.
         not will-1sg   always only Mari-with talk-inf   want-inf

We now note that such a CP cannot be focused in the tensed clause.

(7) *[FP[CP (MINDIG) CSAK MARIVAL   BESZÉLNI] fogok   akarni].
          always only Mari-with talk-inf   will-1sg want-inf

This indicates that CP cannot be focused; therefore, in the cases discussed above PredP is focused on its own. These data suggest the following generalization:

(8) In addition to the well-known focusable categories (DP, PP, etc.), PredP can be focused (but CP, LP(cp), InfP+, etc., cannot).

The observation that only PredP is a focusable category also explains why non-VM dependents of the focused verb cannot accompany it to focus: they will have moved to their own LP(xp) positions, all of which fall outside PredP.

Now, the diagram in (2) reveals that individual auxiliaries in the English infinitival sequence are also dominated by PredP. This predicts that they must also be focusable. This prediction is borne out. As was first observed in Szabolcsi 1996, individual auxiliaries in the English order can indeed be focused.

(9) KEZDENI$_i$ fogok   t$_i$ akarni   haza menni.
     begin-inf will-1sg   want-inf home go-inf
     'I will BEGIN to want to go home.'

(10) AKARNI$_i$ fogok   kezdeni t$_i$ haza menni.
     want-inf will-1sg begin-inf   home go-inf
     'I will begin to WANT to go home.'

More precisely, the highest infinitive can be focused either in an emphatic ("indeed") sense or contrastively, and the result sounds entirely natural. A lower infinitive can only be focused contrastively. This makes the focusing of a nonhighest auxiliary a more restricted option: being fairly contentless items, auxiliaries do not easily lend themselves to a contrastive interpretation, in arbitrary combinations. But genuinely ambiguous examples such as (11) can be constructed. (11a) represents the reading where *próbálni* 'try-inf' is the highest infinitive, and (11b) the reading where it is the second highest.

(11) Csak PRÓBÁLNI fogok   akarni   haza menni.
     only try-inf   will-1sg want-inf home go-inf
     a. 'I will only TRY to want to go home (but will not manage to want to go home).'
     b. 'I will want to only TRY to go home (but will not want to succeed in going home).'

On the other hand, the lowest verb (which is not an auxiliary) is not predicted to be focusable without its VM: it is never exclusively dominated by PredP. This is best checked with a prefix that is purely perfective (*haza* 'home' can be also be a directional adjunct if *menni* 'go-inf' is imperfective).

(12) *ENNI$_i$ fogom   akarni   meg t$_i$ a   kenyeret.
     eat-inf will-1sg want-inf perf   the bread-acc
     'I will want to EAT up the bread (and not cut it up).'

The focusing data provide striking support for some of our assumptions.

First, the fact that PredP turns out to be the category in terms of which focusability can be defined supports our assumption that PredP not only is present but in fact is the category whose presence is responsible for English orders in general.

Second, the fact that individual members of the English sequence can be focused provides independent support for the claim that the English order is not simply a base order (one unaffected by complex verb formation). If it were, there would be no reason to assume a structure in which the individual infinitives are exclusively dominated by a focusable category.

Third, the fact that individual members of the auxiliary sequence can be focused is one more strong argument for the XP-movement analysis of complex verb formation. If such sequences were formed by head movement, before or after Spell-Out, it would be impossible to extract a component from the middle of the complex head— impossible, that is, if the formation of complex heads is to be achieved by a reasonably restricted theory of head movement.

Having shown that the focusing data fully support the constituent structures our analysis assigns to inverted and English sequences, let us briefly consider how they are derived.

We propose to analyze the contrastive focusing of PredPs (whether they dominate inverted sequences or individual auxiliaries) by successive-cyclic movement.

Consider first (4d), repeated here, where the entire infinitival sequence is focused.

(4) d. BE MENNI AKARNI KEZDENI fogok.   [FP 5 4 3 2] 1
        in go-inf want-inf begin-inf will-1sg
        'It is to begin to want to go in that I will [do] (I will not cry, etc.).'

As (1) shows, this sequence is dominated by the PredP of the tensed clause. PredP extracts to FP without a problem.

More interesting is the derivation of cases where less than the full infinitival sequence is focused—for example, (4c), repeated here.

(4) c. BE MENNI AKARNI fogok   kezdeni.   [FP 5 4 3] 1 2
        in go-inf want-inf will-1sg begin-inf
        'It is to want to go in that I will begin (I will not begin to cry, etc.).'

The VP+ dominating 5 4 3 needs to satisfy V2 on the one hand and move to FP on the other. According to the practice we have followed so far, the two tasks seem incompatible: auxiliaries are satisfied by VP+ (InfP+) or CP, but what is focused is PredP. This might seem to force VP+, dominated by PredP, to pied-pipe CP to VP+2 and to extract PredP from there—which is impossible, however, because it is buried low down in the specifier.

In fact, the impasse is only apparent, as pointed out in section 4.4. Any category pied-piped by VP+ may satisfy the auxiliary, and the Hungarian Complexity Filter requires only that if this category is more complex than InfP+, it move on. In the cases discussed so far, only CP was able to move on—to LP(cp). But in the present case PredP can move on. It must move on, too, because it has a [focus] feature to check in FP. Thus, the PredP dominating *bemenni akarni* 'in-go-inf want inf' can extract from the specifier of its own CP and satisfy the auxiliary *kezd* 'begin' without pied-piping CP.

What ensures that the auxiliaries not affected by focusing line up in the English order? The presence of PredP. In (66) of chapter 4, we assumed that whenever VP+ has either CP or PredP in its specifier, as in (13), its InfP+ cannot extract from PredP.

(13)

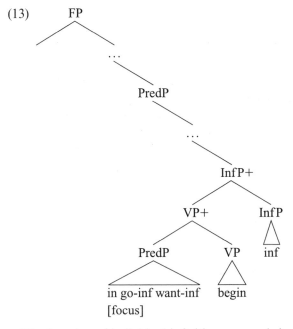

The focusing of individual infinitives proceeds in an entirely analogous fashion.

There is one aspect of the data that our proposal does not capture: the fact that the highest infinitive can be focused either emphatically or contrastively, whereas the others can only be focused contrastively (see the discussion of (9)–(11)). Brody (1997, sec. 4.3, 2000) makes crucial use of this datum in arguing for an alternative approach to inverted orders. Within the framework of Mirror Theory, Brody proposes that inverted sequences form morphological words: entities involving strictly local, head chain–type relations. Brody proposes that contrastive (or exhaustive) focusing is always phrasal, but emphatic focusing is not. In the case of emphatic focusing, the focus-marked category is a lexical/morphological specifier of (the specifier of ...) the F (focus) head. That is, underlying the emphatic interpretation of (9), a morphological word "kezde → ni → fog → ok → F" is formed. If head chains are local and there is no excorporation, then the fact that only the highest infinitive can be focused emphatically follows in Mirror Theory. No such prediction concerning locality can be made if inversion is invariably phrasal movement.

Brody (1997, 2000) does not explicitly define the notion "word." However, it seems to us that the above analysis of emphatic focus will encounter the same problem that we mentioned in section 2.2 in connection with V-to-F movement: namely, emphatic *is* 'indeed, lit. too', which can intervene between a contrastively focused phrase and the finite verb, can equally naturally intervene between an emphatically focused infinitive and the finite verb.

(14) Ha azt   ígértem,   hogy 6-kor már   kezdeni fogok   dolgozni, akkor kezdeni is   fogok.
     if   it-acc promised-1sg that 6-at already begin-inf will-1sg work-inf then   begin-inf too will-1sg
     'If I promised that at 6, I will already begin to work, then I'll begin to, too.'

On Koopman's (1994, 1995b) interpretation of the locality of head movement, the intervention of this particle, which heads an independent projection, indicates that the relation of *kezdeni* 'begin-inf' to *fogok* 'will-1sg' is not local, and that emphatic focusing in general is therefore not contingent on strict locality. If so, the distribution of emphatic and contrastive foci remains unexplained; but in any event it does not constitute an uncontroversial argument in favor of invoking head chain–type relations in the analysis of inversion.

5.2   VM-Climbing in Neutral Sentences

5.2.1   The Basic Idea

As mentioned at the outset, there are two types of Hungarian sentences: neutral and nonneutral. Nonneutral sentences contain at least one FP or NegP; neutral sentences contain none (although they may contain RefP and DistP). The most striking difference between the two types is that in neutral sentences the VM of the finite verb—or, in case the finite verb is an auxiliary, the VM of its infinitival complement—*must* immediately precede the finite verb. This is the process that we called VM-climbing.

(15) Be mentem.   2 1
      in went-1sg
      'I went in.'

(16) Be fogok   akarni   menni.   4 1 2 3
      in will-1sg want-inf go-inf
      'I will want to go in.'

It is natural to assume that VM-climbing targets an Ā-position that is in complementary distribution with FP and NegP (see (17)).[2] We will call this position *NeutP*.

(17) a.

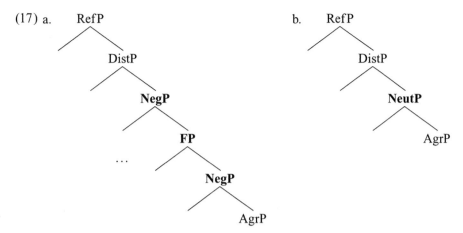

One difference is that whereas NegP and FP occur in finite as well as infinitival clauses, NeutP occurs only in finite ones (recall the discussion in section 2.3). Formally, this can be ensured by requiring that NeutP be related to tense, but at this point we have no substantial suggestion about why this is so. In section 5.2.4, however, we return to the issue of how to represent this requirement.[3]

Our task is to develop a unified account of neutral and nonneutral sentences. This is necessary because essentially the same set of auxiliaries that participate in inversion allow VM-climbing (in fact, Kálmán et al. (1989) identify the set of auxiliaries on the basis of climbing data; they never discuss inversion).

(18) In climbing structures only auxiliaries can intervene between the surface position (NeutP) and the source position of the VM. Nonauxiliaries block VM-climbing from their CP complement.

To account for inversion, we have assumed that auxiliaries require a VP+ (or a category pied-piped by VP+) in their [Spec, VP+]. Since this is a lexical requirement, it must be satisfied by all occurrences of the auxiliary. The discussion of English orders above has shown that it is both possible and rewarding to assume that it is indeed satisfied, regardless of whether or not complex verb formation is visible to the naked eye. Therefore, the analysis of neutral sentences that we propose below consists of (1) everything that we have said and will say about auxiliaries, nonauxiliaries, and other beasts in the course of accounting for nonneutral orders, (2) the assumption that NeutP exists and the requirement that it be filled appropriately (see (19)), and (3) one stipulation about VPs in the domain of NeutP (see (25)). In other words, the analysis of neutral sentences differs from that of nonneutral sentences as little as possible.

The proposal is as follows. Since auxiliaries need VP+, a complex is formed at the level of every clause, just as above. The VM that climbs is located in [*Spec, VP+].

Since climbing targets NeutP, neutral sentences involve an extra final step: the VP+ that satisfies the tensed auxiliary moves to NeutP. This boils down to the following statement:

(19) NeutP is licensed by a VP+ that has overt material in its specifier.

But as things stand, this VP+ contains as many remnant VPs (verbs) as were satisfied by VP+, whereas we know that the only overt material that shows up in NeutP is the VM. It is worth contrasting neutral (climbing) data with focusing data such as (20) (= (4b)).

(20) BE MENNI fogok   kezdeni akarni.   (focusing)
     in go-inf will-1sg begin-inf want-inf   5 4 1 2 3
     'It is to go in that I will begin to want (I will not begin to want to cry, etc.).'

(21) *Be* fogok   kezdeni akarni   menni.   (climbing in neutral)
     in will-1sg begin-inf want-inf go-inf   5 1 2 3 4
     'I will begin to want to go in.'

(22) **Be menni* fogok   kezdeni akarni.   (climbing in neutral)
     in go-inf will-1sg begin-inf want-inf   5 4 1 2 3

The apparently conflicting requirements that VP+ move but only VM end up high can be reconciled by assuming that in neutral sentences VP is ousted from VP+ at every level. That is, the structure of NeutP is not (23a), but at least as big as (23b).

(23) a.   * NeutP   b.   NeutP

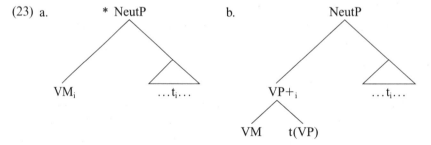

Any inverted sequence can be focused, because the nested VP+s that are carried up all contain their VPs; but only the lowest element climbs, because the nested VP+s that are carried up all lose their VPs along the way. Specifically, the structure of (16) will be roughly as shown in (24) (see section 5.2.4 for a modification).

(24)

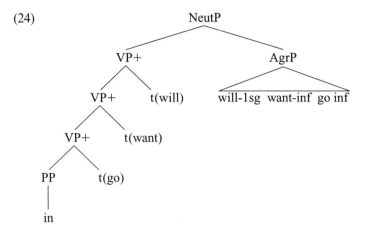

Why is VP ousted from VP+ in neutral sentences? To date we have no specific explanation. Recall, however, that in section 4.1 we pointed out that one crucial parameter responsible for ordering differences between languages and between constructions in the same language is the presence or absence of VP+/VP splitting. VP+/VP splitting occurs quite generally in Dutch, and it occurs in tensed clauses in German. For Hungarian we have already appealed to VP+/VP splitting in nonneutral tensed clauses. We are suggesting that the fact that VP leaves VP+ in infinitival clauses in Hungarian neutral sentences is essentially an instance of VP+/VP splitting.

(25) *The VP Condition in Neutral Clauses* (to be refined in section 6.2)
Within the domain of NeutP, VP splits out of VP+.
The domain of NeutP is its c-command domain, minus the clauses *below* the first nonauxiliary infinitival complement taker.[4]

Where does VP go? Recall that in nonneutral tensed clauses VP splits out of VP+ and moves to TP+. In the same spirit, in infinitival clauses VP splits out of VP+ and moves to InfP+. InfP+ subsequently moves to CP, as usual. That is, a CP complement in the domain of NeutP has the structure shown in (26).

(26)

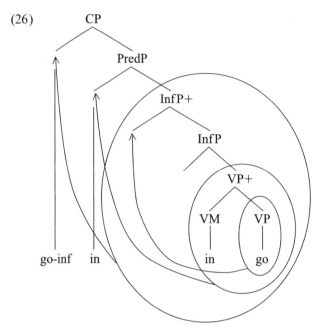

The VP Condition in Neutral Clauses works well when the lowest infinitive has a VM but, understood in an unqualified manner, it wreaks havoc when that verb is VM-less (e.g., *dolgoz-* 'work'). In section 4.7 we argued that VP+ is present in every clause, and when no VM or infinitival VP+ moves into it, it is activated by its complement VP itself. One (but not the only) argument in favor of this analysis was that when the lowest infinitive is VM-less, it climbs like a VM.

(27) Dolgozni fogok   akarni.
     work-inf will-1sg work-inf
     'I will want to work.'

But if VP splits out of VP+ (either from its original complement position or transiting through [Spec, VP+]), the above analysis cannot extend to this piece of data: *dolgozni* is not carried up. In fact, in chapter 8 we will show that Dutch and Hungarian differ precisely on this count: VMs climb in both languages, but the lowest infinitive climbs only in Hungarian. In fact, we already have the requisite modification of VP+/VP splitting at our disposal. In the course of presenting a sample derivation for the nonneutral English order, we proposed the following qualification:

(28) *Nonvacuous VP+/VP splitting* ((94) of chapter 4)
     In Hungarian VP+/VP splitting applies only when [Spec, VP+] is filled (with material distinct from VP) at the relevant stage of the derivation. Otherwise, VP stays inside VP+ and VP+ moves.

If the VP Condition in Neutral Clauses is subject to the same nonvacuity constraint (which is the null hypothesis), the VP dominating a VM-less verb does not split out of VP+ and thus is carried up to NeutP, as desired.

There is one striking fact about climbing that we have not commented on yet: the auxiliaries intervening between NeutP and the base position of the climber are invariably lined up in the English order.[5]

(21) a. *Be* fogok   kezdeni   akarni   menni.   (climbing)
          in will-1sg begin-inf want-inf go-inf   5 1 2 3 4
          'I will begin to want to go in.'

      b. *Be* fogok   kezdeni   menni akarni.   (climbing)
          in will-1sg begin-inf go-inf want-inf   5 1 2 4 3

      c. *Be* fogok   menni akarni   kezdeni.   (climbing)
          in will-1sg go-inf want-inf begin-inf   5 1 4 3 2

In the domains of data considered so far, English orders were always a result of the fact that the specifier of PredP does not extract but instead pied-pipes PredP to CP. As the sample derivation in section 5.2.4 will show, this is not necessary in neutral sentences: because VP moves to InfP+ and then to CP, the infinitival verb will be clause-initial anyway. At first blush this observation might raise the following question. Is it necessary to assume CP pied-piping at all? Could we not account for all English orders by VP+/VP splitting, that is, by having VP move to InfP+ and CP? The answer is that CP pied-piping cannot be eliminated. Recall that the crucial difference between neutral and nonneutral clauses that both have English orders is that the lowest VM is carried up to the tensed level in the former but stays glued to its selector in the latter. The two cannot be collapsed.

5.2.2 Remnant Movement versus Long Head Movement

At this point it is useful to contrast our remnant movement analysis with the standardly pursued analysis for this type of phenomenon. Infinitival VM climbing in Hungarian and in other languages has typically been analyzed in terms of long head movement (Rivero 1994, Roberts 1994, 1997) and not in terms of restructuring. Long head movement analyses take the weak phonological property of tensed auxiliaries as central: tensed auxiliaries are clitics, which must be preceded by a stress-bearing element. In contexts where this condition is not met, a head is attracted to precede the finite auxiliary. Defining the contexts is not an easy task. Some contexts provide an appropriate constituent for the tensed auxiliary—in Hungarian, a focused phrase or negation. Other contexts, such as focus on the tensed auxiliary, override the cliticlike property of auxiliaries. Still other contexts, like DistP or RefP, do not provide an appropriate context for finite auxiliaries, even if they precede the tensed auxiliary. In these cases, as well as in cases where no constituent precedes at all, a VM undergoes movement to provide a host for the clitic.

If the VM is an infinitive, this type of movement is generally argued to be a species of head movement, because dependents are not carried along. More specifically, it is argued to be a special brand of movement, long head movement, because it skips (certain) intervening heads. In such analyses long-moved heads are in complementary distribution with phrases. Long head movement is generally argued to be blocked by an intervening negation. The long head movement account encounters numerous problems. A particularly difficult one is this: given the altruistic motivation for long head movement, why is it not the structurally closest head that procliticizes (*$begin$-inf_i want-1sg t_i swim-inf)? How are we to account for the fact that it is a very specific element that moves, and that this is not the most local one?

Our remnant movement and restructuring analysis accounts for these features quite straightforwardly and parsimoniously. That tensed auxiliaries are preceded by a VM is a property of certain clause types (neutral clauses—i.e., ones without focus or negation), not of tensed auxiliaries: neutral tensed clauses require a particular type of constituent (VP+) in [Spec, NeutP]. This is a phrasal constituent, not a head: infinitival VMs are in complementary distribution with all other VMs and hence are not moved heads but remnant VPs. This phrasal constituent receives main sentence stress. This is in line with Cinque's (1993) proposal, according to which the most deeply embedded constituent in VP is assigned main stress: as inspection of our structures shows, the most deeply embedded constituent that is capable of bearing stress (i.e., that is overt) is [Spec, VP+]. Tensed auxiliaries end up in the projection below NeutP, in AgrP+, because that is where tensed verbs are pronounced. If this is a configuration to which no stress is assigned, then tensed auxiliaries are phonologically weak because of their syntactic position, not because of an inherent phonological property. Contexts with or without VM-climbing are defined in terms of clause type, not in terms of phonology: the only context in which VM-climbing is required appeals to an independently necessary characterization of neutral sentences. Negation blocks VM-climbing for two reasons. First, in clauses with NegP there is no NeutP, and second, there is no (small) VM-climbing (phrasal) movement out of negative infinitivals or subjunctives (i.e., this is not a problem that bears on the mechanics of head movement). Tensed auxiliaries cannot start neutral clauses, not because they are clitics, but because they cannot appear in NeutP. Since they are VPs that must combine with another VM in their VP+, they are simply never able to occur in [Spec, VP+]. Finally, our proposal accounts directly for the fact that it is the closest VP+ with overt material in VP+ that raises to NeutP: none of the intermediate auxiliaries yield configurations that would satisfy NeutP, and all of the intermediate auxiliaries allow VP+ to be passed up in the tree to finally reach NeutP.

5.2.3   Across-the-Board Climbing and TP in NeutP

Earlier analyses of climbing (É. Kiss 1987, Szabolcsi 1996, Brody 1997, 2000)
assumed that the lowest VM moves qua PP to some specifier position in the tensed
clause. As É. Kiss (1998a,b) points out, such an analysis would predict that the following across-the-board (ATB) extraction is grammatical:

(29) *[Be$_i$ [fogok   t$_i$ menni és   akarom t$_i$ vinni   a   könyvet]].
       in   will-1sg go-inf and want-1sg take-inf the book-acc
       'I will go, and want to take the book, inside.'

The fact that (29)—or indeed any example of this format—is sharply ungrammatical
leads É. Kiss to conclude that in neutral sentences the fronted VM actually forms a
constituent with the finite verb (*be fogok*) to the exclusion of the rest of the sentence.
Since É. Kiss proposes to analyze climbing as head movement, this constituent is a
complex head (Y), as shown in (30).

(30)

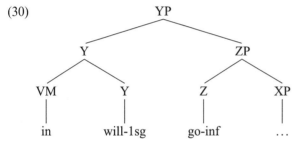

This excludes (29) because the fronted VM is too low to c-command its traces.

   Our current proposal also predicts (29) to be grammatical. A VP+ dominating the
VM and a series of VP traces reaches the tensed clause in both conjuncts; the AgrP+s
are conjoined, and VP+ extracts to NeutP from both (or, following Munn (1993), an
analysis to the same effect can be devised using an empty operator in the second
conjunct). In fact, in Koopman and Szabolcsi 1999 we suggested that remnant
movement itself excluded (29). The idea was that for ATB climbing to be possible,
each VP trace in the fronted remnant VP+ should be linked to two antecedents (two
different verbs in the two conjuncts). As Bob Frank (personal communication) has
pointed out, however, the same reasoning would exclude standard "nonconstituent
conjunction" cases like (31). The reason is that *beszélni* 'talk-inf' is an infinitival VP+
that contains the trace(s) of VP-internal arguments.

(31) a. Beszélni fogok   Marival   a   könyvről   és   Katival   a   filmről.
         talk-inf will-1sg Mari-with the book-about and Kati-with the film-about
         'I will talk with Mari about the book and with Kati about the film.'
      b. Beszélni akarok   Marival   a   piacon   és   Katival   az   iskolában.
         talk-inf want-1sg Mari-with the market-at and Kati-with the school-in
         'I want to talk with Mari at the market and with Kati at school.'

The grammaticality of (31a) contrasts with the ungrammaticality of (32).

(32) *Beszélni fogok Marival a könyvről és *akarok* Katival a filmről.
     talk-inf will-1sg Mari-with the book-about and want-1sg Kati-with the film-about

This contrast indicates that the problem with (29) and (32) is caused not by improper trace binding but by something else.[6] We contend that É. Kiss (1998a,b) is probably correct in attributing the ungrammaticality of (29) to constituent structure. We insert the qualification *probably* because although ATB climbing out of conjunctions is indeed robustly ungrammatical, certain comparable disjunctions are perfect. (É. Kiss (personal communication) shares this judgment.) Consider, for example, the ATB extraction of the VM *át* 'over' (cf. *átjavít* 'over-correct', *átfest* 'over-paint').

(33) Ha át   akarsz   javítani   vagy festeni   egy szót   (ott az asztalom).
     if over want-2sg correct-inf or   paint-inf a   word-acc (there's my desk)
     'If you want to correct over or paint over a word = if you want to change a word by writing over it or by using correcting fluid . . .'

For the time being we put the problem of disjunctions aside and make a tentative proposal to replicate É. Kiss's insight.

    Within the framework of our own remnant movement analysis, we may take the ungrammaticality of (29) and (32) to indicate that the node that moves to NeutP is not just VP+ (or PredP). Instead, the last VP+/VP splitting does not take place and TP+ (or perhaps the whole of AgrP+) is pied-piped to NeutP. In other words, the structure is roughly as shown in (34).

(34)

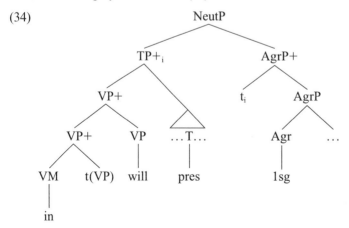

This structure will prevent *be* 'in' from binding a trace in the second conjunct in essentially the same way as É. Kiss's head adjunction structure does: *be* ends up forming a constituent with the tensed verb in NeutP.

Note, by the way, that the following, nonneutral example is equally impossible: *be* cannot be interpreted as the VM of both verbs:

(35) Nem mentem be és vittem   a   könyvet.
     not   went-1sg in and took-1sg the book-acc
     *'I didn't go inside and take the book inside.'

However, this already follows from the analysis we have proposed. The only point in the derivation where *be* moves is when it leaves its base-generated position and raises to [Spec, VP+]. Thus, short of direct V-conjunction (which is excluded by (among other things) the fact that each of the two verbs bears its own inflectional morpheme), there is no chance for *be* to move across the board.

Returning to the main issue of this section, what might be the reason for pied-piping TP+? Recall that, according to Kenesei's (1989) observation discussed in section 2.3, climbing cannot stop lower than the tensed clause. In the ungrammatical (36) *be* 'in' is separated from its verb *menni* 'go-inf'—evidence that the phenomenon must be climbing, as opposed to inversion. But *be* stops in the infinitival clause with *akarni* 'want-inf'.

(36) *Nem fogok   be akarni   menni.
     not   will-1sg in want-inf go-inf
     'I will not want to go in.'

We do not know the deeper reason why VMs in climbing structures are inescapably headed for the tensed clause. We can, however, represent this requirement in our grammar, by assuming that NeutP requires both VP+ with overt material and TP within its specifier. The only way to satisfy this dual requirement is for VP+ to occur in [Spec, TP+] and pied-pipe TP+ to NeutP.

Besides adding the requirement that NeutP must have a [tense] feature in its specifier, the creation of (34) requires an optimality-style modification of our grammar.

(37) VP+/VP splitting occurs only if it does not prevent the satisfaction of some absolute requirement (e.g., that TP occur in [Spec, NeutP]).

This will have the effect that VP+/VP splitting occurs only within the infinitival clauses in the domain of NeutP.

The assumption that TP+ is pied-piped to NeutP is independently needed in at least one case that we will discuss in some detail in section 5.2.4. Consider (38).

(38) Dolgoztam a   cikken.
     worked-1sg the paper-on
     'I worked on the paper.'

This is a neutral sentence, and nothing but the tensed verb can occur in NeutP. As we will spell out in section 5.2.4, the structure of its TP+ is as shown in (39).

(39)

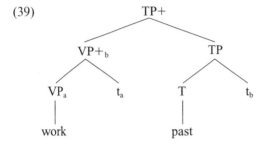

Since TP+ must move on to pick up agreement morphology, VP+ will end up in the specifier of a specifier; that is, it will not be able to extract to NeutP on its own. The only option is for it to pied-pipe TP+ or AgrP+ to NeutP.

Taken together, these considerations suggest that the tensed verb is always part of the category that lands in [Spec, NeutP].

5.2.4   Climbing: Some Sample Derivations

In this section we demonstrate a climbing derivation. (We simplify the task by choosing a verb that has no dependent apart from its VM.)

(40) Be fogok   kezdeni   akarni   menni.
      in will-1sg begin-inf want-inf go-inf
      'I will begin to want to go in.'

For transparency, we will keep track of the traces of VPs throughout the derivation.
  The VM checks a lexical feature in VP+ (41).

(41)

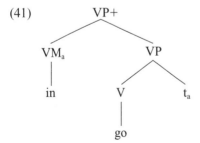

In view of (25), VP splits out of VP+ and moves to InfP+, as shown in (42). If splitting did not take place, the derivation would crash when NeutP is introduced on top of the domain.

(42)

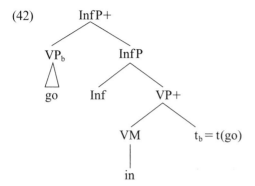

As shown in (43) and (44), VP+ moves to PredP and InfP+ to CP.

(43)

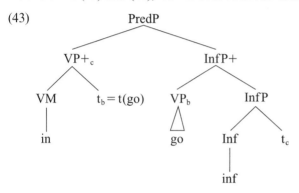

(44)

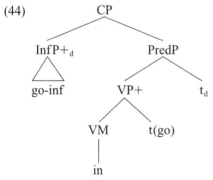

The auxiliary 'want' is merged. To form a complex, VP+ extracts from PredP to the VP+ of 'want', as shown in (45), and we assume, as earlier, that a PredP whose complement and specifier are both removed remains dangling from CP and does not hinder the movement of CP in view of the "move one category at a time" convention.

(45)

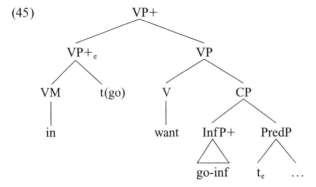

It is already clear that, because VP+ is a remnant, only its VM is visibly carried up. Now CP is licensed in LP(cp), as in (46).

(46)

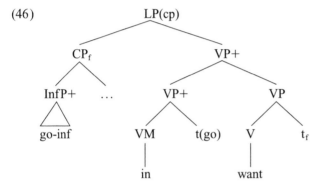

As shown in (47), VP splits out of VP+ and picks up the infinitival suffix.

(47)

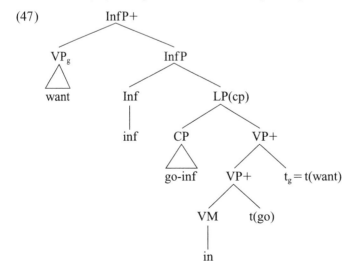

VP+ moves to PredP and LP(cp) is pushed up (48); InfP+ moves to CP (49).

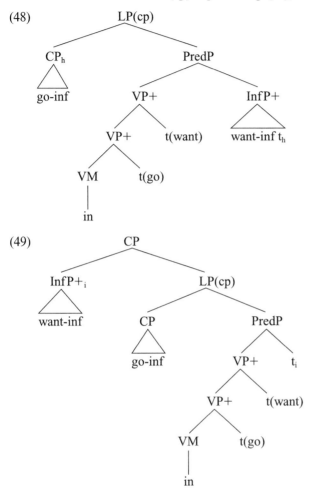

(48)

(49)

The auxiliary 'begin' is merged and the maximal VP+ in [Spec, PredP] extracts to its VP+. As shown in (50), this VP+ now carries the traces of two VPs.

(50)

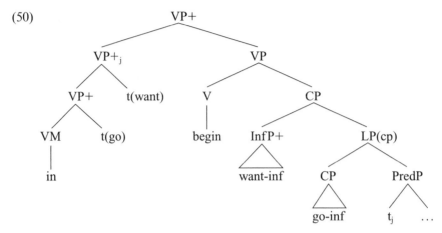

By now it is clear how the mechanism works, both in terms of VP+ carrying up nothing but the VM and in terms of the auxiliaries lining up in the English order. To save space, we skip writing out the following steps: LP(cp) 'go-inf' is pushed up, CP 'want-inf' moves to LP(cp) to get licensed, VP 'begin' moves to InfP+ to pick up infinitival morphology, VP+ moves to PredP, the two LP(cp)s are pushed up, InfP+ 'begin-inf' moves to CP, the auxiliary 'will' is merged, and VP+ 'in' extracts to its VP+. The result is shown in (51).

(51)

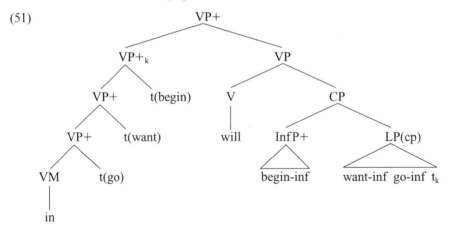

Now the members of the sequence 'want-inf go-inf' are pushed up and the CP 'begin-inf' moves to LP(cp) to get licensed. As discussed in section 5.2.3, in the tensed clause the VP 'will' does not split out of VP+, because that would make it impossible for both VP+ and TP to occur in NeutP. As shown in (52), a VP+ that now dominates the material 'in will' moves to TP+.

(52)

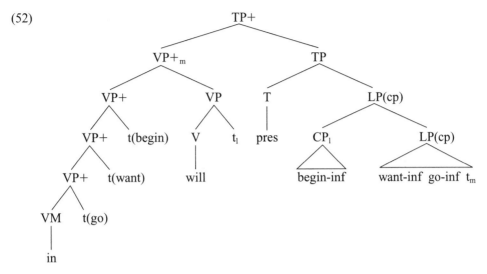

PredP is merged, and VP+ pied-pipes TP+ to PredP to get licensed. AgrP is merged, and TP+ moves to AgrP+ to pick up agreement morphology. Finally, NeutP is merged, and at least TP+ moves to [Spec, NeutP]. This movement satisfies two requirements: VP+ with overt material licenses NeutP, and TP occurs in NeutP. At each step the LP(cp)s are pushed up. The simplest end result is shown in (53).

(53)

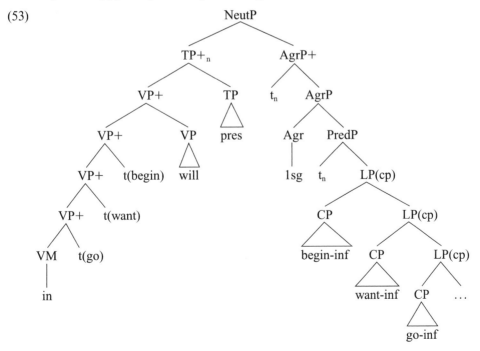

Let us now consider two further relevant cases. When the lowest infinitive has no VM, it climbs.

(54) Dolgozni fogok   akarni.
     work-inf will-1sg want-inf
     'I will want to work.'

We have already assumed that in the absence of a VM, VP activates VP+. Since VP+/VP splitting needs to be nonvacuous, VP does not extract from [Spec, VP+]. The fact that VP constitutes the specifier of VP+ explains the ability of the lowest (VM-less) infinitive to climb. The first steps create the structure shown in (55).

(55)

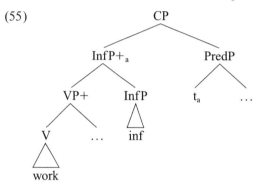

Here VP+ pied-pipes InfP+ to the VP+ of 'want', and from there on the derivation proceeds as above: the VP dominating 'want' splits out of VP+, and so on.
   Consider, finally, the case where the licenser of NeutP is the finite verb.

(56) Dolgoztam a   cikken.
     worked-1sg the paper-on
     'I worked on the paper.'

Up to a certain point, shown in (57), the derivation is uncontroversial.

(57)

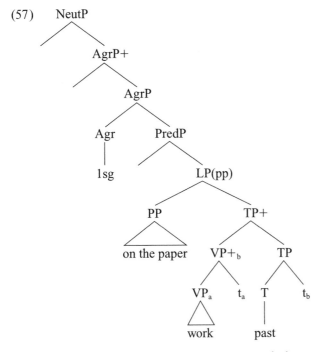

Now TP+ must pick up its agreement morphology, which is standardly done in AgrP+. VP+, on the other hand, must license NeutP. There are several possible scenarios. One is that after making a stop in PredP, TP+ moves to AgrP+. Since VP+ cannot extract to NeutP (it is part of a specifier), it may pied-pipe TP+ to NeutP+. TP+ and Agr do not become separated, although their direct constituency is broken. Another possibility is to omit the AgrP+ level and move TP+ to NeutP directly. Notice that we only postulated AgrP+ to avoid a violation of the Doubly Filled Comp Filter. Since we do not assume that all the components of a word must occur within a single phrase, TP+ in [Spec, NeutP] and AgrP may well form a word. Finally, even AgrP+ might pied-pipe to NeutP (after LP(pp) is pushed up). In this book we do not need to choose between these analyses.

On the other hand, it is interesting to note that this example would be problematic if we assumed that the verb picks up its suffixes in a series of head movements. Suppose V-to-T and V + T-to-Agr movement were to take place. The activation of NeutP with overt material and the licensing of NeutP with VP+ would then have to be separated. We might posit V + T + Agr-to-Neut movement to activate NeutP and relax (19) to say that even a phonetically empty VP+ may license NeutP that is independently activated. This alternative seems less attractive. In this sense, the properties of this construction support the assumption that not only complex verb formation but also the picking up of suffixes is executed by phrasal movement.

5.3   Nonauxiliary Infinitival Complement Takers

Having seen how auxiliaries participate in the formation of verbal complexes, let us turn to those verbs that take infinitival complements but are not auxiliaries. (Note that our label *nonauxiliary* does not cover verbs like *dolgoz-* 'work' that do not take infinitival complements, although they are obviously not auxiliaries.)

(58) *Nonauxiliary infinitival complement takers* (an open class of subject control verbs that carry main accent in neutral sentences)
elfelejt 'away-forget = forget', elkezd 'away-begin = begin', megpróbál 'perf-try = try', fél 'is afraid', habozik 'hesitate', szégyell 'is ashamed', utál 'hate', szeret 'like', imád 'love', siet 'hasten', and so on

Two representative members of this class are prefixless *utál* 'hate' and prefixed *elkezd* 'away-begin' (where *el* functions as a perfective, not a directional, prefix). A verb of the latter type is always the prefixed counterpart of some auxiliary (but not all auxiliaries have prefixed counterparts: de-auxiliarization is not a productive process).

The two properties that qualify these verbs as nonauxiliaries are illustrated in (59) and (60). First, a nonauxiliary does not allow the VP+ of its complement to invert. The *543 pattern is ungrammatical.

(59) a. utálni   be menni   *be menni utálni
         hate-inf in go-inf   in go-inf hate-inf
         'to hate to go in'
     b. el   kezdeni be menni   *be menni el   kezdeni
         perf begin-inf in go-inf   in go-inf perf begin-inf
         'to begin to go in'

Second, in neutral sentences a nonauxiliary blocks the climbing of a lower VM; instead, it (or its prefix) climbs. The pattern is 2143.

(60) a. *Be fogok   utálni   menni.   Utálni fogok   be menni.
         in will-1sg hate-inf go-inf   hate-inf will-1sg in go-inf
         'I will hate to go in.'
     b. *Be fogok   el   kezdeni menni.   El   fogok   kezdeni   be menni.
         in will-1sg perf begin-inf go-inf perf will-1sg begin-inf in go-inf
         'I will begin to go in.'

Given the null hypothesis of our system, these fundamental properties are easily accounted for. Let us assume that nonauxiliary infinitival complement takers differ minimally from auxiliaries in that they do not form a complex with the VP+ of their complement, because they lack the pertinent lexical requirement. In the case of *elkezd* 'perf-begin', the reason is, simply, that *kezd* has its own particle *el* in the specifier of its VP+. In the case of VM-less *utál* 'hate', VP activates VP+. In other words, we are assuming that the behavior of *elkezd* 'perf-begin' is entirely analogous to that of *szétszed* 'apart-take', and the behavior of *utál* 'hate' is entirely analogous to that of *dolgoz-* 'work'. Both *elkezd* and *utál* block inversion and climbing, because these processes involve attraction of the complement VP+ to the VP+ of the selecting verb, and both *elkezd* and *utál* lack the relevant lexical property on the one hand and have an independently filled [Spec, VP+] on the other. Furthermore, the prefix of *elkezdeni* climbs exactly like that of *szétszedni*, and VM-less *utálni* climbs exactly like VM-less *dolgozni*.[7]

In other words, the null hypothesis goes a long way in explaining the properties of nonauxiliaries. But it does not go all the way. There is a third property of nonauxiliaries that is not shared by plain verbs that do not take infinitival complements: namely, that a nonauxiliary does not invert with the selecting auxiliary. The *3254 pattern is ungrammatical.

(61) a. akarni   utálni   be menni   *utálni$_i$ akarni   t$_i$ be menni
         want-inf hate-inf in go-inf   hate-inf want-inf   in go-inf
         'to want to hate to go in'

     b. akarni   el   kezdeni   be menni   *el   kezdeni$_i$ akarni   t$_i$ be menni
         want-inf perf begin-inf in go-inf   perf begin-inf want-inf   in go-inf
         'to want to begin to go in'

This is clearly a difference: both *dolgozni* 'work-inf' and *szétszedni* 'apart-take-inf' can invert with the auxiliary that selects them. Likewise, when *utálni* 'hate-inf' selects a DP, not a CP, it behaves like *dolgozni* 'work-inf', not like the nonauxiliary *utálni*. Thus, resisting inversion is a property of nonauxiliary infinitival complement takers, not of particular lexical items.

This combination of properties is puzzling. If inversion and climbing are essentially the same process, how can *utálni* climb but not invert? Recall that for *dolgozni*, the derivations of the inverted order and the climbing order start out alike, as shown in (62).

(62)

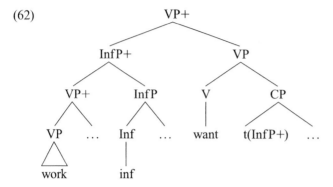

It is only after this point that the two derivations begin to diverge: in the inversion structure the VP+ 'work-inf want' as a whole moves to InfP+, whereas in the climbing structure the VP 'want' splits out and moves to InfP+ on its own. But at this very level there is no tangible difference between 'work-inf' and 'hate-inf'. Therefore, if the derivation involving 'hate-inf' gets this far, there is no way for it not to invert.

Thus, the contradictory properties of 'hate-inf' appear to defy our most basic assumptions. Instead of despairing, however, we may observe that there is another class of expressions that exhibits exactly the same properties: big VMs.

We know that big VMs climb just as small VMs do.

(63) Ostobának fogok   bizonyulni.
       stupid-dat will-1sg prove-inf
       'I will prove to be stupid.'

On the other hand, although big VMs invert with their own selector, they bleed the inversion of the VP+ so obtained in the next clause up.

(64) *Nem fogok   [ostobának bizonyulni] akarni.
        not   will-1sg stupid-dat prove-inf   want-inf
        'I will not want to prove to be stupid.'

This is exactly the property that *utál* 'hate' has. Both the big VM and the remnant VP dominating *utál* move to the specifier of the VP+ within their own clause, but the VP+ so obtained does not escape from that clause to form a complex with the selecting auxiliary on its own; in other words, that VP+ does not invert.

The fact that *utál* shares these properties with big VMs is fortunate in two respects. One, it shows that the problem we encountered is not simply an artifact of our analysis. Two, it suggests a way out. The reason is that we have committed ourselves to the assumption that the second property of big VMs, namely, the fact that they bleed inversion in the next clause up, is to be accounted for by assuming that their InfP+ does not extract from [Spec, PredP]. To capture the parallelism, we may stipulate the same for nonauxiliaries.

(65) VP$_{nonaux}$ in [Spec, VP+] blocks specifier extraction from PredP.

If so, the question is not how inversion by *utál* can be prevented; rather, it is how categories that do not extract from PredP (both big VMs and *utál*) can climb.

To recap, consider the preclimbing structure shown in (66), where α is either (67a) or (67b).

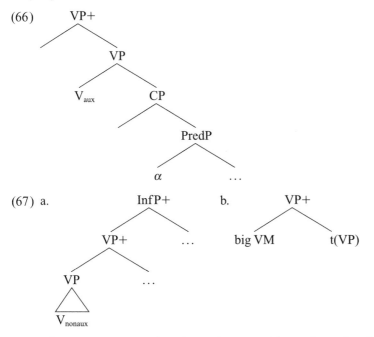

According to the assumptions in section 4.4, this configuration inescapably leads to the pied-piping of PredP or CP. α cannot extract from PredP; therefore, it pied-pipes PredP (in the (67a) case, possibly also CP). Furthermore, we assumed that although either CP or PredP may satisfy the selecting auxiliary, both must immediately leave its VP+, by virtue of the Hungarian Complexity Filter. If so, the α that is contained in PredP/CP is removed from VP+ and has no chance to climb. This conclusion is avoidable if we change either of the two premises.

(68) In the structure (66), α may climb if
    a. in neutral sentences, α can extract from PredP, or
    b. the Hungarian Complexity Filter allows PredP to stay in VP+.

Let us consider these options in turn.

Recall that our theory of extraction does not, by itself, prevent the extraction of α, a full specifier, from PredP. In section 4.4 we ascribed the inability of certain infinitival VP+s to invert to their inability to extract from [Spec, PredP]; this is a mechani-

cally simple stipulation that serves to describe the facts correctly and that we will
have to eliminate as soon as we gain a better understanding of the inverting abilities
of different kinds of VP+s. In any case option (68a) would amount to saying that the
range of categories that can extract from [Spec, PredP] is broader in neutral sentences
than in nonneutral ones; specifically, it includes, besides VP+s with a small VM or
a plain VM-less verb like *dolgoz-* 'work', VP+s with big VMs and nonauxiliaries.
Although this solution is mechanically feasible, it seems to make an existing stipulation even worse.

Alternatively, we may maintain that the αs above never extract from PredP and
revise the Hungarian Complexity Filter ((69) in chapter 4) in such a way that it forces
PredP to move out of VP+ in nonneutral sentences but allows it to stay in neutral
ones. The requisite modification is not difficult.

(69) *Hungarian Complexity Filter* (old)
     VP+ may pied-pipe any *β*P to the auxiliary in the next clause, but *β*P must
     move on if it is more complex than InfP+.

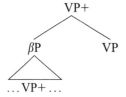

(70) *Hungarian Complexity Filter* (revised)
     At the end of the derivation VP+ may not contain both a category more
     complex than InfP+ in its specifier and overt material in its complement VP.

What (70) says, in effect, is that if VP splits out of VP+ (as it does in neutral sentences), the specifier of VP+ can be complex, but if VP stays, the specifier must be
kept simple.[8] The revised version seems no less natural than the old version was. This
is what we adopt.

The structure in (66), in conjunction with our standard assumptions and the
revised Hungarian Complexity Filter (70), yields the structures shown in (71) for VP+
in the auxiliary clause. VP+/VP splitting takes place in the next step, and the remnant
VP+ climbs to the tensed clause, as desired.

(71) a.

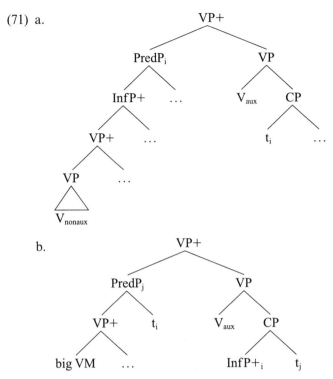

Notice that in Hungarian there are only two contexts where VP+/VP splitting occurs: in the tensed clause and in the domain of NeutP. Since the revision of the Hungarian Complexity Filter makes a difference only in VP+/VP splitting clauses, it will not affect our analyses of infinitival complements in nonneutral sentences. What we need to check is whether it is innocuous in tensed clauses. The example illustrated in (72) shows that it is. In this example we choose PredP to dominate an English order, the kind of material that normally must not stay inside VP+.

(72)

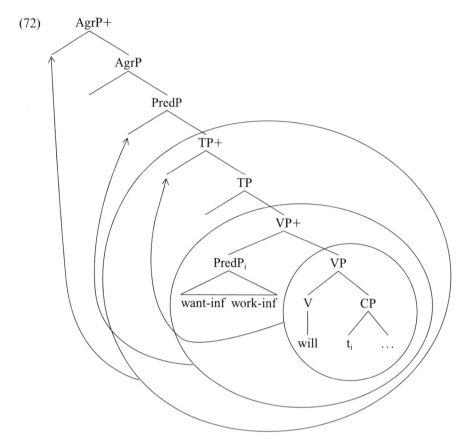

Here VP splits to TP+ to pick up its tense morphology, the remnant VP+ with PredP in its specifier moves to PredP, and TP+ moves to AgrP+. This is perfectly accept-able. For pertinent discussion, see the end of section 4.6.

Chapter 6
Are Infinitival Clauses Full CPs?

The argument we have presented so far has the following major ingredients:

(1) Verbal complex formation is triggered by auxiliaries' need to have a carrier of the [vp+] feature in the specifier of their own VP+. This is a lexical requirement of auxiliaries that must be overtly satisfied in all clauses, whether or not they exhibit any overt signs of "restructuring."

(2) The carrier of the [vp+] feature is VP+. VP+ may move to satisfy the auxiliary in the next higher clause on its own (extracting from [Spec, CP]) or it may pied-pipe the clause that contains it (PredP or CP).

(3) The movement of VP+/PredP/CP to VP+ inverts the order of the auxiliary and its complement. This is made invisible by a further movement, that of VP+ to InfP+, if at the point when it occurs the infinitival verb is already located in LP(cp) or is on its way to focus, and the VP+ that moves to InfP+ dominates only the auxiliary. This is how an English order results.

In executing these ideas, we posited a highly uniform structure for all clauses, including the assumption that all auxiliaries take CP complements. As we noted, the fact that climbing occurs out of subjunctive complements with the overt complementizer *hogy* provides direct support for this assumption. In what follows we first sketch the derivation of the subjunctive examples (section 6.1). We then consider how further data, pertaining to the presence or absence of operator positions (section 6.2), object agreement climbing (section 6.3), and verbal co-occurrence restrictions (section 6.4), are compatible with this position.

There are two types of proposals about the size of restructured infinitival complements (for general discussion and an overview of the literature, see Wurmbrand 1998, in particular the appendix). The first type of proposal argues that such complements are the same size as all other infinitivals. This is the CP approach we have been arguing for (see, e.g., Burzio 1986, Baker 1988, Kayne 1989, Hinterhölzl 1998). Transparency is achieved by some mechanism (head movement, VP-movement, TP-movement, etc.). The second type of proposal relates transparency of infinitival complements to smaller-than-CP size of these infinitives. This is the issue we address in this section: what is the evidence that Hungarian constituents that involve climbing are CPs? If one assumes that these infinitival complements lack (at least) the CP level, then constituents can escape from them. This effect is achieved either by making the CP disappear (as in Evers's (1975) pruning analysis and Rizzi's (1978) restructuring analysis) or by having complements of restructuring predicates simply start out as smaller (VP-like) complements (the double subcategorization analyses of, e.g., Zagona 1982, Rosen 1989). Under the latter type of analysis, predicates that optionally restructure have a double subcategorization frame: either they select a VP complement, and restructuring effects are observed, or they subcategorize for a CP complement, and no restructuring effects are possible. Cinque's (1998b) proposal discussed in section 6.4 is a particular implementation of the double subcategorization analysis.

6.1   Auxiliaries with Subjunctive Complements

Some Hungarian auxiliaries take either infinitival or subjunctive complements; the latter have an overt complementizer (*hogy*). As É. Kiss (1994) observes, climbing is possible out of subjunctives. Let us take a closer look at the data.

(4) a. Szét kell, hogy szedjem   a rádiót.
       apart must that take-subj-1sg the radio-acc
       'I must take apart the radio.'
    b. El   kell, hogy menjek.
       away must that go-subj-1sg
       'I must go away (leave).'

These examples are both impeccably grammatical and fully acceptable according to the norms of the written language. Climbing involving *szabad* 'permitted' is not quite as good.

(5) a. Szét szabad, hogy szedjem   a rádiót?
       apart permitted that take-subj-1sg the radio-acc
       'May I take apart the radio?'
    b. ?El   szabad, hogy menjek   moziba?
       away permitted that go-subj-1sg movie-to
       'May I go to the movies?'

Other examples may be slightly questionable and are in any case restricted to the spoken language.[1,2]

(6) a. ?Szét akarod, hogy szedjem   a   rádiót?
       apart want-2sg that   take-subj-1sg the radio-acc
       'Do you want me to take apart the radio?'

    b. ?El   akarod, hogy menjek   hozzá?
       away want-2sg that   go-subj-1sg to-him
       'Do you want me to go see him?'

It is conceivable that the examples with *akar* 'want' are as grammatical as the examples with *kell/szabad* 'must/permitted' and that the availability of an alternative construction has a blocking effect.[3] We will not examine this issue in detail but note that allowing climbing out of a subjunctive complement is by no means an idiosyncrasy of the predicate *kell*.

Climbing out of subjunctives with an overt complementizer is not restricted to particles: all the expected units climb. For example:

(7) a. Igaznak kellett,   hogy tartsam.
       true-dat must-past that   hold-subj-1sg
       'I had to think it true.'

    b. A   városba kell, hogy költözzünk.
       the city-into must that   move-subj-2pl
       'We must move to the city.'

    c. Aludni   kell, hogy menjek.
       sleep-inf must that   go-subj-1sg
       'I must go to sleep.'

On the other hand, subjunctives do not participate in overt inversion, either by dragging the complementizer *hogy* along (8a) or by stranding it (8b). Only the English order is possible (8c).

(8) a. *Nem fog [hogy el   menjél]   kelleni.
       not   will that   away go-subj-2sg must-inf

    b. *Nem fog el   menjél   kelleni hogy.
       not   will away go-subj-2sg must-inf that

    c. Nem fog kelleni, hogy el   menjél.
       not   will must-inf that   away go-subj-2sg
       'You will not need to leave.'

Since our analysis of climbing does not in any way rely on the fact that the complement is infinitival, the climbing data are not difficult to derive. But what might explain the impossibility of inversion? Since AgrP+ is certainly more complex than InfP+, the Hungarian Complexity Filter effectively forces pied-piping already; but there may be an additional, more interesting reason. In what follows we will explore an application of a proposal in Kayne 1998a.

Kayne proposes that the complementizer is not generated immediately above IP; instead, IP merges with C in the course of movement. In chapter 4 we mentioned that our LP(cp) might be construed as the site where such merger takes place; but since Hungarian infinitives do not have an overt complementizer, adopting this analysis would not have made any descriptive difference. Adopting this analysis does make a difference when we turn to the complementizer *hogy*.

Hogy is an invariant subordinator that introduces indicative and interrogative clauses alike. Bhatt and Yoon (1992) observe that whereas languages like English conflate subordinators with clause-type indicators, languages like Japanese, Korean, Hindi, Bengali, and Hungarian lexicalize them as separate C morphemes.

(9) a. Tudod,   hogy el   mentem.
       know-2sg that away went-1sg
       'You know that I left.'
    b. Tudod,   hogy ki   ment   el.
       know-2sg that who went-3sg away
       'You know who left.'
    c. Tudod,   hogy el   mentem-e   Marihoz.
       know-2sg that away went-1sg-interrog Mari-to
       'You know whether I visited Mari.'

We will assume that *hogy* is the head of SubordP. SubordP is in the place of LP(cp), and a tensed clause must raise to [Spec, SubordP]. Subsequently, *hogy* adjoins to the head of SubordP+, yielding the order *hogy CP*. This last step is forced by Koopman's (1996) modified LCA (Doubly Filled Comp Filter) and replaces Kayne's head adjunction to W.

Notice that this proposal allows complement selection (indicative, subjunctive, interrogative CP) by the matrix predicate to be local: V takes a CP complement and *hogy* does not intervene; it unites with CP later.

As the derivation below indicates, (8a,b) are excluded by the fact that subjunctive material must unite with *hogy* above VP+. In other words, the impossibility of inversion is reduced to an independent reason. These data might also shed some light on the fact that in Romance languages overt complementizers like *que* are incompatible with restructuring but infinitival complementizers like *a* or *de* are compatible.[4]

Below, we first derive the relevant portion of the nonneutral example (8c), repeated here, and then derive a climbing example.

(8) c. Nem fog kelleni, hogy el   menjél.
       not   will must-inf that away go-subj-2sg
       'You will not need to leave.'

The first steps proceed exactly as in the case of infinitival complements, except that (as shown in (10)) InfP+ is replaced by SubjP+.

(10)

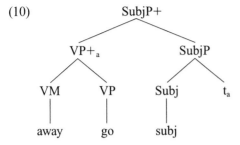

As (11) shows, SubjP+ moves to PredP, as usual, and PredP to AgrP+.

(11)

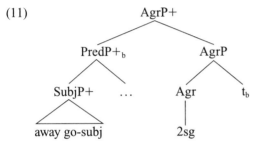

Since SubjP+ already occupies [Spec, AgrP+], the selecting verb will automatically be assured of the subjunctive character of the complement. However, since interrogative complements are clearly CPs (with C a clause-type indicator), *hogy* presumably wants to unite with CP, not AgrP+. Thus, C is merged and AgrP+ moves to its specifier, as shown in (12), to let V know that CP is subjunctival.

(12)

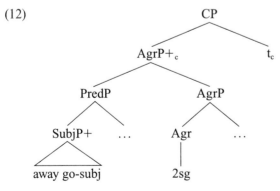

Now the auxiliary *kell* 'must' is merged and CP moves to its VP+, as shown in (13).

(13)

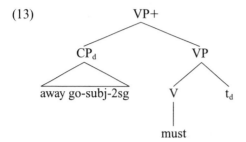

Subord *hogy* 'that' is merged and CP moves into its specifier, whereupon *hogy* moves to Subord+ as shown in (14) to avoid a violation of the Doubly Filled Comp Filter.

(14)

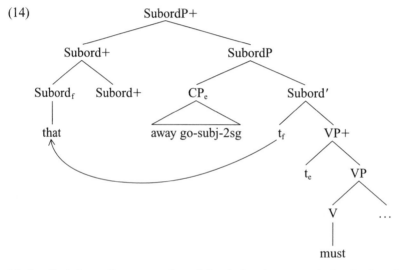

Notice that, from the perspective of the derivation as a whole, the fact that CP moves to SubordP has the same effect as infinitival CP moving to LP(cp). When VP+ moves to InfP+ in the next step, it dominates only the auxiliary *kell* 'must', and the English order arises. We do not spell out these steps, since they are identical to the ones reviewed in previous chapters.

The reason why (8a) does not come about is that *hogy elmenjél* 'that you leave' is not a constituent below VP+ and therefore cannot be moved to VP+; and (8b) does not come about because *hogy* 'that' is not generated below V and therefore cannot be stranded there.

Now, in the same spirit, let us return to climbing. In this derivation the presence of NeutP in the tensed clause forces VP+/VP splitting resulting in (15).

(15)

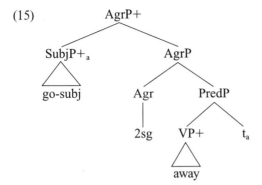

C and the auxiliary are merged and VP+ moves to VP+ (we skip the stacking of VP+); the result is shown in (16).

(16)

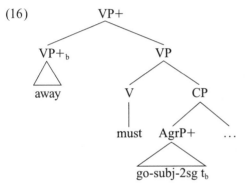

CP unites with *hogy* 'that' and *hogy* moves to Subord+, resulting in the structure in (17).

(17)

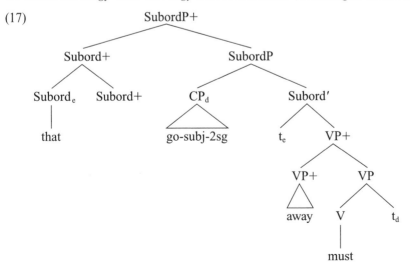

Now the neutral character of the sentence triggers VP+/VP splitting again: VP moves to InfP+. The climbing of VP+, dominating nothing but *el* 'away', proceeds as with infinitival complements.

6.2 Operator Projections

If the infinitival clause may contain all the operator projections that finite clauses do, we can reasonably conclude that it is a CP, or something almost that big.

Hungarian does not have infinitival interrogatives comparable to *I didn't know what to do*. A superficially similar construction unambiguously involves existential/negative quantification.

(18) a. (Nem) tudtam   mit   tenni ellene.
         not   could-1sg what-acc do-inf against-3sg
         'I was able to do something/nothing against it.'
     b. (Nem) volt hol   aludnunk.
         not   was where sleep-inf-2pl
         'We had somewhere/nowhere to sleep.'

Infinitives also lack emphatic IsP (*is* 'indeed'), perhaps because infinitivals have no independent polarity in the relevant sense.

Apart from these constructions, nonneutral sentences with English order may contain the sequence RefP-DistP-NegP-FP-NegP. The infinitival structures in (19) and (20) exactly match the finite structures in (2) and (3) of section 2.1.

(19) PÉTER fog   akarni [$_{RefP}$ két fiúval   [$_{DistP}$ minden problémáról
     Peter will-3sg want-inf   two boy-with   every   problem-about
     [$_{FP}$ EGY LÁNY jelenlétében   beszélni]]].
          a   girl   presence-poss.3sg-in talk-inf
     'It is Peter who will want, for two boys *x*, for every problem *y*, for it to be in the presence of a girl that he talks with *x* about *y*.'

(20) PÉTER fog   akarni [$_{NegP}$ nem [$_{FP}$ MARIVAL [$_{NegP}$ nem beszélni]]].
     Peter will-3sg want-inf   not   Mari-with   not talk-inf
     'It is Peter who will want for it to be not Mari that he does not talk with.'

The above characterizes English orders. In contrast, at least NegP and FP block both inversion and climbing. These facts might seem to suggest that inverted and climbing orders involve truncated structures that do not make room for those operator projections. But that cannot be the whole story. For instance, NegP and FP also block climbing out of subjunctives, but subjunctives with complementizers are probably not truncated structures.

(21) a. *Szét akarom, hogy *ne* szedd   a   rádiót.
          apart want-1sg that   not take-subj.2sg the radio-acc
     b. *Szét akarom, hogy *MOST* szedd   a   rádiót.
          apart want-1sg that   now take-subj.2sg the radio-acc

We will not consider whether some version of a truncation analysis is in principle possible. We will simply argue that the relevant facts can be accounted for given our assumption that auxiliaries take essentially CP-size complements in all three constructions.

We first discuss climbing. Negation and focus in the infinitival or subjunctive clause are completely unacceptable (22). The negation fact was observed by Farkas and Sadock (1989); generally, restructuring is known to be blocked by negation. Names and universals are tolerable (23); they would be better in either initial or final position, but this is likely the result of the stricter order requirements of neutral sentences in general.

(22) a. *_Haza_ fogok   akarni   nem menni.
          home will-1sg want-inf not go-inf
          'I will want not to go home.'
     b. *_Haza_ fogok   akarni   (csak) MOST menni.
          home will-1sg want-inf (only) now go-inf
          'I will want to go home only now.'

(23) a. (?)_Haza_ fogom   akarni   Julit   vinni.
          home will-1sg want-inf Juli-acc take-inf
          'I will want to take Juli home.'
     b. (?)_Haza_ fogok   akarni   mindent   vinni.
          home will-1sg want-inf everything-acc take-inf
          'I will want to take everything home.'

The unacceptability of (22) can then be accounted for if we redefine the notion of "the domain of NeutP." Recall that VM-climbing is contingent on VP+/VP splitting in this domain. Since NeutP is in complementary distribution with NegP and FP in tensed clauses, it is quite natural to say that these projections delimit the domain of NeutP. Hence, in the clauses 'not to go home' and 'to go home only now', VP does not move out of VP+ and _haza_ 'home' has no chance to climb on its own. Since RefP and DistP are present in neutral clauses, they do not delimit the domain of NeutP, and (23a,b) are allowed. (Note, however, that although this modification will do for Hungarian, it will not account for similar Neg intervention effects in Dutch and Italian.)

(24) *The VP Condition in Neutral Clauses* (refined version of (25) in chapter 5)
     Within the domain of NeutP, VP splits out of VP+.

The domain of NeutP is its c-command domain, delimited by any NegP, FP, and the infinitival complement of a nonauxiliary infinitival complement taker.

The fact that RefP and DistP are compatible with climbing would make it somewhat difficult to develop an alternative truncation analysis, but perhaps their presence might be attributed to scrambling.

Now consider inversion. In the case of NegP and FP we find very interesting evidence for the blocking effect. As Brody (1995) observes, NegP and FP in the infinitival clause trigger optional verb movement. This can be illustrated with the English order: note the relative position of *haza* 'home' and *menni* 'go-inf'.

(25) a. Nem fogok   akarni   [MOST haza menni].
         not   will-1sg want-inf now home go-inf
         'I will not want for it to be now when I go home.'
     b. Nem fogok   akarni   [MOST menni haza].
         not   will-1sg want-inf now go-inf home
         'I will not want for it to be now when I go home.'

Brody argues that this is V-to-F movement; we have argued that it is probably PF movement. Whatever the analysis might be, the phenomenon is local and thus serves as a descriptive diagnostic: it tells us that *most* 'now' in (26) is the focus of *menni haza* 'go-inf home', not of *menni haza akarni* 'go-inf home want-inf'. We see, then, that when an infinitival clause contains NegP/FP, it cannot invert with its selecting auxiliary.

(26) *Nem fogok   [MOST menni haza] akarni.
         not   will-1sg now go-inf home want-inf
         'I will not want for it to be now when I go home.'

In the absence of "V-to-F movement," the judgment is more subtle. Let us focus the accusative-marked measure phrase *egy órát* 'one hour', as in (27). The inverted string can in principle be bracketed in two ways, with 'one hour' in the focus of the infinitival clause that contains just 'sleep' (27a) or within the clause whose VP+ is 'want to sleep' (27b). In the first case the measure phrase specifies the duration of sleeping; in the second it specifies the duration of wanting to sleep. Now, it appears that the sentence can only have the latter interpretation; that is, (27b) is the correct bracketing. Moreover, those speakers who accept the accusative-marked measure phrase as a modifier of 'sleep' but require the postpositional phrase *egy órán át* 'for an hour, lit. through an hour' as a modifier of 'want' find the sentence marginal to begin with, again indicating that the correct bracketing is (27b).

(27) a. *Nem fogok   [[EGY ÓRÁT   aludni] akarni].
         not   will-1sg one hour-acc sleep-inf want-inf
         'I will not want for it to be the case that I sleep an hour.'

   b. Nem fogok [EGY ÓRÁT   [aludni   akarni]].
       not   will-1sg one hour-acc sleep-inf want-inf
       'I will not have a one-hour-long desire to sleep.'

Likewise, when we find a name or a universal in the same linear position, the judgment is subtle, because RefP and DistP never trigger V-movement in any event. It appears that interpretation favors the same bracketing as in the case of FP and NegP.

Our theory as it stands predicts the ungrammaticality of (26), as was in fact discussed in note 1 to chapter 5. Recall that anything with the feature [vp+] can satisfy the auxiliary (here: *akarni* 'want-inf'), but nothing larger than InfP+ can end up in its [Spec, VP+] at Spell-Out. (26) could only arise with MOST *menni haza* 'now go-inf home' in [Spec, VP+]. But since this phrase contains focus, it is minimally an FP, that is, a category much larger than VP+. Thus, the Hungarian Complexity Filter straightforwardly rules it out. The same filter predicts that (27) can only have the bracketing in (27b); similarly with a name (RefP) or a universal (DistP) in the place of focus/negation.

In other words, our proposal predicts that no operator can be dragged along by inversion, even if the infinitival clause is invariably analyzed as CP.

6.3   Transparency Effects: Object Agreement Climbing

Let us now turn to data that involve transparency effects. One such effect is *object agreement climbing* (OAC).

Hungarian has overt object agreement. Finite verbs have two distinct conjugations: one used, roughly, when the direct object is definite, and the other used when the direct object is indefinite or there is no direct object. (Szabolcsi (1994) and Bartos (2000) argue explicitly that the definite/indefinite distinction is only an approximation and that the relevant factor cannot be purely semantic; this is immaterial here.)

Infinitival verbs assign accusative case (to definite and indefinite direct objects alike) but do not carry object agreement morphology themselves. In the subject control construction, the finite verb agrees with the direct object of (the infinitival complement of . . .) its infinitival complement. The nonagreeing forms corresponding to the agreeing forms in (28) would be *látott*, *akart*, and *fog*.

(28) a. Mari látta   ezt.
         Mari saw-3sg+def.obj this-acc
         'Mari saw this.'
     b. Mari látni   akarta   ezt.
         Mari see-inf wanted-3sg+def.obj this-acc
         'Mari wanted to see this.'

   c. Mari látni fogja   akarni ezt.
      Mari see-inf will-3sg+def.obj want-inf this-acc
      'Mari will want to see this.'

OAC is functionally reminiscent of pronominal clitic climbing in Italian, for instance. Szabolcsi (1983), the first to subject OAC to theoretical scrutiny, analyzed it using restructuring, inspired by Rizzi's (1978) analysis of clitic climbing in Italian. É. Kiss (1987) proposed a revision in the spirit of Zubizarreta 1982, involving a dual structure whose monoclausal side caters to OAC.

The main point to be made here is that, whatever the correct analysis of OAC might be, it is orthogonal to our present concerns, as previously observed by Farkas and Sadock (1989). The main reason is that all subject control verbs exhibit OAC. Most importantly, OAC obtains in all three construction types with auxiliaries, and it also obtains with nonauxiliary subject control verbs (e.g., *elkezd* 'away-begin', *utál* 'hate'). The only restriction is that the verb should be lexically able to carry object agreement morphology. For instance, because *fog* 'will' is historically 'take, grab', it is able to do so; verbs of coming and going may or may not be, depending on regional dialect. We may also note that unlike Italian clitic climbing, which is optional, OAC is obligatory.

As far as we can tell, at least the examples with nonauxiliaries and those with auxiliaries in the nonneutral English order must involve CPs. Thus, OAC must be compatible with CP-hood and we therefore omit it from consideration.[5]

6.4 Transparency Effects: Co-occurrence Restrictions

Cinque (1998a,b) has proposed an analysis of restructuring in Romance inspired by earlier results eventually published in Cinque 1999. The analysis is reminiscent of, but not identical to, the double subcategorization analysis proposed by Strozer (1976, 1981), Picallo (1991), and others. In sentences without transparency effects, modal, aspectual, and movement verbs take normal CP complements. In sentences that exhibit transparency effects (long NP-preposing, auxiliary selection, and, less diagnostically, clitic climbing), these verbs are base-generated in functional heads of the extended projection of the lexical verb. The inventory and order of the relevant functional heads are revealed by the distribution of adverbs, which appear in their specifiers. In restructured contexts only functional projections of a single clause are available; with CP embedding each clause has the whole range of functional projections.

Are there contrasts in Hungarian between nonneutral English orders and inverted/ VM-climbing structures that indicate that the latters' auxiliaries are in fact functional heads? This question is especially natural since Hungarian auxiliaries are by and large a proper subset of Romance restructuring verbs.

One of the most straightforward predictions that Cinque's specific restructuring proposal makes is this. When all the restructuring verbs take a CP complement, their order is free. When they are functional heads, their order is determined by the order of the functional projections in a single clause. Let us examine how these predictions fare in Hungarian.

We indeed find restrictions, although they are not easy to evaluate. The main reason is that there are fewer Hungarian auxiliaries than Italian restructuring verbs, and of those, even fewer may occur in the infinitive. Since Kálmán et al. (1989) checked the entire stock of Hungarian verbs for VM-climbing, it is possible to give an exhaustive list.

(29) *Hungarian auxiliaries that allow VM-climbing*
  a. Must be finite: fog 'will', lehet 'may', szokott 'used to', tetszik 'auxiliary of politeness, lit. please', szabad 'be permitted', szeretne 'would like', szokás 'be customary'
  b. If infinitive, must be highest: kell 'must'
  c. Possible anywhere: akar 'want', bír 'be able', kezd 'begin', kíván 'desire', mer 'dare', óhajt 'wish', próbál 'try', szándékozik 'intend', talál 'happen to', tud 'be able to/know how to'
  d. Possible only for some speakers: hagy 'let', hajlandó 'willing', igyekszik 'strive', iparkodik 'hurry, strive', képes 'be able', készül 'prepare, be about', köteles 'be obliged', segít 'help', sikerül 'succeed', szeret 'like', tartozik 'be obliged', törekszik 'try' (only finite: muszáj 'must', szükséges 'necessary')

The positional restrictions in (29a,b) apply in nonneutral sentences with the English order as well as in VM-climbing contexts; thus, no interesting contrasts can be built on them. But many other co-occurrence restrictions also apply regardless of construction type. (30) offers just a small sample—note again that these examples involve neither inversion nor climbing.

(30) a. *Nem volt szabad   találni   haza menni.
           not   was permitted happen-inf home go-inf
           'It was not permitted to happen to go home.'
     b. *Nem akart   kívánni   haza menni.
           not   wanted desire-inf home go-inf
           'He didn't want to desire to go home.'
     c. *Nem próbált szándékozni haza menni.
           not   tried   intend-inf   home go-inf
           'He didn't try to intend to go home.'
     d. *Nem kezdett tudni   haza menni.
           not   began   be-able-inf home go-inf
           'He didn't begin to be able to go home.'

The English translations are also rather incoherent although, in all probability, they involve full CP complements. Exactly what component of the grammar should account for this incoherence is not clear. Most likely, CPs must map onto the functional hierarchy, just as negative constituents move to NegP, and the ill-formedness of such cases reflects restrictions on the derivations. What is clear is that various co-occurrence restrictions exist quite independently of restructuring. Moreover, given the small number of auxiliaries in Hungarian, those restrictions do not leave us many combinations to work with.

The relevant combinations should involve a carefully chosen sequence of auxiliaries from (29c). An immediate difficulty is that some speakers do not accept VM-climbing across more than one (29c)-type auxiliary, regardless of their order (we thank László Kálmán and Huba Bartos for the judgments).

(31) *"Dialect A"*
    a. Haza fogok   akarni   menni.
        home will-1sg want-inf go-inf
        'I will want to go home.'
    b. *Haza fogok   akarni   kezdeni menni.
        home will-1sg want-inf begin-inf go-inf
        'I will want to begin to go home.'
    c. *Haza fogok   kezdeni akarni   menni.
        home will-1sg begin-inf want-inf go-inf
        'I will begin to want to go home.'

Other speakers, the second-named author of this book among them, find both (31b) and (31c) grammatical, though not to the same degree.

(32) *"Dialect B"*
    b. Haza fogok   akarni   kezdeni menni.
        home will-1sg want-inf begin-inf go-inf
        'I will want to begin to go home.'
    c. ??Haza fogok   kezdeni akarni   menni.
        home will-1sg begin-inf want-inf go-inf
        'I will begin to want to go home.'

It is true that "psychologically speaking," wanting to begin may be more plausible than beginning to want, as a result of which the order *kezdeni akarni* is independently more difficult, see (33c), but the contrast with VM-climbing seems stronger than what this alone would predict.

(33) b. Nem fogok   akarni   kezdeni haza menni.
        not   will-1sg want-inf begin-inf home go-inf
        'I will not want to begin to go home.'

c. (?)Nem fogok kezdeni akarni   haza menni.
   not   will-1sg begin-inf want-inf home go-inf
   'I will not begin to want to go home.'

Now, the contrast in "dialect B" is exactly the kind that Cinque's proposal predicts. Compare:

(34) a. Lo ha voluto smettere di frequentare.
         him (I) wanted to-stop frequenting
     b. *Lo ha smesso di voler frequentare.
         him (I) stopped wanting to-frequent

On the other hand, no proposal (ours, Cinque's, or anyone else's we are aware of) seems to predict "dialect A"—that is, that some speakers do not tolerate climbing across two class (29c) auxiliaries, in either order. Specifically, Cinque's proposal would not predict it, because the items that fall into this class are semantically quite varied and therefore would not head the same functional projection.

In sum, examining data inspired by Cinque has helped us identify an issue that requires further research, but the data do not seem to strongly call for Cinque's theory as an explanation.

6.5   Conclusion

Let us take stock. We have considered the following types of data: auxiliaries with subjunctive complements in section 6.1, the absence of operator positions from inverted and climbing structures in section 6.2, object agreement climbing in section 6.3, and verbal co-occurrence restrictions in section 6.4. We have found that the data in section 6.1 strongly argue for the assumption that the complements of auxiliaries are always CP-size projections. The data in section 6.2 are at least totally compatible with this assumption. Those in section 6.3 are irrelevant to this matter. Finally, in section 6.4 we indeed found that there are verbal co-occurrence restrictions that our theory does not predict, but they do not seem to pertain uniquely to the "restructuring" versus "English" division.

In view of these facts, we conclude that the unified analysis explored in the preceding chapters is justified.

Chapter 7
The Structure of Dutch

7.1 Introduction

In order to discuss Dutch, German, and Hungarian verbal complexes and the ways they are similar or different, we must first establish a structure that allows us to compare Hungarian with Dutch and German. In this chapter we discuss the location of the nodes that play a role in the syntax of verbal complexes in Dutch (i.e., VP, VP+, InfP+, PredP, TP, Agr$_S$P, and CP) and the distribution of overt material over these nodes. Unless explicitly noted, we assume that German and Dutch are basically identical.

It is also important to check how the analysis developed for Hungarian works crosslinguistically. Given the assumption in section 1.2 that the hierarchy of categories is universal, a precondition is to establish that the portion of the Hungarian hierarchy that is independent of verbal complexes is conceivably crosslinguistically valid. In this chapter we take preliminary steps toward making this claim plausible.

7.2 Standard Assumptions about the Structure of Dutch

We cast the problem of verbal complexes within a more general analysis of the structure of Dutch. Given the structure of Hungarian, the standard assumptions about the structure of Dutch and how linear orders are derived are incompatible with the general theory underlying this book, regardless of whether they are OV or VO based. Standard OV analyses are incompatible with the antisymmetry of phrase structure (Kayne 1994). Standard VO analyses are compatible with antisymmetry, but incompatible with the universal base hypothesis, the overt movement theory, and the incorporation of morphology into the syntax. There are projections in Hungarian (RefP, DistP, FP) that are not identified for Dutch, or that do not seem to contain phonological material.

Standard VO analyses, as developed for example by Zwart (1993, 1997), Koster (1994), and Den Dikken (1996), assume the following. In nonroot environments the finite verb is lower than the Case positions. DPs and small clause predicates co-occurring with V individually raise to licensing positions to the left of the finite verb: DPs raise to AgrP, and small clause predicates to PredP (Zwart 1993, 1997, Koster 1994). Because of the obligatory raising, neither small clauses nor DPs ever occur after the finite verb in nonroot contexts. CPs are stranded in the VP in post-verbal position, since they do not need to be licensed. This analysis is illustrated in (1), where *SC* stands for small clauses and particles, and V_f for the finite verb.

(1) *Nonroot context*

7.3   The Position of the Finite Verb

Dutch finite verbs carry tense and agreement morphology. According to our assumptions, this morphology is picked up in the corresponding projections. A projection containing the finite verb must therefore have moved to at least Agr_SP (see also Hallman 1999, Kayne 1994, 52, and Haegeman 2000 for proposals that the finite verb in nonroot environments is in fact quite high). We are therefore forced to reject the standard head-initial analysis sketched in (1), and we instead assume the following (for Agr_SP+, see (21) in chapter 4 and (14) in appendix A).

(2) The finite verb is (at least) in Agr_SP+.

The finite verb in Hungarian dominates the Case positions and the licensing positions for DPs, both dubbed LP(dp), and the licensing position for CPs, LP(cp). (Recall that we argued extensively that CPs obligatorily move to licensing positions.) The Hungarian complementizer *hogy* is merged into the derivation in such a position (SubordP) (see (22) in appendix A). Given the hypothesis that the hierarchy of categories is universal, the same hierarchy should hold for Dutch as well. Therefore, contrary to standard assumptions, V_f is higher than LP(dp) and LP(cp). Dutch CPs are either topicalized and occur in the first position in root environments, or follow the finite verb: their distribution is briefly discussed in section 7.9. Dutch DPs can never surface to the right of the finite verb in nonroot environments; instead, they must surface to its left. They must therefore have moved there, either individually or as part of a larger constituent, as proposed by Hinterhölzl (1998) and Pearson (2000), for example. Thus, (2), in conjunction with the universal hierarchy, minimally entails that the structure splits obligatorily somewhere below the landing site position of the finite verb.

(3) a. $[_{\text{Agr}_S\text{P}}\ [_{V_f}\ \text{zie}]_i\ \Downarrow split\ [_{\text{YP}}\ [\text{ik}\ [_V\ e]_i\ \text{Jan straks}]]]]$
                                              see   I   Jan shortly

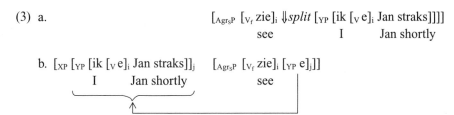

   b. $[_{XP}\ [_{YP}\ [\text{ik}\ [_V\ e]_i\ \text{Jan straks}]]_j\quad [_{\text{Agr}_S\text{P}}\ [_{V_f}\ \text{zie}]_i\ [_{YP}\ e]_j]]$
              I   Jan shortly   see

This analysis raises many questions. What is the landing site for the leftward-moved remnant? Are there several landing sites higher than Agr$_S$, or is there a single landing site? If there are several landing sites, what are they, and what overt material do they contain? What precisely is the derived constituent structure in the middle field? We do not have a fully worked-out account. However, we will suggest that there are several projections higher than Agr$_S$: the left periphery of the Hungarian structure (RefP, DistP, FP, NegP) is present in German and Dutch as well.

Let us start with the problem of the landing site for the verbal remnant. Hinter-hölzl (1998) proposes that the surface material to the left of V raises as a single TP to PredP, followed by scrambling of individual constituents out of this constituent.

(4) $[\text{DP}_i\ [_{\text{PredP}}\ [_{TP}\cdots\ [_{DP}\ e]_i\cdots]_j\ [_{\text{Agr}_S\text{P}}\ [_{TP}\ e]_j]]]$

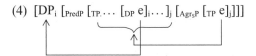

This analysis is not available to us. First, PredP is the landing site for VP+. Second, once a constituent has moved to some specifier position, no elements may be extracted out of it. We assume a variant of this analysis below, where individual constituents raise to particular landing sites higher than Agr$_S$ and pied-pipe some remnant verbal projection. We will simply assume that there is always some remnant constituent with a verbal trace moving leftward. This constituent must contain the licensing positions for clitics and for DPs, since DPs are always preverbal. In (5) we sketch one possible derived structure for a string that contains a clitic pronoun ('*t* ... *leest* 'reads it', from the embedded sentence *dat zij 't iedere dag leest* 'that she reads it each day').

(5)

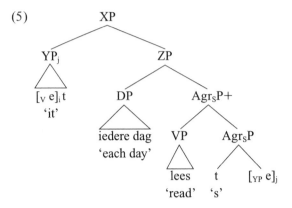

   This derived constituent structure suggests that the Dutch/English OV/VO difference is a matter of whether or not the VP has split out of the constituent that undergoes further movement (see Pearson 2000 for a general proposal in these terms). That
is, the Dutch/English OV/VO difference is a matter, not of whether English has an
additional rule of VP-movement that Dutch lacks, as Kayne (1998b) proposes, but of
whether the verb is inside the constituent that moves (English) or outside it (Dutch).
As this structure suggests, clitics do not move independently to some high position,
but are carried along with another constituent.
   Haegeman (2000) independently argues for a remnant movement analysis. If the
finite verb is high, she points out, Dutch no longer violates Holmberg's (1986) generalization, which states that object shift is possible only if the verb has moved to a
higher position. If the finite verb is in Agr$_S$ in nonroot environments as well, "object
shift" is possible if a remnant constituent containing the trace verb moves past this
position. The object ends up linearly preceding the finite verb, because it is carried up
by a further leftward movement.

7.4   The Pre-V Domain

In Hungarian a sequence of categories dominates Agr$_S$: RefP* > DistP > FP >
NegP (Szabolcsi 1997, and section 2.1). These categories are seemingly absent from
Dutch. However, given the hypotheses that the hierarchy is universal and that all
movement is overt, it becomes natural to suggest that leftward movement in Dutch
can target RefP* (= Top), DistP, and FP as well. Specific constituents move to RefP,
universal quantifiers move to DistP, and focused constituents move to FP.
   In the sections below we sketch this analysis. At several points it remains suggestive: each projection raises issues that are generally not well understood. In a narrow
sense these sections are unrelated to the analysis of the verbal complex, since what we

need for these is an understanding of the distribution of the finite verb, small clauses, and CP complements. Therefore, the open questions will not hinder the presentation of the core claims in chapter 8. In a broader sense these issues are intimately linked to the more general research program.

7.5   The Position of Negation

The Dutch negation *niet* obligatorily precedes the finite verb. *Niet* must be overtly associated with NegP. This points to NegP > AgrP, as in Hungarian. We return in section 7.8 to the distribution of small clauses (VMs) that are sandwiched between NegP and V.

(6) NegP ... Agr_SP+

For the present discussion it is irrelevant whether *niet* spells out the negative head (NegP) or whether it is a negative quantifier that pied-pipes a remnant constituent to NegP (as in Nkemnji's (1995) analysis for Nweh and Kayne's (1998b) proposal regarding *not*).

7.6   The Position of Focus

FP in Hungarian is projected above negation and the finite verbs. Certain facts point to a similarly positioned FP projection in Dutch. There is also evidence for an additional presubject FP, close to C, which we leave aside.

According to the only-overt-movement theory, constituents that are interpreted as focused must appear in FP. This is not obviously correct for Dutch, since focused constituents may be followed or preceded by different types of constituents, even when they are not in the immediate vicinity of FP.

(7) omdat   ik DEZE boeken vanavond niet wil   lezen
     because I   these books   tonight   not want read
     'because I don't want to read THESE books tonight'

We must interpret such cases as involving a derived constituent structure that is consistent with focused constituents' being in FP (see (13)).

The following facts suggest that FP is higher than Agr_S. First, neutral focus is argued to be preverbal, that is, in the VP of the traditional OV analysis (Reinhart 1997). This points to FP > Agr_S. Second, a focused constituent must precede the finite verb, though the two need not be immediately adjacent.

(8) omdat   ik gisteren   met JAN gepraat heb   (?*met JAN)
     because I yesterday   with Jan talked   have (?*with Jan)

Third, the focus particle *maar* (literally 'but') occurs in a fixed position. It immediately precedes negation, suggesting FP > NegP > Agr$_S$P+.

(9) omdat ik morgen   *maar*   niet zal tennissen
    because I tomorrow focus-particle not will play-tennis
    'because I won't play tennis tomorrow'

Given this hierarchy, focused XP constituents should be able to precede NegP, as indeed they can.

(10) omdat   ik [$_{FP}$ ZULKE BOEKEN [$_{NegP}$ niet [$_{Agr_S P+}$ wil   lezen [. . .]]]
      because I   such   books   not   want read
      'because I don't want to read SUCH BOOKS'

However, focused XPs can also follow Neg, giving rise to constituent negation.

(11) omdat ik Jan niet DIT boek heb voorgelezen
      because I Jan not this book have for-read
      'because I did not read THIS book to Jan'

(12) omdat ik aan Marie niet DIT boek wil   geven (maar DAT boek)
      because I to Marie not this book want give   (but   that book)
      'because I don't want to give THIS book to Marie, (but THAT book)'

In Hungarian FP can be sandwiched between two NegPs. This seems to hold for Dutch as well. At least marginally, the two NegPs can co-occur, yielding a complex sentence where the two negations cancel each other out. Therefore, NegP > FP > NegP.

A serious problem for the overt-movement-only approach is that focused XPs need not precede NegP immediately: nonfocused material may intervene. This suggests a pied-piping analysis of the focused constituent, as in the bracketing in (13).[1]

(13) omdat [$_{RefP}$ ik [$_{FP}$ DEZE boeken vanavond [$_{NegP}$ niet wil   lezen]]]
      because   I   these books   tonight   not want read
      'because I don't want to read THESE books tonight'

Whether this derived constituent structure is indeed correct is a question for future research.

In conclusion, although problematic cases exist, there is solid evidence for a structural FP higher than Agr$_S$ in Dutch, as in Hungarian.[2]

This yields the following clausal architecture, where *XP* refers to the landing site of the remnant YP constituent that pied-pipes the clitics:

(14) C . . . XP . . . NegP FP NegP . . . [$_{Agr_S}$ V$_f$] . . . LP(dp)* . . . Adv* . . .

7.7 The Prefocus Field

A remnant constituent with a clitic pronoun undergoes leftward movement to a position higher than FP in Dutch. Is all prefocused material in fact pied-piped with this constituent, or are there individual landing sites attracting smaller parts of the structure? Below we suggest the latter: there are specific landing sites, which correspond to the Hungarian RefP and DistP projections. Nonfocused subjects, objects, and adverbs might end up in one (or more) landing site(s) to the left of FP, probably RefP and DistP, depending on the interpretations of the DPs or adverbs. This suggests roughly the following bracketing, with the subject pied-piping the YP constituent to RefP:

(15) dat $[_{RefP}[_{YP}$ ik $[_V$ e$]$ [gisteren …] $[_{RefP}$ deze tekeningen, na   lang aarzelen,
        that   I   yesterday   these drawings   after long hesitation
      $[_{FP}$ alleen aan Marie (heb   laten zien)$]]]]$
           only   to   Marie (have let   see)
      'that I showed these drawings only to Marie yesterday after hesitating for a
      long time'

(16) dat $[_{RefP}[_{YP}$ dat meisje $[_V$ e$]$ …] $[_{DistP}$ over elk   probleem maar $[_{FP}$ met
        that   that girl   about each problem foc(but)   with
      twee vriendinnen [heeft gepraat]$]]]$
      two friends   has   talked
      'that that girl talked about each problem with only two friends'

If this analysis is on the right track, "topic" and "focus" determine the order in the middle field. The most topiclike elements occur to the left, and focused elements to the right, as many grammarians have claimed (for Dutch, Blom and Daalder (1977), Verhagen (1979), and for German, Höhle (1986), among others). Constituents move to designated positions, depending on their interpretation.[3]

Given the gist of this analysis, some puzzling interactions between scrambling and focus fall into place. In "standard" analyses, certain DPs (roughly, the specific DPs) are forced to scramble out of the domain of the VP. There are two kinds of proposals for why this is so. The first holds that scrambling is triggered by the need to acquire Case (see De Hoop 1992, Mahajan 1990 for A-scrambling). This is problematic, since scrambling is not necessary when the specific DPs can be interpreted as focused. In our proposal there is no anomaly with respect to Case. Movement of DP to FP is regular movement from a Case position to [Spec, FP]; that is, the focused constituent picks up Case before moving to FP.

(17) $[_{RefP}[_{FP}$ DP$_i$ $[_{Agr_SP+}$ V$_f$ [. . . $[_{LP(dp)}$ e]$_i$ . . .]]]]

$$\text{[−Case]} \qquad\qquad\qquad \text{[+Case]}$$

"Scrambling" is not related to Case; it is the movement of a constituent dominated by Agr$_S$ to a RefP position higher than FP.

(18) $[_{RefP}$ DP$_i$ $[_{FP}[_{Agr_SP+}$ V$_f$ [. . . $[_{LP(dp)}$ e]$_i$ . . .]]]]

$$\text{[+topic]} \qquad\qquad\qquad \text{[+Case]}$$

The second type of proposal holds that scrambling is a defocalization process (Reinhart 1997): it is forced by the need to remove the nonfocused material from the domain of focus. Under our proposal there is no need to assume a defocalization rule, since the result simply follows from the tree geometry. Being specific, scrambled constituents end up in RefP, and not in FP. Therefore, they are defocused.[4]

7.8 The Position of Small Clauses, Incorporated Particles, Nouns, and Adjectives

The distribution of small clauses and "incorporated" particles, adjectives, and nouns (i.e., the class of elements corresponding to big and small VMs in Hungarian) plays a central role in our analysis. They are in the VP+ constituent that auxiliaries (e.g., verb raisers or restructuring verbs) need to form a complex with. Their distribution reveals where VP+ is located.

We established for Hungarian that VP+ is licensed in PredP and that PredP is located between Agr$_S$ and TP+.

(19) a. Big and small VMs must occur in [Spec, VP+]
    b. VP+ is licensed in [Spec, PredP]
    c. Agr$_S$P+ > PredP > TP+

In Dutch tensed clauses, big and small VMs (we will use the Hungarian terminology for Dutch too) must immediately precede the finite verb they combine with. This is true for all tensed clauses, regardless of whether they contain neutral focus, negation, or focus.

(20) a. dat hij (alleen) huizen schoonmaakt
        that he (only)   houses clean-makes
        'that he only cleans houses'
    b. omdat ik de muren niet geel   verf
        because I the walls not yellow paint
        'because I am not painting the walls yellow'

VMs are in VP+, and VP+ is in PredP. Assuming that VP splits out of VP+ in all tensed clauses, we arrive at the PredP structure shown in (21), with VP+ a remnant constituent in PredP.

(21)

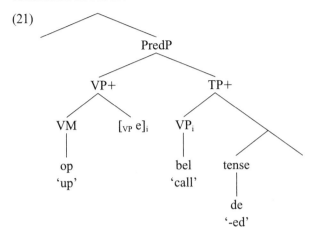

This PredP analysis is in fact close to the analysis proposed by Koster (1994) and Zwart (1994, 1997), who move the predicate of small clauses to PredP, although not via remnant movement.

The structure in (21) raises a problem with respect to Agr_S and the universal hierarchy. In Hungarian we were led to assume $Agr_S > PredP > TP+$, with TP+ moving to Agr_S. When VP splits out of VP+, the linear order V_f VM results. In Dutch nonroot clauses the linear order is VM V_f. In root clauses it is V_f ... VM. We can adopt the same hierarchy for Dutch as for Hungarian, if PredP pied-pipes TP+ to Agr_SP+ in nonroot contexts.

(22)

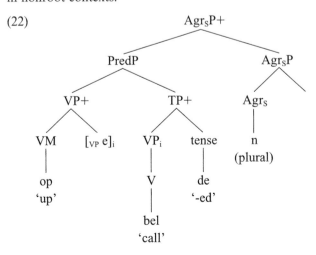

This derivation is unproblematic for nonroot clauses but does not yield the right constituency for verb-second in root clauses. If we assume that TP+ splits out of PredP/TP+ in root clauses, we can maintain the base-generated Agr$_S$ > PredP > TP. Thus, in root clauses TP+ splits out of PredP and moves to Agr$_S$P+ on its own, leaving its VM behind in PredP. In effect, then, PredP/TP+ do not split, except in root clauses. This type of variability generally characterizes the splitting parameters that we need elsewhere, as in VP+/VP splitting.

7.9 The Distribution of CPs

A final ingredient for the account of verbal complexes is the distribution of CPs. Dutch tensed CP complements occur *after* the finite verb. All infinitives follow the finite verb as well, regardless of the extent to which they participate in restructuring. In this respect Dutch infinitival clauses fall into three classes: "extraposition" infinitivals, "remnant extraposition" (or third construction) infinitivals, and verb-raising complements. (We will characterize them as nonsplittable, partially splittable, and maximally splittable CPs, respectively.) The fact that all CPs follow the finite verb is illustrated in (23). (Remnant) CPs are boldfaced, and parts of the infinitive that "belong" together are italicized.

(23) a. *Tensed clausal complements*
           omdat hij tegen mij zei ***dat hij het boek zou   uitlezen***
           because he against me said that he the book would out-read
           'because he said to me that he would finish reading the book'
       b. *"Extraposition" infinitivals*
           omdat   hij probeert ***om dat boek uit te lezen***
           because he tries   for that book out to read
       c. *"Remant extraposition" infinitivals*
           omdat   hij (*dat boek*) probeert (***dat boek***) ***uit te lezen***
           because he (that book) tries   (that book) out to read
       d. *"Verb-raising" infinitivals*
           omdat   hij *dat boek uit* probeert ***te lezen***
           because he that book out tries   to read

The postverbal position of CPs was initially taken to be strong evidence for a verb-initial VP in Dutch (see Zwart 1994, 1997): CP complements could be treated as being stranded in the VP. This simple solution to the CP distribution problem was probably instrumental in how easily many Dutch (as opposed to, say, Japanese) linguists embraced the head-initial analysis for VPs. This analysis is incompatible with our theory. We have argued that CPs must move to licensing positions as well, and that this must be universally true. Hinterhölzl (1998) discusses an empirical argument for CP-movement under a head-initial analysis. AP constituents with dependent CP complements move without their CPs. This order can only be achieved if CPs have previously vacated the AP, that is, if they have undergone movement to some licensing position.

(24) dat ik [$_{AP}$ erg blij   [$_{CP}$ e]$_i$] ben [$_{CP}$ dat ...]$_i$
      that I   very happy   am   that
      'that I am very happy that ...'

We leave for future research the question of exactly how the positions of all CPs should be accounted for.[5] Given Hungarian, it is clear that they are least in LP(cp). The V1 V2 order will be used as a diagnostic that V2 is inside the CP complement, which in turn is at least in LP(cp).

(25) A V1 V2 order (in a nonroot environment) signals that V2 is inside the CP complement.

7.10   Summary

We have suggested the following hierarchical structure for Dutch and German:

(26) C (FP) RefP* DistP NegP FP NegP Agr$_S$P+ PredP TP+ LP(xp)* ...

In addition, we have assumed the following structure-splitting parameter:

(27) PredP/TP+ do not split, except in root environments (see section 7.8).

Central to the analysis of verbal complexes are the position of the finite verb, the position of PredP, and the position of CPs. The syntax of RefPs, DistPs, NegP, and FP is a matter of considerable interest, but of secondary importance for the analysis of verbal complexes. If the research program is on the right track, an analysis along the lines outlined in this chapter seems unavoidable.

Chapter 8
Dutch and German Verbal Complexes

8.1 Introduction

In this chapter we extend our proposed theory and analysis to Dutch and German restructuring verbs. Dutch and German verbal complexes have been studied extensively,[1] but many puzzles remain. The analysis of Dutch and German verbal complexes is made particularly challenging by considerable and seemingly unstructured crosslinguistic and dialectal variation.

The main analytical issues addressed in this chapter (and briefly illustrated in the rest of this section) are the possible and impossible orders of Dutch and German restructuring verbs, the exceptional behavior of Dutch infinitives, the syntax of the infinitival marker *te/zu*, the different behavior of *te/zu*-infinitives in Dutch and German, and the distribution of participles and the so-called IPP (*infinitivus pro participio*) effect.

Dutch restructuring verbs in general line up in English orders, German verbs in inverted orders (*D* stands for *Dutch* and *G* for *German*).

(1) a. omdat Peter wil   kunnen zwemmen   (D) 1 2 3
    because Peter wants can-inf swim-inf
    'because Peter wants to be able to swim'

     b. weil   Peter schwimmen können will   (G) 3 2 1
    because Peter swim-inf   can-inf want
    'because Peter wants to be able to swim'

Dutch also has inverted orders, and German has mixed orders.

(2) omdat   Peter zwemmen wil   (D) 2 1
    because Peter swim-inf   wants
    'because Peter wants to swim'

(3) omdat   Peter gezwommen heeft   (D) 2 1
    because Peter ge-swim-part has
    'because Peter swam'

(4) weil   Peter hat schwimmen wollen   (G) 1 3 2
     because Peter has swim-inf   want-inf
     'because Peter wanted to swim'

Dutch infinitives are subject to severe and quite curious restrictions on inversion, which can be stated as follows:

(5) Infinitives may invert iff they are in a V1 V2 environment, V1 is a tensed restructuring V, and V2 is a bare infinitive.

Current theories do not adequately account for this restriction. We will show that our theory provides the tools to do so.

The German mixed order is a property of the IPP context. An infinitive shows up instead of an expected participle when the participle combines with a restructuring infinitive. In this case the usual inverted order is no longer available, and the auxiliary must precede the infinitive(s). Our theory provides particular insight into this problem.

Dutch has remnant VP+ movement with intermediate infinitives lining up in an English order. Although all categories can occur in the remnant VP+, infinitives cannot. Remnant VP+s are italicized for clarity.

(6) a.   ... *op* zal (willen)   bellen   (VP+ remnant with overt PP)
          up will (want-inf) call-inf
          'will want to call up'

     b.   ... *aardig* zal vinden   (VP+ remnant with overt AP)
          nice   will find-inf
          'will find ... nice'

     c.   ... *naar huis* zal gaan   (VP+ remnant with overt PP)
          to   home will go-inf
          'will go home'

     d.   ... *piano* zal spelen   (VP remnant with overt NP)
          piano will play-inf
          'will play piano'

     e.   ... *gezwommen* zal hebben   (VP remnant with overt participle)
          ge-swim-part will have-inf
          'will have swum'

     f. *... *zwemmen* zal willen   (*VP remnant with overt infinitive)
          swim-inf will want-inf
          'will want to swim'

Our account of restrictions on inverted infinitives captures this categorial asymmetry in Dutch as well. Quite generally, our proposal captures the exceptional behavior of Dutch infinitives. It also extends to the syntax of *te-* and *zu*-infinitives in Dutch and

German and sheds light on salient differences between Dutch *te*-infinitives and German *zu*-infinitives. For example, it explains why Dutch *te*-infinitives neither invert nor topicalize, whereas German *zu*-infinitives both invert and topicalize.

(7) a. *dat hij niet te zwemmen probeert   (D)
         that he not to swim-inf tries

    b. *te ZWEMMEN probeert hij niet
         to swim-inf tries   he not
         (lit. 'to swim he does not try')

(8) a. weil   er zu schwimmen versuchte   (G)
         because he to swim-inf   tried
         'because he tried to swim'

    b. zu schwimmen versuchte er nicht
         to swim-inf   tried   he not
         (lit. 'to swim he did not try')

How can the crosslinguistic and cross-categorial variation be handled in a theory that assumes a universal hierarchy and overt feature-driven movement? Under our proposal there are no differences in underlying structure or in basic type of derivation: Dutch, German, Hungarian—and for that matter Italian, English, Japanese, and Bantu—are all part of the same system. In chapter 4 we pointed out that variation in linear order can only be due to variation in the size of the constituents that move or survive. The different patterns in Hungarian are accounted for in such terms: specifier extraction versus pied-piping, inflection of VP+ versus VP, and complexity restrictions on the output. We will follow the same strategy here. In our account of crosslinguistic and crosscategorial variation, several new complexity filters will play an especially important role. Our primary goal is to show that these filters are descriptively insightful in that they correctly predict intricate patterns of data. If they indeed do so, they also offer evidence for the general structures and processes developed in this book, because these structures and processes provide the very terms in which the filters can be stated.

8.2   Background Information on Dutch Restructuring Verbs

We start with some background information on Dutch verbal complexes. Dutch forms verbal complexes with infinitives and participles.

(9) a. *Restructuring verbs that select for infinitives (nonexhaustive list)*
         Modals: kunnen 'can, be able to', willen 'want', zullen 'will (future)', mogen
         'be allowed to', hoeven '(not) have to', durven (te) 'dare'
         Aspectual verbs: blijven 'continue', gaan 'go to'

Causative verbs and perception verbs: laten 'let, make', zien 'see', horen
'hear', voelen 'feel'
Others: proberen 'try'
b. *Restructuring verbs that take participles*
hebben 'have', zijn 'be'[2]

Restructuring verbs that take infinitival complements and manifest the IPP effect
in participial constructions (see (10)) are called *verb raisers* in the literature on Dutch.
Most of these verbs combine with "bare" infinitival complements. Some select infinitival complements with the infinitival marker *te*.

The class of verb raisers is the same core class of verbs that trigger restructuring in
Romance and inversion in Hungarian: we are dealing with verbs that must combine
with VP+ in their VP+ projection. As a morphosyntactic property, these verbs combine with a bare infinitive, or with a *te*-infinitive. We continue to assume that this
property is checked under sisterhood by the restructuring verb ((9) in chapter 4).

Hebben 'have' and *zijn* 'be' take participial complements and form verbal complexes with their participles. In their distribution, Dutch participles resemble Hungarian infinitives somewhat more closely than Dutch infinitives do, as we will show in
section 8.9. These verbs also participate in the IPP (*infinitivus pro participio*) effect,
where an infinitive appears instead of an (expected) participial form. This happens if
the "participle" itself is a verb raiser combining with an infinitival complement.

(10) omdat ik met Jan heb willen/*gewild   praten
     because I with Jan have want-inf/*ge-want-part talk-inf
     'because I wanted to talk with Jan'

We return to the IPP effect in Dutch and German in sections 8.9.4 and 8.10.

We restrict the discussion to verb-raising constructions, that is, those restructuring
verbs that induce the IPP effect in Dutch. Basically the same class of verbs behaves
distinctively in German as well, though Dutch and German vary slightly with respect
to the exact configurations in which the IPP effect obtains. Neither remnant extraposition infinitives (Broekhuis et al. 1995), also known as the third construction, nor
extraposition infinitivals will be discussed in this chapter.

8.3 Infinitival Sequences

We distinguish between sequences with VM-less infinitives (e.g., *zwemmen* 'swim')
and sequences with VM-taking infinitives (e.g., *opbellen* 'call up; lit. up-call'). Small
VMs (particles, incorporated nouns, and adjectives) and big VMs (small clauses) occur in [Spec, VP+], the constituent that restructuring verbs attract. Their distribution
forms an integral part of complex verb formation.

8.4   Simple Patterns

We start with the simple patterns and develop an account of the restrictions they display. Ideally, more complex patterns follow from the grammar that accounts for the simple patterns. Indeed, this is what we will argue: the possible and impossible patterns in longer sequences follow naturally, modulo independently motivated analyses for *te*-infinitives and participles.

8.4.1   Order of a Finite Restructuring Verb and a VM-less Infinitive
In Dutch a finite verb and a VM-less infinitive can occur either in a V1 V2 order or in a V2 V1 order.

(11) a. ... wil   zwemmen $V1_f$ $V2_{inf}$
          want swim-inf
      b. ... zwemmen wil $V2_{inf}$ $V1_f$
          swim-inf   want

The English order (11a) suggests that the infinitival verb is in the infinitival CP and satisfies the VP+ of the modal by CP pied-piping. The inverted order (11b) suggests that the infinitival verb has escaped from the infinitival complement and occupies the VP+ of the modal. Since VP+ ends up in PredP, the infinitive should be able to be topicalized, that is, appear in the first position in root clauses and receive contrastive focus interpretation. This is indeed the case.

(12) ZWEMMEN kan hij niet.
      swim-inf can he not
      'He cannot SWIM.'

The English order represents the normal pattern for Dutch verbal complexes; the inverted order does not. In fact, inversion is severely restricted and is often set aside as a special case. In a 1998 manuscript version of this book, we pursued an analysis that treated cases of inversion as falling outside the "core grammar" of verbal complexes. In particular, we argued that inverted infinitives were not in PredP, but in a slightly higher FP position, reserved for contrastively focused XPs. This analysis turns out to be untenable. As Marcel den Dikken (personal communication) points out, inversion and contrastive focus can co-occur. Furthermore, inversion should be available in infinitival complements, since these may have contrastively focused elements lower than NegP. Yet these cases are sharply excluded (see (15c)).

Here, instead of setting aside the restrictions on these patterns, we develop an account for them. The possible and impossible patterns in longer sequences follow naturally, modulo independently needed analyses for *te*-infinitives and participles.

8.4.2   Restrictions on Inversion

Dutch exhibits several curious restrictions on inversion with VM-less infinitives.

First, inversion is restricted to two restructuring verbs (V1 V2), where V1 is a tensed verb. Thus, a string of more than two restructuring verbs can only occur in V1 V2 V3 order.

(13) ... zal kunnen zwemmen   V1(finite) V2 V3
          will can-inf swim-inf

None of the following orders are possible, whether fully inverted (14a), partially inverted (14b), or the result of remnant VP+ climbing and VP/VP+ splitting (14c):

(14) a. *... zwemmen kunnen zal $*V3_{inf}$ $V2_{inf}$ $V1_f$
             swim-inf can-inf will

      b. *... zal zwemmen kunnen $*V1_f$ $V3_{inf}$ $V2_{inf}$
             will swim-inf can-inf

      c. *... zwemmen zal kunnen $*V3_{inf}$ $V1_f$ $V2_{inf}$
             swim-inf will can-inf

Second, inversion is restricted to V1 V2 sequences where V1 is a tensed verb (15a). It is impossible in infinitival clauses (15c).

(15) a. ... zwemmen kan/kan zwemmen $V2_{inf}$ $V1_f$/$V1_f$ $V2_{inf}$
             swim-inf can/can swim-inf

      b. (om) ... te kunnen zwemmen   te $V1_{inf}$ $V2_{inf}$
          (for)   to can-inf swim-inf

      c. *(om) ... zwemmen te kunnen $*V2_{inf}$ te $V1_{inf}$
          (for)   swim-inf to can-inf

Third, inversion is possible only with bare infinitival complements, not with *te*-infinitives.

(16) a. ... probeert te zwemmen $V1_f$[te $V2_{inf}$]
             tries   to swim-inf

      b. *... te zwemmen probeert   *[te $V2_{inf}$] $V1_f$
             to swim-inf   tries

And fourth, bare infinitives topicalize, but *te*-infinitives do not.

(17)   ZWEMMEN kan hij niet.
        swim-inf can he not
        'He cannot SWIM.'

(18) *Te zwemmen probeert hij niet.
        to swim-inf tries   he not

The latter two behaviors may not be surprising from a Dutch perspective: after all, *te* always remains in the infinitival complement. They are surprising, however, from the perspective of German. German *zu*-infinitives behave exactly like bare infinitives with respect to both inversion and topicalization (see section 8.7.2).

(19) a. weil   er zu schwimmen versuchte
         because he to swim-inf   tried
         'because he tried to swim'
     b. Zu schwimmen versuchte er nicht.
         to swim-inf   tried   he not

In analytical terms, Dutch *te*-infinitives neither extract to the VP+ of the modal nor display PredP behavior. German *zu*-infinitives do. We therefore need to account for the fact that Dutch *te*-infinitives remain stuck in CP but German *zu*-infinitives do not. This is the subject of section 8.6.2.

8.4.3   Preliminaries: Restrictions on Specifier Extraction and Parameters in Hungarian
How to view crosslinguistic variation within the theoretical assumptions we have adopted?

We cast the discussion in terms of derivations involving a VM-less infinitive and consider the options that we developed for Hungarian.

Within infinitives, the derivations proceed as in Hungarian, up to PredP, yielding the representation in (20). VP and VP+ have strictly speaking not yet been merged into the derivation and are enclosed in parentheses.

(20)   (VP+)   [must combine with a carrier of [vp+]]

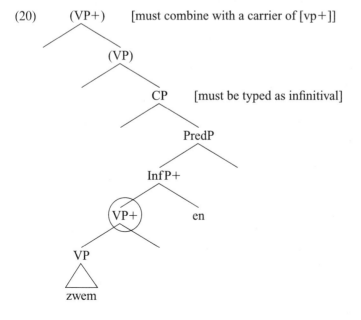

As indicated in this tree, CP and VP+ have particular needs.

(21) a. CP needs to be typed as (bare) infinitival.
    b. A carrier of the [vp+] feature is attracted to VP+ of the restructuring verb.

How can these needs be satisfied? Let us discuss the options we have defined for Hungarian, which (if we are correct) must be generally available. We will argue that the parameters can be set differently, but that Dutch needs one parameter fewer.

The problem we encountered for Hungarian is that the different orders, described in terms of specifier extraction versus CP pied-piping, are not free, but depend on a variety of factors. We captured these by means of splitting parameters, by specifying certain derivational options, and by complexity filters that restrict certain representations at the end of the derivation. More specifically:

(22) *Parameters, specific derivational options, and complexity filters in Hungarian*
    1. Splitting parameter: does VP+/VP split in infinitives?
        Yes in neutral sentences, no in nonneutral sentences; see (25) in chapter 5.
    2. Pied-piping and specifier extraction
        A. How does InfP+ get to CP?
            a. (Light) InfP+ specifier-extracts from PredP.
            b. InfP+ pied-pipes PredP.
        B. How does VP+ get to VP+ of a restructuring verb?
            B1. VP+ is embedded in InfP+.
                a. InfP+ specifier-extracts from CP (yielding inversion).
                b. PredP specifier-extracts from CP (if it can continue to FP).
                c. InfP+ pied-pipes CP (yielding an English order).
                d. PredP pied-pipes CP (yielding an English order).
            B2. VP has split out of VP+ and occupies InfP+. VP+ is a remnant.
                a. VP+ specifier-extracts from PredP to VP+.
    3. Hungarian Complexity Filter (at the end of the derivation)
        "At the end of the derivation VP+ may not contain both a category more complex than InfP+ in its specifier and overt material in its complement VP." (See (70) in chapter 5.)

With VM-less infinitives the VP+/VP-splitting parameter does not come into play, because VP+/VP splitting must be nonvacuous (see (94) in chapter 4). With VM infinitives it does, as we will show in section 8.4.5.

Hungarian (22) makes use of a structural parameter (1: does a particular structure split or not?), a movement parameter (2A: can a particular constituent extract from a particular specifier?), and a complexity filter (3: how complex can the internal structure of particular category in a particular location be?). Given 1 and 2A, VP+ can move by either specifier extraction or pied-piping in various logically possible ways listed in 2B, all of which are acceptable.

We will argue that the analysis of Dutch verbal complexes requires only a VP+/ VP-splitting parameter and a complexity filter. These determine the particular specifier extractions for Dutch and account for the asymmetric behavior of Dutch VM-less infinitives. It is not necessary to invoke a separate movement parameter; the pertinent effects follow naturally from the existing account.

8.4.4   The "No-Complex-InfP+-in-PredP" Filter

We now turn to the question in 2A of (22): how does InfP+ get to CP to type it as an infinitival? In Hungarian a VM-less infinitive can either escape from PredP or pied-pipe PredP to CP. Such an infinitive can escape in Dutch as well, yielding inversion (see (11b)). The question arises whether or not InfP+ in Dutch occupies PredP. Dutch infinitives that must remain in the infinitival CP do not show PredP behavior: they cannot be topicalized (i.e., they cannot be focused and appear in first position in root clauses; see (79)). We take this to show that InfP+ can always specifier-extract from the infinitival PredP, on its way to CP, regardless of its internal structure, and we formulate the following descriptive generalization:

(23) *Dutch*

   In infinitives InfP+ can specifier-extract from PredP to CP.

All InfP+s can trigger CP pied-piping, the unmarked case. On the other hand, specifier extraction of InfP+s from CP is restricted, and only certain types of InfP+s can escape, yielding inversion. Only bare infinitives in InfP+s can invert, hence extract from CP. No other InfP+s can, including *te*-infinitives. These facts can be stated as follows:

(24) *Dutch: Specifier extraction from CP*

   InfP+ may extract from CP only if InfP+ is no more complex than this:

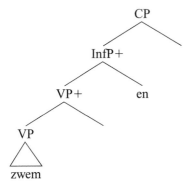

The intention here is to let only "light" InfP+s specifier-extract from CP, and hence invert. Light InfP+s contain VP+s of the form in (24), but none with more complex structure (*te*-InfP+, or VP+ with big VMs (see section 8.4.6), or VP+ with trace of [Spec, CP] in [Spec, VP+] (see section 8.6.2)). In section 8.6 we will discuss why *te*-infinitives do not count as light InfP+s, developing the idea that *te* involves a restructuring predicate: sequences involving *te* pattern exactly like sequences involving three restructuring verbs, not like sequences involving two restructuring verbs.

(24) ensures CP pied-piping for all sequences of infinitives that have a more complex internal structure, including *te*-infinitival complements (see sections 8.6 and 8.7.2).

(23) and (24) together result in pushing all InfP+s out of PredP within the infinitival (later we will show that a slightly weaker statement holds: only InfP+s with a certain complex internal structure are pushed out) and allowing only light InfP+s to extract from CP. Thus, other InfP+s (i.e., those whose internal structure is too complex to allow them to extract from [Spec, CP]) remain stuck in the infinitival CP and trigger pied-piping. At the same time these InfP+s are still outside PredP.

As a result, at the end of the derivation the VP+ or the PredP of the tensed clause never contains an InfP+ in a structure more complex than the ones shown in (25).

(25) At the end of the derivation no VP+ or PredP contains a structure more complex than these:

a.

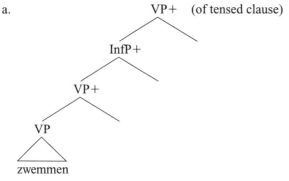

b.

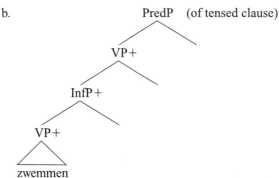

This raises the question whether (25) should be seen as a consequence of the descriptive generalizations on extractability, or whether (25) itself is the source of the conditions on extractability.

We adopt the latter view: only InfP+s of a certain degree of structural complexity may extract, because only they conform to (25). For Hungarian we formulated a restriction on derived complexity as a filter on VP+. For Dutch we formulate it as a filter on the maximal allowable structural complexity of PredP at the end of the derivation. In this way, (23) will force obligatory InfP+ extraction from PredP in infinitival complements for all nonlight InfP+s. In other words, the grammar of Dutch employs specifier extraction for InfP+s, to keep the derived structure as simple as possible.

In conclusion, Dutch has a filter on PredP that only tolerates InfP+s of a certain internal structural complexity. We will refer to it as the *No-Complex-InfP+-in-PredP Filter*, or the *Complexity Filter on PredP*.

(26) *No-Complex-InfP+-in-PredP Filter* (Dutch)
      At the end of the derivation [Spec, PredP] may contain at most a light InfP+
      in a structure no more complex than this:

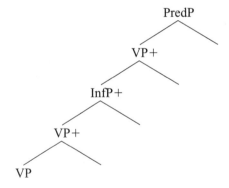

This filter in effect only allows infinitival molecules of a certain size to "stay" in the [Spec, PredP] slot.

This filter looks very strange. It refers to a particular category, InfP+, but it does not impose a complete ban on InfP+ in PredP. In the sections below we argue that this is correct: certain InfP+s do survive in PredP. The filter does not generally rule out complex derived structures in PredP; it only rules out complex derived structures that happen to contain an InfP+. Again, this might seem strange, but it captures a basic asymmetry in the data: the filter rules out remnant VP+ movement only if InfP+ contains an InfP+, allowing it for any other type of VP+, including participles (27e). (The examples in (27) encode the derived internal structure of the remnant VP+ constituent in PredP; silent material has been crossed out.)

(27) a.   ... [PredP[VP+[VP+ [op] [~~bel~~]] ~~zal~~]] zal bellen
                              up   will call-inf

   b.   ... [PredP[VP+[VP+ [aardig] [~~vind~~]] ~~zal~~]] zal vinden
                              nice   will find-inf

   c.   ... [PredP[VP+[VP+ [naar huis] [~~ga~~]] ~~zal~~]] zal gaan
                              to   home   will go-inf

   d.   ... [PredP[VP+[VP+ [piano] [~~speel~~]] ~~zal~~]] zal spelen
                              piano   will play-inf

   e. *... [PredP[VP+[VP+ [zwemmen] ~~wil~~] ~~zal~~]] zal willen
                              swim-inf   will want-inf

   f.   ... [PredP[VP+[VP+ [gezwommen] ~~heb~~] ~~zal~~]] zal hebben
                              ge-swim-part   will have-inf

The paradigm in Dutch is symmetric except for infinitives. In languages like German and Hungarian, which lack this specific filter, similar paradigms are entirely symmetric. Thus, the equivalent of (27e) is possible in Hungarian neutral clauses and in German *zu*-infinitives (*schwimmen zu können* 'swim-inf to can-inf'). We will argue that this difference between Dutch and Hungarian/German is due to the presence of this language-specific and (as far as we can see) idiosyncratic filter on InfP+s in PredP in Dutch.

We end this section by comparing the grammars of Dutch and Hungarian. In Hungarian, we assumed, light InfP+ can extract from PredP (see (66) in chapter 4) and thereby from CP. In Dutch all InfP+s extract from PredP, but their extraction from CP is subject to a similar lightness constraint. This, we will argue, is due to the fact that only certain InfP+s can survive in PredP. Unlike in Hungarian, in Dutch no InfP+ that remains inside the infinitival CP gets focused. Light InfP+s, which may escape from the infinitival and invert, are in effect able to get focused qua PredP. Assuming that PredP is the relevant category for focusing in Dutch as well, this indicates that InfP+s remaining in the infinitival are not in PredP. Dutch thus yields a slightly different picture from Hungarian. In Hungarian the structures that are light enough to extract from PredP and CP and the ones that may remain in VP+ at the end of the derivation are not identical. The revised Hungarian Complexity Filter ((70) of chapter 5) captures this; for example, a big VM bleeds extraction from PredP but is tolerated in VP+ when VP splits out. In Dutch a big VM infinitive is never tolerated in PredP.

8.4.5   Simple Patterns with VM-Taking Infinitives
In Dutch the order of a finite verb and a VM-taking infinitive differs, depending on the "size" of the VM. These orders are equally possible in neutral clauses and in clauses with contrastive focus or negation; none depends on clause type, unlike in Hungarian.

(28) exemplifies patterns with small-VM-taking infinitives.

(28) a.   ... op wil   bellen   VM$_{small}$ V$_f$ V$_{inf}$
            up want call-inf

   b.   ... wil   opbellen   V$_f$ VM$_{small}$ V$_{inf}$
          want up-call-inf

   c. (%) ... opbellen   wil   VM$_{small}$ V$_{inf}$ V$_f$
          up-call-inf want

Small VMs can occur either in VM V1 V2 order (28a) or in V1 VM V2 order (28b). This shows that VP+/VP optionally splits in infinitival complements when the VM is small. Splitting VP+/VP yields remnant VP+ climbing; not splitting VP+/VP feeds either CP pied-piping (28b) or inversion (28c). (We return to the % mark, which signals dialectal variation, in section 8.4.6.2.)

The patterns with big VMs differ from those with small VMs.

(29) a.   ... naar huis   wil   gaan   VM$_{big}$ V$_f$ V$_{inf}$
            to   home want go-inf

   b. *... wil   naar huis   gaan   *V$_f$ VM$_{big}$ V$_{inf}$
          want to   home go-inf

   c. ??*... naar huis   gaan   wil   VM$_{big}$ V$_{inf}$ V$_f$
          to   home go-inf want

With big VMs, VP+/VP splitting is obligatory; compare (29a) with (29b,c).[3]

8.4.6   The VP+/VP-Splitting Parameter

The parallelism between Dutch VM-climbing cases and patterns in Hungarian neutral clauses is due to the presence of a similar VP+/VP-splitting parameter. We formulate this parameter as follows, using *small VMs* and *big VMs* as descriptive labels:

(30) In infinitives VP splits out of VP+ only if [Spec, VP+] is filled with material distinct from VP. VP+/VP splitting is (a) optional if VP+ contains a small VM, (b) obligatory if VP+ contains a big VM.

As in Hungarian, in Dutch the condition that [Spec, VP+] be filled with material distinct from VP ensures that non-VM-taking VPs like *zwemmen* 'swim-inf' remain in VP+; clause (30a) allows infinitives with small VMs (*op* 'up') to remain in the VP+ (yielding *opbellen* 'up-call-inf' after VP+ moves to InfP+). Clause (30b) forces VP+ splitting, with VP moving to InfP+, retaining big VMs in VP+.

Since splitting VP out of VP+ creates a remnant VP+, obligatory VP+/VP splitting yields obligatory VM "climbing" in Dutch, shown in (31), the same way it does in neutral clauses in Hungarian.

(31) *Patterns that arise when VP+ splits* (if VP+ splits, VM-climbing is obligatory)

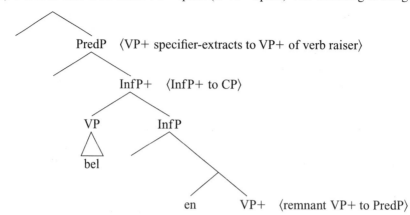

VP's move to InfP+ (i.e., VP+/VP splitting) entails that InfP+ moves to CP, without VP+. The VP+ that the restructuring verb needs is too low in the infinitival complement to trigger CP pied-piping; hence, it must move directly from PredP to the VP+ of the restructuring verb, yielding obligatory VM-climbing, as indicated in (32).

(32)

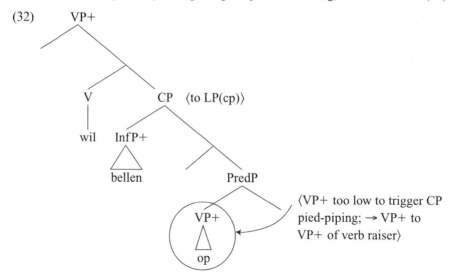

At the end of the derivation the Complexity Filter on PredP will be respected. As (33) shows, PredP contains no InfP+, either silent or overt.

(33)

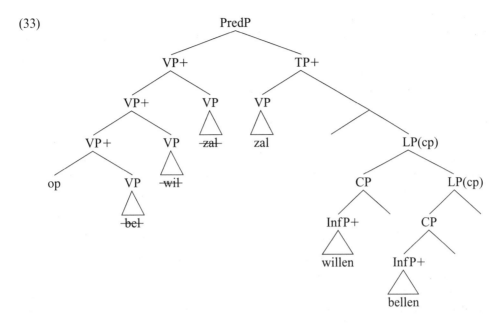

8.4.6.1 On the Independence of the No-Complex-InfP+-in-PredP Filter and the VP+/VP-Splitting Parameter   We have so far motivated one filter (InfP+ cannot be inside a too-complex structure in PredP) and one parameter (the VP+/VP-splitting parameter). Since VP+/VP splitting overlaps with the filter in some cases, we may ask whether they are both needed. For example, (27c), *naar huis gaan wil* 'to home go-inf want', could also be excluded by the filter, since it contains an InfP+ with a heavy VM. That type of InfP+ behaves like an InfP+ with a big VM in Hungarian. The filter could in effect force VP+ splitting inside the infinitive in this case, yielding *naar huis wil gaan* 'to home want go-inf' as the only possible outcome. This is generally true for cases of obligatory VP+/VP splitting, like (27a) and (27c). However, this account says nothing about the unacceptability of (27b), *wil naar huis gaan* 'want to home go-inf'. Since InfP+s may extract from PredP, the filter has nothing to say about this case, and one must therefore capture independently what constituents may remain in the infinitival CP. This is what the VP+/VP-splitting parameter does, since as we have shown, obligatory VP+/VP splitting leaves no other option than remnant VP+ climbing.

We therefore conclude that the data pattern results from the interaction of two independent mechanisms: a parameter on VP+/VP splitting in the infinitival CP and a complexity filter on PredP. The latter disallows complex InfP+s in PredP, as a result of which only noncomplex InfP+s may extract from the infinitival CP.

8.4.6.2   Dialectal Variation: The No-Complex-InfP+-in-PredP Filter and the VP+/ VP-Splitting Parameter   Dialectal variation in Dutch might be traced to variation in the No-Complex-InfP+-in-PredP Filter (the Complexity Filter on PredP) and the VP+/VP-splitting parameter.

Some speakers accept inversion with infinitives with small VMs (*opbellen wil* 'up-call-inf wants' (28c)); others do not. This variation can be captured as a slight variation in the form of the Complexity Filter on PredP. The grammar of speakers who accept (28c) counts small VM-VP sequences as light enough to pass the filter. The grammar of speakers who do not accept it counts such InfP+s as not light enough.[4]

As is well known, examples like (29b), repeated here, were possible in quite recent stages of Dutch and are still attested in certain southern dialects (Hoeksema 1993).

(29) b. *... wil   naar huis   gaan   *V_f VM_{big} V_{inf}
         want to   home go-inf   (* because of VP+/VP splitting)

This dialectal variation reflects slightly different settings for the VP+/VP-splitting parameter. In dialects that allow (29b) next to strings like *naar huis wil gaan* 'to home wants go-inf', VP+/VP splitting must be optional with big VMs. The splitting point is thus defined on a slightly bigger constituent—namely, VP+—with big VMs. If the setting of this parameter involves determining exactly where the split must occur,[5] VP+ constituents below the split should not be splittable in these dialects. Thus, small VMs and infinitives must be kept together, whereas big VMs and infinitives may split. This may be correct, as the following remark suggests:

Many regard the splitting of particles from their accompanying verbs as a typical special trait of northern, Hollandic Dutch; Belgian speakers are not fond of sentences like ... [(29b)]. (Den Besten and Edmondson 1983, 193)

Splitting parameters quite generally must be involved in the distinction between so-called verb-raising languages (languages that allow only a small remnant infinitival in the CP) and VP-projection-raising languages (languages that allow a big remnant in the infinitival CP) (e.g., Den Besten and Edmondson 1983, Haegeman and Van Riemsdijk 1986, Den Dikken 1996). This distinction is usually described in terms of the size of the constituent that can undergo verb raising. Given our perspective, it should be described in terms of the size of the constituent that the remnant CP may contain (Hinterhölzl 1998). This in turn might involve the interaction of several splitting parameters. The different distribution of small clauses results from a different setting in the VP+/VP-splitting parameter. A very similar parameter seems to hold for InfP+/PredP and TP+/PredP splitting, determining whether an InfP+ or a TP+ may split out of PredP or not. In Dutch InfP+ must split out of PredP, yielding an infinitive as the sole remnant in the CP complement of restructuring verbs. In West Flemish the remnant CP may be at least as big as NegP and FP (Haegeman

1998). This suggests that in this case InfP+ has not split out of PredP, but has pied-piped PredP and higher projections to CP, exactly as in Hungarian (section 6.2). Recall that for Dutch we had to assume that TP+ splits out of PredP in root environments, but not in nonroot environments.

These parameters can vary slightly and are independent of each other. This predicts a very precise constellation of data, with the distribution of different VMs forming an integral part of the pattern. We thus make precise predictions regarding individual speakers' patterns of judgments. This in turn should provide insight into the considerable existing dialectal variation and allow us to move from the inventory of possible patterns to the actual patterns attested in different dialects.

8.4.6.3 Restructuring: Sample Derivations of VM-Taking Verbs Involving the Stacking Positions As is well known, in the course of a derivation the dependents of the infinitive end up in the matrix clause: this is obligatory, even in case the infinitive triggers CP pied-piping.

Obligatory restructuring follows naturally from the mechanics of the derivation in case VP+ extracts from the infinitival CP. It is simply a consequence of the way we have defined movements in conjunction with stacking positions, which we had to invoke in order to obey the cycle (see (27) and (28) in chapter 4).

We illustrate this in the derivations below. Although these derivations look complex, we want to draw attention to their mechanical nature and the fact that the same patterns repeat. The parts that make up the final string are pushed up in the tree in quite boring, repetitive ways. The strings become larger as more overt material is merged into the derivation. The items always remain close to each other, and the basic structure repeats again and again. We extract these basic recurring strings in (38).

Of necessity, the derivations are cut into three smaller parts, (35)–(37). They should be read upward from the lowest position. We indicate what movement each node undergoes. We do not write out the remnant structure, nor do we show how the subject is merged into the structure; all operator positions are merged in the matrix clause. The string that we derive is this:

(34) (dat ik) Marie op zal   willen   bellen
      (that I) Marie up will(finite) want-inf call-inf
      'that I will want to call Marie up'

(35) *First part: derivation up to the VP+ of the* willen *clause*

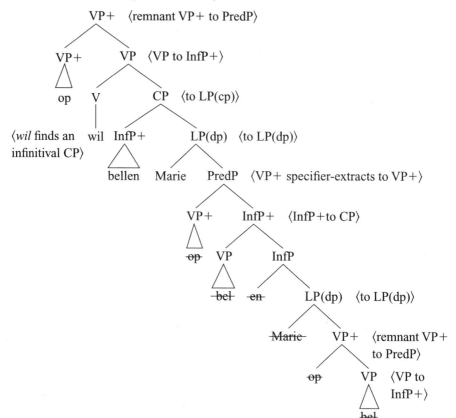

(36) *Second part: derivation up to the VP+ of the future auxiliary* zullen *in the tensed clause*

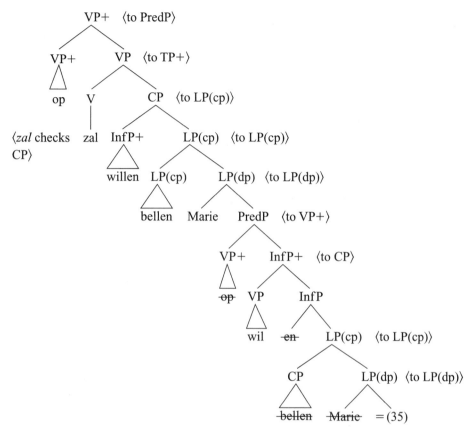

(37) *Third part: continuation of the derivation up to RefP*

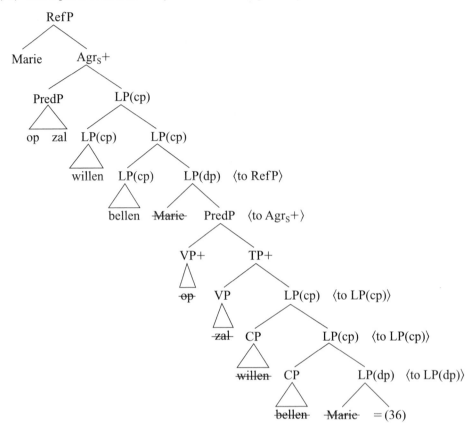

(38) *Recurring strings*
      Marie op bel
      Marie op bel+en
      Marie op wil bellen
      Marie op wil+en bellen
      Marie op zul willen bellen
      Marie op zul+T willen bellen (zul+T is spelled out as *zal*)
      Marie op zal+T+Agr willen bellen

These derivations demonstrate how the verb is gradually built up. Some of the stacking positions could possibly represent projections where other categories are built up or "grown." This would be consistent with proposals by Kayne (1994, 1998a) and Sportiche (1997). Sportiche argues that a D does not form an underlying constituent with its NP; instead, the two get together in the course of the derivation. Kayne argues that this is true for *of* (1994) and for infinitival complementizers like *de/di* in French and Italian (1998a). Similarly, a P and a DP (e.g., *of DP* in *a picture of DP*) are not necessarily merged in the derivation as a constituent, but give the appearance of being one because of the way the derivation puts the parts together. A P does not form a constituent with DP, but moves into a local relation with it somewhere in the course of the derivation (Kayne 1999).

Dutch verb-raising complements obligatorily restructure, even if a small VM remains in the infinitival CP, and the restructuring verb's needs are satisfied by CP pied-piping. The only material that may remain in the infinitival CP is the infinitive or a small VM infinitive. The question arises how restructuring follows when the small VM remains in the infinitival and CP pied-piping is forced. We do not have an account to offer at present. The problem is related to the puzzle of how to exclude **wil opbellen Marie* and **wil Marie opbellen*, where *Marie* remains in the infinitival. These examples show that there must be a point in the derivation where *opbellen* is the sole remnant in the CP. If *Marie* is in a stacking position just above CP (see (39)), as in Hungarian, it is assured of climbing into the matrix clause, because of the "move one category at a time" strategy.

(39)

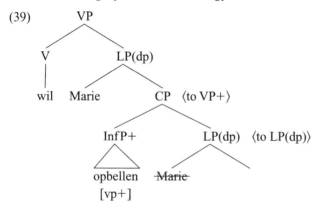

8.5   More Complex Patterns

8.5.1   Longer Sequences with VM-less Infinitives
In Dutch a series of more than two restructuring verbs can occur only in an English order.

(40) dat je   met Jan *zal moeten kunnen lachen*   V1(finite) V2 V3 V4
     that you with Jan will must-inf can-inf laugh-inf
     'that you will certainly have to be able to laugh with Jan' (i.e., that it definitely
     must be the case that you should be able to have some fun with Jan)

None of the following orders are possible, though they are in principle available and are attested in other languages:

(41) a. *... zal moeten lachen   kunnen   *V1$_f$ V2$_{inf}$ V4$_{inf}$ V3$_{inf}$
         will must-inf laugh-inf can-inf

   b. *... zal lachen   kunnen moeten   *V1$_f$ V4$_{inf}$ V3$_{inf}$ V2$_{inf}$
         will laugh-inf can-inf must-inf

   c. *... lachen   kunnen moeten zal   *V4$_{inf}$ V3$_{inf}$ V2$_{inf}$ V1$_f$
         laugh-inf can-inf must-inf will

   d. *... lachen   zal moeten kunnen   *V4$_{inf}$ V1$_f$ V2$_{inf}$ V3$_{inf}$
         laugh-inf will must-inf can-inf

   e. *... lachen   kunnen zal moeten   *V4$_{inf}$ V3$_{inf}$ V1$_f$ V2$_{inf}$
         laugh-inf can-inf will must-inf

   f. *... moeten zal kunnen lachen   *V2$_{inf}$ V1$_f$ V3$_{inf}$ V4$_{inf}$
         must-inf will can-inf laugh-inf

As we will show in section 8.7.1, the ungrammaticality of all these patterns can be explained in a unified manner. In section 8.5.3 we will focus on how to exclude the order in (41d), *lachen zal moeten kunnen 'laugh-inf will must-inf can-inf'. The ungrammaticality of this string becomes all the more puzzling in light of the general availability of remnant VP+ climbing, discussed in the following section.

8.5.2 Longer Sequences with VM-Taking Verbs

The possible orders for longer sequences with VM-taking verbs are identical to the ones discussed in section 8.4.5.

   If [Spec, VP+] and VP contain distinct material, VP splits out of VP+ and moves to InfP+. This yields remnant VP+ climbing and places InfP+ in CP.

(42) a. ... op wil   kunnen bellen   VM$_{small}$ V1$_f$ V2$_{inf}$ V3$_{inf}$
         up want can-inf call-inf

   b. ... naar huis zal willen   gaan   VM$_{big}$ V1$_f$ V2$_{inf}$ V3$_{inf}$
         to   home will want-inf go-inf

VP/VP+ splitting is optional with small VMs, hence the pattern in (43a). VP/VP+ splitting is obligatory with big VMs, hence the impossibility of (43b).

(43) a. ... wil   kunnen opbellen   V1$_f$ V2$_{inf}$ VM$_{small}$ V3$_{inf}$
         want can-inf up-call-inf

   b. *... zal willen   naar huis gaan   *V1$_f$ V2$_{inf}$ VM$_{big}$ V3$_{inf}$
         will want-inf to   home go-inf

If VP does not split out of VP+, and VP+ pied-pipes InfP+, the result is ungrammatical, just as (41d) is.

(44) a. *... opbellen   wil   kunnen $*V3_{inf}\ V1_f\ V2_{inf}$
          up-call-inf want can-inf

     b. *... lachen   wil   kunnen $*V3_{inf}\ V1_f\ V2_{inf}$
          laugh-inf want can-inf

8.5.3   An Infinitive/Noninfinitive Asymmetry

If we compare the categorial status of the VMs that may climb in longer sequences, we observe a systematic asymmetry. As before, constituents that have been removed from VP+ in the course of the derivation are crossed out.

(45) a.   ... [$_{PredP}$[$_{VP+}$[$_{VP+}$[$_{PP}$ op] [~~bel~~]] [~~zal~~]]] zal bellen   ([Spec, VP+] contains PP)
                                     up   will call-inf

     b.   ... [$_{PredP}$[$_{VP+}$[$_{VP+}$[$_{AP}$ aardig] [~~vind~~]] [~~zal~~]]] zal vinden   ([Spec, VP+] contains AP)
                                     nice   will find-inf

     c.   ... [$_{PredP}$[$_{VP+}$[$_{VP+}$[$_{PP}$ naar huis] [~~ga~~]] [~~zal~~]]] zal gaan   ([Spec, VP+] contains PP)
                                     to   home   will go-inf

     d.   ... [$_{PredP}$[$_{VP+}$[$_{VP+}$[[$_{DP}$ piano] ~~speel~~]] [~~zal~~]]] zal spelen   ([Spec, VP+] contains NP)
                                     piano   will play-inf

     e. *... [$_{PredP}$[$_{VP+}$[$_{VP+}$[$_{InfP+}$ zwemmen] ~~wil~~]] [~~zal~~]]] zal willen   ([Spec, VP+] contains InfP+)
                                     swim-inf   will want-inf

Recall that it is not the case that a InfP+ never inverts: it may invert if it is the unique complement of a finite restructuring verb. ((46) repeats (11b).)

(46) ... zwemmen wil $V2_{inf}\ V1_f$
         swim-inf   want

   This categorial asymmetry resurfaces in the possibilities for topicalization under contrastive focus interpretation.[6] VP+s that may climb can be topicalized, as can InfP+s that may invert. InfP+s that do not invert do not topicalize, either.[7]

(47) a.   Erg aardig zal je   dit toch niet moeten   vinden.
          very nice   will you this prt not must-inf find-inf
          'You certainly should not find this very nice.'

     b.   Naar Groningen zal je   vast wel willen   gaan.
          to   Groningen will you certainly want-inf go-inf
          'You will certainly want to go to Groningen.'

     c.   Piano zal zij zeker   niet willen   spelen.
          piano will she certainly not want-inf play-inf
          'She certainly will not want to play the piano.'

     d. ?*Zwemmen zal hij zeker   niet willen.
          swim-inf will he certainly not want-inf

    e. *Lachen zal je zeker   niet moeten/kunnen/willen.
        laugh-inf will you certainly not must-inf/can-inf/want-inf

    f.   Lachen   kan hij niet.
        laugh-inf can he not
        'He cannot laugh.'

    g. Zwemmen kan hij zeker   niet.
        swim-inf   can he certainly not
        'He certainly does not know how to swim.'

This asymmetry follows from the Complexity Filter on PredP, which tolerates InfP+s only in a relatively shallow structure. This can be brought out by considering the derived structures that our analysis assigns. A simple extraction as in (47) yields the following representation:

(48) $[_{PredP}[_{VP+}[_{InfP+}$ [zwemmen] ~~wil~~]]] wil $V2_{inf}$ $V1_f$
              swim-inf   want

Since this string is obviously allowed, it passes the Complexity Filter on PredP. However, any InfP+s embedded in more complex structure violate the filter. Since VP+ climbing involves larger and larger structures, further remnant VP+ climbing of a VP containing an InfP+ will inevitably embed the InfP+ in a more complex structure and thereby violate the filter.

(49) a. *$[_{PredP}[_{VP+}[_{VP+}[_{InfP+}$ zwemmen] [~~wil~~]] [~~zal~~]]] zal willen   *$V3_{inf}$ $V1_f$ $V2_{inf}$
                        swim-inf   will want-inf

     b. *$[_{PredP}[_{VP+}[_{VP+}[_{VP+}[_{InfP+}$ [zwemmen] [~~kun~~]]   *$V4_{inf}$ $V1_f$ $V2_{inf}$ $V3_{inf}$
                        swim-inf
  [~~moet~~]]] ~~zul~~]]] zal moeten kunnen
               will must-inf can-inf

The Complexity Filter on PredP therefore allows only one step of InfP+ extraction.

    Only InfP+s, which may survive in PredP, may be topicalized qua PredP. InfP+s, which do not pass the Complexity Filter on PredP, may not be topicalized qua PredP. Removing the offending InfP+ to FP on the way to RefP will not help, because InfP+ is not a focusable projection, but PredP is.

    The Complexity Filter on PredP does not exclude complex VP+s in general—only those that contain an InfP+. As the representations in (45) show, other categories can occur without any problem in complex structures in PredP.[8] ((50) repeats (45a).)

(50) ... $[_{PredP}[_{VP+}[_{VP+}[_{PP}$ op] [~~bel~~]] [~~zal~~]]] zal bellen
                     up   will call-inf

What is important is that the remnant VP+ never contains the InfP+: InfP+ is always merged outside VP+, with VP moving to InfP+ in these cases.

In sum, then, the Complexity Filter on PredP restricts inversion of InfP+. It allows a single step of inversion and rules out all other cases of inversion for InfP+. As a consequence, it keeps InfP+ within CP in such cases and leaves CP pied-piping as the only option. An English order is obligatory in precisely those cases where the filter would be violated.

8.5.3.1 Sample Derivation of *V3 V1 V2 We illustrate the derivation of the ungrammatical string **lachen zal willen* 'laugh-inf will want-inf', *V3 V1 V2 (stacking positions omitted). In the lowest infinitive VP+ does not have to split because [Spec, VP+] and VP do not contain distinct material (*lachen* 'laugh-inf' is a VM-less infinitive). InfP+ in [Spec, CP] may therefore escape to VP+ of the restructuring verb *willen* 'want-inf'. Then VP splits out of VP+ and moves to InfP+. The remnant VP+ is attracted to PredP. This yields the structure in (51) at the point where the verb of the tensed clause is merged (the history of the derivation can be read from the crossed-out part).

(51) *First part of derivation*

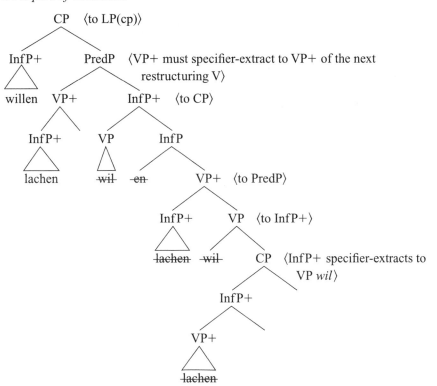

At this point the restructuring verb *zul* 'will' is merged into the derivation. The remnant VP+ moves to VP+, CP moves to LP(cp), the remnant VP moves to TP+, and the remnant VP+ moves to PredP. The derived constituent structure violates the Complexity Filter on PredP. As (52) shows, it contains an InfP+ dominated by two VP+ nodes, where only one is allowed.

(52) *Second part of the derivation*

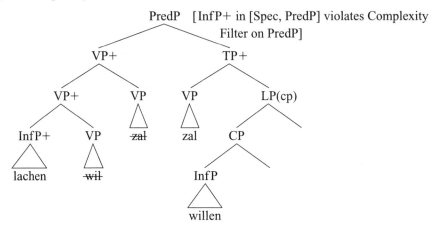

InfP+ extraction from the lowest CP, followed by VP+/VP splitting, therefore always results in a violation of the Complexity Filter on PredP. Hence, InfP+ must remain in the lowest CP, and CP pied-piping is the only remaining possibility.

8.5.3.2 Sample Derivation of VM V1 V2 The derivations of Dutch *op will bellen* 'up want call-inf', VM V1 V2, closely resemble the derivations for Hungarian neutral clauses. As indicated in (53), VP+/VP splitting creates a VP+ remnant, which contains nothing but an overt VM; InfP+ ends up in the infinitival CP. VP+ is too low to trigger CP pied-piping in this context and must extract from PredP to VP+. (Stacking positions are not shown.)

(53) *The most deeply embedded infinitive*

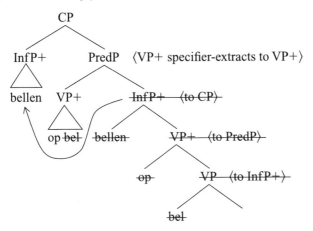

In all intermediate infinitives VP+ must split: VP+ splitting is obligatory when [Spec, VP+] and VP contain different overt material. The derivation continues in (54).

(54) *The intermediate infinitive* (VP+ splitting is obligatory)

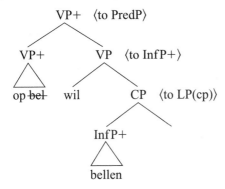

The VP+ is carried successive-cyclically to the PredP of the highest restructuring verb. This yields the derived constituent structure shown in (55).

(55) *The tensed clause* (only PredP and TP+ shown)

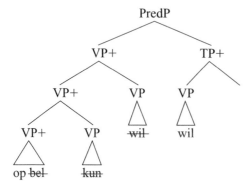

Obligatory VP splitting thus accounts for the fact that the lowest VP+ is carried all the way up through a series of restructuring verbs and cannot be stranded in intermediate infinitives.[9]

8.6   *Te*- and *Zu*-Infinitives

We turn next to *te*- and *zu*-infinitives, a thorny problem of Dutch and German syntax. Our goal is to show that *te/zu* behave like restructuring predicates: a *te*-infinitive sequence thus contains two VP+s, not one VP+. This fact plays a crucial role in explaining the patterns described in section 8.4.2: if a *te*-infinitive is embedded under another restructuring predicate, a violation of the Complexity Filter on PredP will result.

8.6.1   The Structure of *Te*-Infinitives

Like participial *ge*, *te* behaves like a restructuring predicate in the sense that it attracts a remnant VP+ to its left.

(56) a. i. (om Jan) op te bellen
             (for Jan) up to call-inf
             'to call up Jan'
         ii. (dat ik Jan) op wil   bellen
             (that I   Jan) up want call-inf
             'that I want to call up Jan'
     b. i. (om de kamer) schoon te maken
             (for the room)   clean   to make-inf
             'to clean the room'
         ii. (dat ik de kamer) schoon wil   maken
             (that I   the room)   clean   want make-inf
             'that I want to clean the room'

c. i. (om) naar Venetie te varen
      (for) to   Venice to go-by-boat-inf
      'to go to Venice by boat'
   ii. (dat hij) naar Venetie wil   varen
      (that he) to   Venice wants go-by-boat-inf
      'that he wants to go to Venice by boat'

A non-VM-taking infinitive shows up to the right of *te*.

(57) a. (om) te zwemmen
      (for) to swim-inf
      'to swim'
   b. (dat jij) wil   zwemmen
      (that you) want swim-inf
      'that you want to swim'

Te-infinitives differ in two ways from restructuring verbs. First, infinitival verbs with small VMs cannot follow *te* (*wil opbellen* vs. **te opbellen*). Second, some infinitival verb always follows *te;* that is, infinitives do not invert with *te*.

(58) a. i. *zwemmen te
         swim-inf   to
      ii. (dat hij) zwemmen wil
         (that he) swim-inf   wants
         'that he wants to swim'
   b. i. *te opbellen
         to up-call-inf
      ii. (dat jij) wil   opbellen
         (that you) want up-call-inf
         'that you want to call up'

This suggests the following analysis: *te*—or, as we will show, some other, hidden predicate—is a restructuring predicate, projecting VP+ and requiring a VP+ in its VP+. It is this predicate that is responsible for the differing behavior of *te*-infinitives and bare infinitives (section 8.6.2).

Te always requires an InfP+ to its right. This InfP+ may not be structurally complex (58b). We account for this fact as follows. *Te* selects for an InfP+, since that is what it co-occurs with. This property does not distinguish *te* from, say, *willen* 'want-inf'. What does distinguish them is that the InfP+ that follows *te* must be "small." We implement this restriction as a complexity filter on some specifier position. Since this property is specifically related to *te*, and not to infinitivals in general, the filter holds of a specifier position of teP: [Spec, teP]. [Spec, teP] attracts InfP+. *Te* causes obligatory VP+/VP splitting, even when the VM in [Spec, VP+] is small (*te opbellen* (58bi)). Dutch and German *te* and *zu* are basically identical in these regards.

(59) [Spec, te/zu] attracts InfP+.

(60) *Complexity Filter on [Spec, te/zu]*
    InfP+ in [Spec, te/zu] may not be more complex than this:

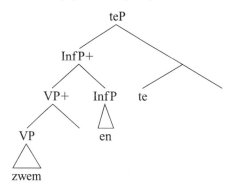

(60) forces VP+/VP splitting with all VM-taking verbs. Hence, only two teP config-urations survive, namely, (61a) and (61b).

(61) a. *With full infinitives*   b. *With VM infinitives*

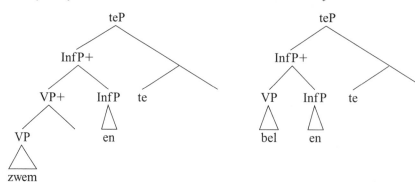

These configurations yield the wrong linear order: *te* must immediately precede the infinitive, revealing the presence of some additional projection that attracts *te*. The surface position of the remnant VP+ (*op te bellen* 'up to call-inf') indicates the pres-ence of a higher VP+ attractor. Putting these two facts together, we conclude that the projection where *te* ends up is a silent restructuring V, which attracts VP+ to its VP+ in the usual fashion. *Te* undergoes head movement to the silent V. This is an allow-able case of head movement since it adjoins overt material to a silent head. VP+ moves to [Spec, VP], as illustrated in (62). (Intermediate licensing and stacking posi-tions are omitted from the derivations below.)

(62) *Continuation of (61b)*

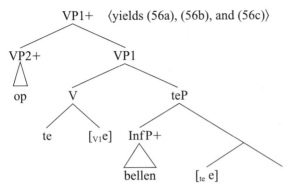

The resulting VP1+ (*op te bellen* 'up to call-inf') behaves like any VP+ of this form: it carries a [vp+] feature that will be attracted by any higher restructuring verb. This is shown in the examples below. With a small VM in VP+, it behaves like VP+s with a small VM, and VP+/VP splitting is optional (63a). With a big VM in VP+, VP splits obligatorily out of VP+ (63b).

(63) a. 〈op〉 schijnt 〈op〉 te bellen
          up   seems   up   to call-inf
      b. 〈naar Venetie〉 schijnt 〈*naar Venetie〉 te gaan
          to   Venice   seems   to   Venice   to go-inf

As we show in the next section, the more complex internal structure of *te*-infinitives accounts for the differing behavior of *te*-infinitives and bare infinitives in Dutch: specifically, the presence of the silent restructuring predicate yields violations of the Complexity Filter on PredP.

8.6.2 Restrictions on Inversion Revisited

In section 8.4.2 we discussed three curious restrictions on the inversion of infinitives. As far as we know, until now these asymmetries remained unaccounted for. However, they follow immediately from the quite independently motivated analysis of *te* and the Complexity Filter on PredP.

First, inversion is possible in tensed clauses, but impossible in infinitival clauses.

(64) a. ... zwemmen kan / kan zwemmen V_{inf} V_f / V_f V_{inf}
          swim-inf can / can swim-inf
      b. (om) ... te kunnen zwemmen / *zwemmen te kunnen   te V1 V2 / *V2 te V1
          (for)   to can-inf swim-inf   swim-inf to can-inf

This follows from the presence of a restructuring predicate associated with *te*. Structures with *te* contain, not one VP+, but two VP+s. As a result, inversion induces violations of Complexity Filter on PredP, just as sequences of three restructuring verbs do, and CP pied-piping is obligatory.

(65) *[$_{PredP}$[$_{VP+}$[$_{VP+}$[$_{InfP+}$ zwemmen] wil]]] te willen   *V3 V1 V2
                                        swim-inf   to want-inf

The other two asymmetries follow in essentially the same way: we are in effect comparing a sequence of two with a sequence of three restructuring verbs.

The second asymmetry is that bare infinitives can invert in a single step under a tensed verb, but *te*-infinitives cannot. This is explained in the same way as the impossibility of inversion with sequences of three restructuring verbs.

(66) a.   probeert te zwemmen
           tries   to swim-inf
           'tries to swim'
      b.   *te [$_{InfP+}$ zwemmen] probeert
           to   swim-inf   tries
      c.   wil   kunnen zwemmen
           wants can-inf swim-inf
           'wants to be able to swim'
      d.   *[$_{InfP+}$[$_{InfP+}$ zwemmen] kunnen] wil
                        swim-inf   can-inf   wants

Writing out the derived structure makes it clear that the InfP+ in (66b) is embedded in a structure too complex to pass the Complexity Filter on PredP.

(67) *[$_{PredP}$[$_{VP1+}$[$_{VP2+}$ te [$_{InfP+}$[$_{VP3+}$ zwemmen] probeer]]]]

The filter thus rules out inversion, and CP pied-piping is forced, yielding the V1 *te* (= V2) V3 order.

The third asymmetry concerns topicalization: bare infinitives topicalize under a contrastive focus reading, but *te*-infinitives do not.

(68) a.   Zwemmen wil   hij niet.
           swim-inf   wants he not
           'lit. swim he does not want'
      b.   *Te zwemmen probeert hij niet.
           to swim-inf   tries   he not
           'lit. to swim he does not try'

The *te*-infinitive may topicalize only if it is contained in PredP. As we have just shown, it may not appear there, because of the Complexity Filter on PredP. Therefore, a *te*-infinitive cannot be topicalized qua PredP.

8.7   Dutch and German: German Verbal Complexes

We capture the difference in behavior between Dutch *te*-infinitives and German *zu*-infinitives quite simply: German tolerates complex InfP+s in PredP and thus lacks the Complexity Filter on PredP. InfP+s therefore show PredP behavior in German.

8.7.1   Absence of VP+ Splitting in German Infinitives

Simple infinitival sequences with restructuring verbs in German are inverted.[10]

(69)   weil   Peter lachen   können will
       because Peter laugh-inf can-inf wants
       'because Peter wants to be able to laugh'

(70)   weil   sie Peter anrufen   müssen wollen
       because they Peter up-call-inf must-inf want-inf
       'because they want to have to call Peter up'

As these examples show, infinitives obligatorily participate in inversion, whether they combine with VMs or not. German therefore does not split VP+/VP in infinitives. Although German does not normally split VP+/VP, there are contexts in which splitting is forced: tensed root clauses, *zu*-infinitives (*lachen zu können* 'laugh-inf to can-inf'), and in some dialects the IPP configuration (*lachen hat können* 'laugh-inf has can-inf') (see section 8.10).

  The inverted infinitives show the characteristic behavior of elements in PredP: they can be topicalized.

(71)   Lachen   können will   er. (Lattewitz 1977, 148)
       laugh-inf can-inf wants he
       'He wants to be able to laugh.'

  German resembles Hungarian in tolerating structurally complex infinitives in PredP and differs from Dutch in lacking the Complexity Filter on PredP. The lack of splitting and the absence of a complexity filter go hand in hand for these cases.

8.7.2   VP+ Splitting in German Infinitives: *Zu*-Infinitives

However, the ban on VP+/VP splitting in German infinitives is not absolute. VP splits out of VP+ in infinitives (or participles) when forced to by the complexity filters imposed by *zu* or *ge*. Like Dutch *te, zu* forces VP to split out of VP+ in the infinitive, because the Complexity Filter on [Spec, te/zu] tolerates only light InfP+s in that position.

  German InfP+s, which contain VP+, distribute like other VMs with respect to the placement of *zu* in longer sequences. In (72) we contrast Dutch and German.

(72)   *German*   *Dutch*
   a. anzurufen   op te bellen   'up to call'
   b. sauber zu machen   schoon te maken   'clean to make'
   c. Klavier zu spielen   piano te spelen   'piano to play'
   d. gehen zu müssen   *gaan te moeten   'go to must'

VP+/VP splitting, and attraction of the remnant VP+ to the VP+ of the silent restructuring predicate associated with *zu,* yields the following VP+ representations for (72a–c):

(73) a. German: $[_{VP+}[_{VP+}$ an ~~ruf~~ $[_{VP}$ zu $[_{InfP+}$ rufen $[_{zu}$ e][. . .
    b. Dutch: $[_{VP+}[_{VP+}$ op ~~bel~~ [te $[_{InfP+}$ bellen $[[_{te}$ e][. . .

VP+ is attracted to PredP. The difference in the placement of infinitives (72d) results from the filter restricting the InfP+s that fit into PredP in Dutch. Since German lacks this filter, the German pattern is symmetric, as expected.

(74) a. German: $[_{PredP}[_{VP+}[_{VP+}[_{InfP+}$ gehen]] ~~müs~~ [zu $[_{InfP+}$ müssen . . .]]]
    b. Dutch: *$[_{PredP}[_{VP+}[_{VP+}[_{InfP+}$ gaan]] ~~moet~~ [te $[_{InfP+}$ moeten . . .]]]

The resulting complex VP+ constituent behaves like a VP+ in its own right. It is attracted by a higher restructuring verb (75a), or it can be topicalized (75b). Both options are excluded in Dutch because of the Complexity Filter on PredP.

(75) a. weil   er zu schwimmen versuchte
      because he to swim-inf   tried
      'because he tried to swim'
    b. Zu schwimmen versuchte er nicht.
      to swim-inf   tried   he not
      'He didn't try to swim.'

This surprising Dutch/German contrast, hitherto unaccounted for, follows from our theory.

8.8 Excluding Other Infinitival Patterns

In (41), repeated here, we listed impossible patterns in longer sequences of Dutch infinitives. Since these patterns are in principle available in other languages, we must discover what excludes them in Dutch. As discussed in section 8.5.3, pattern (41d) is accounted for by the Complexity Filter on PredP; we therefore cross it out here.

(41) a. *. . . zal moeten lachen   kunnen   *$V1_f$ $V2_{inf}$ $V4_{inf}$ $V3_{inf}$
        will must-inf laugh-inf can-inf
    b. *. . . zal lachen   kunnen moeten   *$V1_f$ $V4_{inf}$ $V3_{inf}$ $V2_{inf}$
        will laugh-inf can-inf must-inf

c. *... lachen   kunnen moeten zal $*V4_{inf}$ $V3_{inf}$ $V2_{inf}$ $V1_f$
   laugh-inf can-inf must-inf will

d. *... ~~lachen   zal moeten kunnen~~   ~~$*V4_{inf}$ $V1_f$ $V2_{inf}$ $V3_{inf}$~~
   ~~laugh-inf will must-inf can-inf~~

e. *... lachen   kunnen zal moeten $*V4_{inf}$ $V3_{inf}$ $V1_f$ $V2_{inf}$
   laugh-inf can-inf will must-inf

f. *... moeten   zal kunnen lachen $*V2_{inf}$ $V1_f$ $V3_{inf}$ $V4_{inf}$
   must-inf will can-inf laugh-inf

VM-less infinitives may either remain in the infinitival CP or escape once from [Spec, CP] qua light InfP+s. In the latter case an English V1 V2 V3 V4 order results.

What excludes the other orders? At first sight it looks as if they are excluded because of VP+/VP split in infinitives. VP+/VP splitting turns out to be irrelevant, however: splitting takes place only if [Spec, VP+] and VP contain distinct material, and this is not the case in these derivations. To clarify: In section 8.5.3 we showed that infinitives cannot move qua remnant VP+s. Only in this case would the splitting parameter play a role. Thus, in the first step of the derivation InfP+ may not invert, because—taken together with obligatory VP+/VP splitting in this configuration—such inversion will inevitably yield the ungrammatical surface order in (41a). This implies that the CP pied-piping derivation is the only one that can be entertained.

CP pied-piping to the lowest restructuring verb (V3) results in the configuration in (76).

(76) *CP pied-piping to [Spec, VP+]*

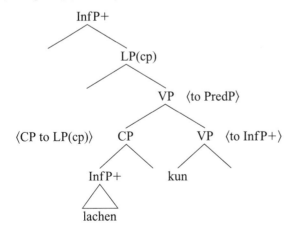

At this point there are three further movements but only two overt constituents: VP, or some projection of VP, must move to InfP+; CP must move to LP(cp); and VP+ must move to PredP. CP moves to LP(cp), as in Hungarian. This movement bleeds VP+/VP splitting, which occurs only if [Spec, VP+] and VP contain distinct overt material. VP therefore remains in VP+; VP+ moves to InfP+, then moves to PredP, and then extracts from [Spec, PredP] to [Spec, CP]. The resulting structure is shown in (77).

(77)

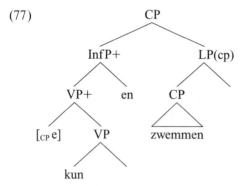

This derivation—the only one available—always yields a V3 V4 (*kunnen zwemmen* 'can-inf swim-inf') order. Therefore, all instances of V4 V3 order are excluded, whence the impossibility of (41a,b,c,e).

This still leaves (41f), a configuration found in "long head movement" phenomena, unexplained.

(41) f. *... moeten zal kunnen lachen   *V2$_{inf}$ V1$_f$ V3$_{inf}$ V4$_{inf}$
        must-inf will can-inf laugh-inf

Here, the problem is ruling out inversion of V2. The CP pied-piping derivations just described yield a configuration where inversion is in principle possible. Intermediate clauses with restructuring verbs will end up with the structure in (77): the carrier of the [vp+] feature is an InfP+ in CP.[11] If indeed InfP+ extracts from [Spec, CP] into the matrix clause, the derived structure in (78) results for (41f).

(78)

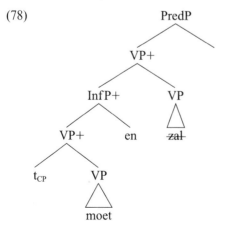

This is because *moeten* 'must-inf' is in the VP+ attracted by *zullen* 'will-inf'. This VP+ has a trace of the infinitival CP (*kunnen* 'can-inf') in its specifier. In Hungarian this configuration is classified as a heavy VP+ (see appendix A, (23)). This classification is instrumental in keeping this type of InfP+ within PredP, and accounts quite generally for its failure to invert. There is no reason to suppose that this configuration would behave any differently in Dutch. Since the Complexity Filter on PredP allows only light InfP+s in PredP, it will exclude all representations of the form (78). Languages that have long head movement V2 V1 V3 should independently allow (78).

Under these terms, then, the Complexity Filter on PredP again ensures pied-piping of CP, instead of extraction of InfP+.

The complexity filter forces InfP+ out of PredP in all intermediate infinitives, since they will always be of the form in (78). If by necessity InfP+ is outside PredP in the infinitival complement, none of the intermediate infinitives should be topicalizable. This seems correct, as the following examples indicate. In this regard Dutch contrasts sharply with Hungarian, where such cases are possible, because InfP+s are in PredP.[12]

(79) a. *WILLEN zal hij waarschijnlijk niet zwemmen.
           want-inf will he probably   not swim-inf
      b. *KUNNEN zal hij zeker   niet lachen.
           can-inf will he certainly not laugh-inf

8.9 Participles

Dutch participles resemble *te*-infinitives, with *ge* comparable to *te*, but differ from them in containing a PartP rather than an InfP+. The distribution of Dutch participles resembles that of Hungarian infinitives as far as climbing options are concerned. Different climbing options for participles and infinitives follow from the Complexity Filter on PredP, which excludes complex InfP+ in PredP but is silent about other categories.

8.9.1 Participial Morphology

Participial morphology in Dutch generally involves a prefix *ge*, the verbal root, and a participle suffix (*ge-bel-d* 'ge-call-part'). We assume that *ge* selects a PartP, in quite the same way as *te* selects an InfP+, and that PartP must occur in a projection of *ge* at some point in the derivation. Like *te*-infinitives, participles involve a restructuring predicate attracting a remnant VP+: *op-ge-bel-d* 'up-ge-call-part', *schoon-ge-maak-t* 'clean-ge-make-part'. From the ungrammaticality of forms like **ge-op-bel-d* 'ge-up-call-part' we conclude that a projection of geP requires a noncomplex PartP in a specifier projection. This filter, stated in (80), is clearly of the same family as the Complexity Filter on [Spec, te/zu] (60).

(80) *Complexity Filter on [Spec, geP]* (Dutch and German)
     [Spec, geP] may not be more complex than this:

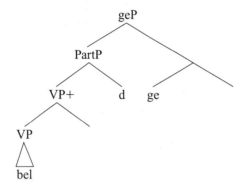

This forces obligatory VP+/VP splitting under the participle and filters out *geopbeld*.
Like *te*, *ge* undergoes further movement to a silent restructuring verb: [ge_i [beld [e]_i
[op...]]]. The silent restructuring predicate attracts the remnant VP+ *op*, forming the
string *opgebeld*. Participles involve a restructuring predicate, but the resulting structure is a participle (PartP), not an infinitive (InfP+).

8.9.2 Participle Climbing

Dutch participles may climb as remnant VP+s, even when they contain big VMs, in
both tensed clauses and infinitives.[13]

(81) *PartP inversion in tensed clauses*
   a. dat ik dat boek om drie uur *gelezen*   *wil   hebben* $V3_{part}$ V1 $V2_{inf}$
      that I that book at three hour ge-read-part want have-inf
      'that I want to have finished reading that book by three o'clock'
   b. dat jij hem voor drie uur *opgebeld*   *moet hebben* $VM4_{small}$ $V3_{part}$ V1 $V2_{inf}$
      that you him before three hour up-ge-call-part must have-inf
      'that you must have called him before three o'clock'
   c. dat jij die film vast   *aardig gevonden* *zou   hebben* $VM4_{big}$ $V3_{part}$ V1 $V2_{inf}$
      that you that movie certainly nice   ge-find-part would have-inf
      'that you certainly would have liked this movie'

Since there is no InfP+ in participial clauses, the resulting structures are not subject
to the Complexity Filter on PredP. Remnant VP+ movement is therefore possible, as
expected. If this is correct, we expect a participle to be possible in all cases where an
infinitive is excluded. Thus, tensed and infinitival clauses should have parallel paradigms—as indeed they do.

(82) a. ... gelezen   zal hebben $V3_{part}$ V1 $V2_{inf}$
            ge-read-part will have-inf
         'will have read ...'

b. ... gelezen   te hebben $V3_{part}$ $V1_{te}$ $V2_{inf}$
   ge-read-part to have-inf
   'to have read ...'

(83) a. ... opgebeld   zal hebben   VM V_{part} V1 $V2_{inf}$
        up-ge-call-part will have-inf
        'will have called up ...'

   b. ... opgebeld   te hebben VM_{small} $V3_{part}$ $V1_{te}$ $V2_{inf}$
        up-ge-call-part to have-inf
        'to have called up ...'

(84) a. ... aardig gevonden   zal hebben VM_{big} $V3_{part}$ V1 $V2_{inf}$
        nice   ge-find-part will have-inf
        'with have found ... nice'

   b. ... aardig gevonden   te hebben VM_{big} $V3_{part}$ $V1_{te}$ $V2_{inf}$
        nice   ge-find-part to have-inf
        'to have found ... nice'

The presence of an additional restructuring predicate in participles simply does not matter, because there is no restriction on derived complexity in PredP. Intermediate infinitives line up in the English order and cannot invert, because the result would violate the Complexity Filter on PredP.

VP+/VP splitting in the PartP clause yields remnant VP+ climbing. As before, the intermediate verb raisers line up in the English order.

(85) *Remnant VP+ climbing*
   a. i. *Tensed clauses*
         op moet hebben   gebeld
         up must have-inf ge-call-part
      ii. *Infinitivals*
         op te hebben   gebeld
         up to have-inf ge-call-part
   b. i. *Tensed clauses*
         aardig zal hebben   gevonden
         nice   will have-inf ge-find-part
      ii. *Infinitivals*
         aardig te hebben   gevonden
         nice   to have-inf ge-find-part

VP+/VP splitting cannot occur in intermediate clauses: by then the VP+ containing both the VM and the *ge*-participle occur in a specifier position and are no longer splittable.

(86) a. *... op wil   gebeld   kunnen hebben
            up want ge-call-part can-inf have-inf
     b. *... wil   op kunnen gebeld   hebben
            want up can-inf ge-call-part have-inf

8.9.3   A Small VM/Big VM Asymmetry

Participles exhibit a further unexpected small VM/big VM asymmetry, revealed by inspecting what may remain in the participial CP and what may escape. Small VMs may stick with the participle, either remaining in the participial CP or escaping from it.

(87) *Small VMs*
     a. zal hebben opgebeld
        will have-inf up-ge-call-part
        'will have called up'
     b. opgebeld   zal hebben
        up-ge-call-part will have-inf
        'will have called up'
     c. (om) ... ⟨opgebeld⟩   te hebben ⟨opgebeld⟩
        (for) ... up-ge-call-part to have-inf up-ge-call-part
        '(for) ... to have called up'

A big VM may not remain inside the participial CP (88a,d), yet a big VM+ participle sequence escapes from the participial CP as an unsplit unit (88b,c).

(88) *Big VMs*
     a. *zal hebben aardig gevonden
         will have-inf nice   ge-find-part
         'will have found nice'
     b. aardig gevonden   zal hebben
        nice   ge-find-part will have-inf
        'will have found nice'
     c. zonder hem aardig gevonden   te hebben
        without him nice   ge-find-part to have-inf
        'without having found him nice'
     d. *zonder hem te hebben   aardig gevonden
         without him to have-inf nice   ge-find-part
         'without having found him nice'

How should the distribution of big VMs be captured? It cannot be due to conditions on the VP+/VP-splitting parameter. If it were, big VMs should behave uniformly: if big VM+ participles may fail to split, (88a) should be fine. The ungrammaticality of (88a) must therefore be due to some other factor. We formulate it as a complexity restriction on [Spec, CP] of the participial CP. Some projection containing the PartP will need to move to CP to type the CP as a participial CP. The above effects follow if we assume the complexity filter in (89).[14]

(89) *Complexity Filter on [Spec, CP]*
At the end of the derivation, [Spec, CP] may not contain a PartP more complex than this, where VM is a small VM:

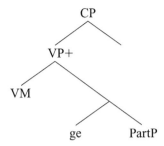

This filter allows at most small-VM participles to survive in CP (87a). Therefore, participles with big VMs must split out of VP+/VP in order to survive in an English order. In other words, VP+/VP splitting is obligatory with big VMs (88a) in an English order, but not in an inverted order (88b).

This implies that we should allow VP+/VP splitting to apply freely. Some derived structures are filtered out because they violate specific complexity filters at the end of the derivation. This correctly allows participles with big VMs to remain unsplit, but only in case they escape from the participial CP and invert ((88b) and (87c)).

Note that we are driven to the Complexity Filter on [Spec, CP] on the basis of asymmetries in the most elementary patterns. It is important to focus on these patterns and the minute asymmetries they reveal, because they are what language learners must be using to determine language-specific properties. They should therefore provide clues for solving the "big" problems. Below, we suggest that this is indeed the case for the Complexity Filter on [Spec, CP]. Rather surprisingly, this filter excludes the participle form in the IPP context (section 8.9.4). In a nutshell, participles may not be intermediate restructuring verbs, because infinitival pied-piping forces CP to VP+ and from there to LP(cp). As a result, the participle, which remains in VP+, ends up in CP and violates the filter.[15]

8.9.4 The Participial CP Filter and the IPP Effect

Dutch and German show the so-called IPP (*infinitivus pro participio*) effect, whereby an infinitival verb appears instead of an expected participial form. This takes place in a well-defined configuration, namely, when the verb that should be a participle is a restructuring verb taking an infinitival complement. (90) shows that verbs like 'have' select for a participial CP and cannot combine with an infinitive. (In this section we give examples from Dutch.)

(90) omdat zij dat wel had gewild/*willen
    because she that prt had ge-want-part/*want-inf
    'because she had indeed wanted that'

(91) shows that the participle cannot surface when the verb itself is a restructuring
verb; the infinitival form must appear instead.

(91) omdat ik die film   graag   had willen/*gewild   zien
    because I that movie voluntary had want-inf/ge-want-part see-inf
    'because I would have liked to see that movie'

   Why is participial morphology excluded? Let us focus on the point in the derivation where participial morphology is merged. As (92) illustrates, the infinitival CP has
pied-piped to VP+, CP has specifier-extracted to LP(cp), and a "heavy" VP+ has
been created.

(92)

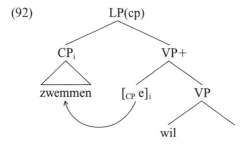

This heavy VP+ should in turn combine with the participial morphology. VP+ does
not split in this context, and the heavy VP+ moves to the morphological projections.
As (93) illustrates, this step is excluded by the Complexity Filter on [Spec, geP] (80):
ge- tolerates only a light VP+ in its specifier, and the VP+ in question is a heavy one.

(93)

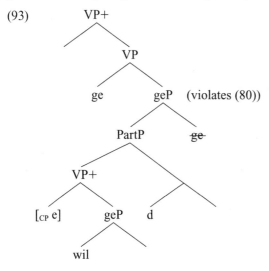

An alternative derivation, in which CP remains in VP+, will not survive either: CP contains an InfP+, which will end up in VP+ and hence ultimately in PredP, violating the Complexity Filter on PredP. Something exceptional needs to happen. Suppose that the problem is resolved by not merging the *ge*-projection. This will remove the effects of the Complexity Filter on [Spec, geP] (80), but it will still lead to a violation of the Complexity Filter on [Spec, CP], (89). In order to remove the effects of this filter, both morphological projections must be absent. Merging the infinitival morphology instead of the participial morphology will not cause any problems since there is no restriction on how complex an InfP+ in [Spec, CP] may be.

How is the selectional property of *hebben* 'have-inf' satisfied when an infinitive appears instead of a participle? As we argued in section 8.9.1, participial morphology involves a silent restructuring V, which selects for geP. geP in turn selects for PartP. Thus, we need only assume that 'have'/'be' always select this silent restructuring predicate and that the latter can exceptionally co-occur with an InfP+ instead of a PartP. Why this is so we leave for future research. Consider the continuation of the derivation in (94).

(94)

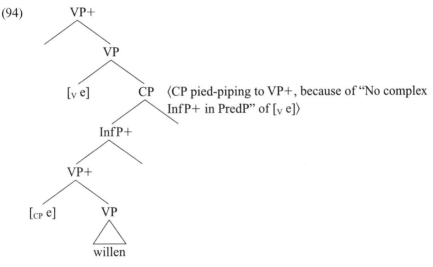

Once in VP+ of the silent verb raiser, the CP cannot specifier-extract to LP(cp): such a move would leave VP+ without any overt material to satisfy the VP+ of *hebben* 'have-inf'. Therefore, CP will cause VP+ to pied-pipe to LP(cp) to PredP in the restructuring predicate selected by *hebben*. This yields a derived structure, (95), wherein VP+ can no longer extract.

(95) *PredP in the restructuring predicate*

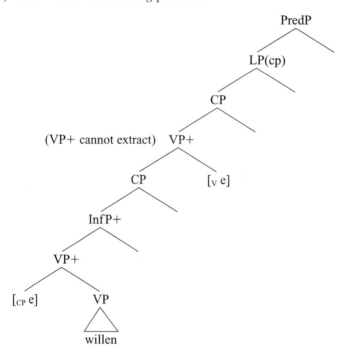

This derivation therefore only allows CP pied-piping, which in turn yields an English order. This English order is not so surprising for Dutch, where there are also other ways to force it: for example, the Complexity Filter on PredP will filter out an InfP in a complex structure and block inversion. However, the effect *is* surprising for German: in precisely this context, an English order arises, as we discuss in the next section.

In sum, the interaction of the two independently motivated complexity filters pertaining to PartP—the Complexity Filter on [Spec, geP] (80) and the Complexity Filter on [Spec, CP] (89)—exclude participial morphology in the very specific context where the participle is an intermediate restructuring verb. CP pied-piping leads to an English order.

8.10   The IPP Effect in German: CP Pied-Piping with or without VP+/VP Splitting

Like Dutch, Standard German exhibits the IPP effect.[16] We focus on the significance of a word order change in German that accompanies this phenomenon.

(96) a.   weil   Peter hat singen   wollen   V1 V3 V2
           because Peter has sing-inf want-inf
           'because Peter wanted to sing'

   b. *weil   Peter singen wollen   hat   *V3 V2 V1
       because Peter sing-inf want-inf has

The triggering auxiliary *must* precede the rest of the verbal complex, indicating that
CP pied-piping is forced at this point in the derivation. The ungrammaticality of the
"normal" inverted order shows that VP+ may not escape from the participial complement in the usual fashion. This particular word order is no longer mysterious in
light of the previous discussion: CP pied-piping is the only option in the IPP context
(see (95)) and CP pied-piping leads to an English order.[17]

   The order of the infinitives inside the CP complement is the normal inverted one,
indicating that up to this point derivations proceed in a regular fashion.

(97) a. weil   Peter *hat* [CP[VP+[VP+ singen] wollen] ...]   V1 V3 V2
        because Peter has   sing-inf want-inf

Small VMs (particles) are glued to their infinitives and do not climb. This follows
from the fact that VP+/VP in infinitives does not split unless it needs to (see section
8.7.1).

(98) weil   Peter Marie *⟨an⟩ *hat* [CP[VP+[VP+⟨an⟩rufen] wollen] ...]   *VM4 V1 V3 V2
        because Peter Marie   up has   up-call-inf want-inf
        'because Peter wanted to call Marie up'

   The CP pied-piping pattern discussed above is one of the characteristic patterns in
IPP contexts. In southern German dialects (Den Besten and Edmondson 1983, 182),
a different pattern obtains: V3 V1 V2 (*singen hat wollen* 'sing-inf has want-inf').[18]
These orders are reminiscent of the patterns with *zu*-infinitives.

(99) a. ... singen   hat wollen   V3 V1 V2 (V3/V2 split)
            sing-inf has want-inf
            'wanted to sing'
      b. singen   zu wollen   V3 V1 V2
            sing-inf to want-inf
            'to want to sing'

In analytical terms we can describe these dialects as using VP+/VP splitting, thus
causing the remnant VP+ to climb. The structure in (100) clarifies why VP+/VP
splitting leads to a V3 V1 V2 sequence. The VP *wol* 'want' gets inflected by splitting
out of VP+/VP. InfP+ moves to [Spec, CP] to type the CP as an infinitival. VP+/VP
splitting creates a remnant VP+, which climbs to the VP+ of the silent verb raiser.

(100)   VP+   ⟨VP+ movement to VP+ of *hab* 'have'⟩

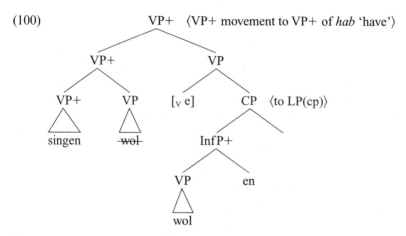

VP+ movement to VP+ of *hab* results in the inverted string *singen wol hab*; CP movement to LP(cp) results in the English order *hat wollen*.

VP+/VP splitting is possible only in the clause under the silent restructuring predicate, and not in any of the more deeply embedded infinitives.

(101) a. weil   ich die Arie singen wollen ~~müssen~~ habe müssen   V4 V3 V1 V2
           because I   the aria sing-inf want-inf   have must-inf
           'because I must have wanted to sing the aria'

       b. *weil   ich die Arie singen ~~wollen müssen~~ habe müssen   wollen   *V4 V1 V2 V3
           because I   the aria sing-inf   have must-inf want-inf

This is because VP+/VP in German does not split unless forced to. The various dialects seem to differ in whether the silent restructuring has properties similar to *zu*, causing VP+/VP splitting or not.

   Given the restricted possibilities of VP+/VP splitting, particles may never climb (102a); instead, they always form a VP+ constituent with the V they depend on (102b).[19]

(102) a. *an hat wollen   rufen
           up has want-inf call-inf

      b. anrufen   hat wollen
          up-call-inf has want-inf
          'has wanted to call up'

In other words, German dialects resort to CP pied-piping without VP+/VP splitting, or to CP pied-piping and VP+/VP splitting in IPP contexts. In either case partial Hungarian or Dutch patterns surface.

8.11   Summary and Discussion: Why CP Pied-Piping or VP+ Splitting?

We have presented Hungarian, Dutch, and German as forming one big system with basically the same structure and movements. The distribution of small clauses is woven into the basic patterns and forms an integral part of the patterns. Differences among Hungarian, German, and Dutch can be reduced to splitting parameters, which can be violated to satisfy other needs, and inviolable complexity filters. We have established the complexity filters in (103) (= (26)) and (104) (= (89)) for Dutch and German, which act on representations given by the derivations.

(103) *No-Complex-InfP+-in PredP Filter* (Dutch)
    At the end of the derivation [Spec, PredP] may contain at most a light InfP+ in a structure no more complex than this:

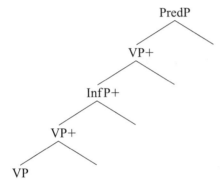

(104) *Complexity Filter on [Spec, CP]*
    At the end of the derivation [Spec, CP] may not contain a PartP more complex than this, where VM is a small VM:

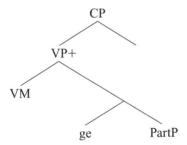

These filters are independently motivated and inviolable.

   Given the independent need for filters that are sensitive to the complexity of the structure at the end of the derivation, we used complexity filters to encode certain well-known restrictions on placement of Dutch and German *te/zu* and *ge*, shown here in (105) (= (60)) and (106) (= (80)).

(105) *Complexity Filter on [Spec, te/zu]* (Dutch and German)
InfP+ in [Spec, te/zu] may not be more complex than this:

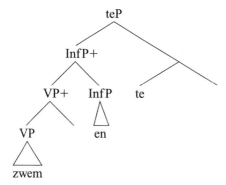

(106) *Complexity Filter on [Spec, geP]* (Dutch and German)
[Spec, geP] may not be more complex than this:

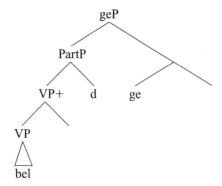

There are recurring themes in Dutch and Hungarian regarding what counts as a complex (or heavy) VP+. We can state these themes in terms of the following scale, from least complex to most complex:

(107) *Scale of complexity of VP+*
   a. VP+ containing a VM-less infinitive (*zwemmen* 'swim-inf')
   b. VP+ with a small VM (*opbellen* 'call up (lit. up-call-inf)')
   c. and d. VP+ with a big VM (*aardig vinden* 'nice find-inf') VP+ with a trace of a clausal complement in [Spec VP+] (*intermediate restructuring Vs*)

If we picture the VP+s, it seems that what matters is not only the "size" of the derived VP+, but also its "orientation" (VP+ with a trace of CP in [Spec, VP+]).

Currently we do not understand why big and small VMs behave differently, and why exactly the classes pattern as they do.

In many cases complexity filters determine particular derivations. They force splitting, which keeps the derived structure as small as possible, and specifier extraction, which further minimizes structural complexity.

The complexity filters can be extracted from the most elementary patterns. They are independently necessary to account for asymmetries in these patterns. The filters can be seen as reflecting the primary data: they are in effect statements of the environments that a particular specifier position allows, measured in terms of derivational complexity. The filters eliminate certain representations generated by the derivations, thus accounting for the acceptable patterns in the grammar of an individual speaker. These filters are a novel addition to the theory of Universal Grammar. They are in fact only possible under the kind of theory outlined in this book, since the theory provides the terms under which they can be stated.

In the theory we have presented, crosslinguistic variation is not uniquely due to variations in lexical properties, or in properties of the inflectional system. In fact, variation in lexical properties seems to play hardly any role in accounting for the considerable variation within West Germanic verbal complexes: by and large, lexical properties and inflectional properties seem to be stable. To a large extent cross-linguistic variation is located in structural properties (splitting parameters) and representations (filters). Structure splitting (whether a particular stretch of structure splits or not, and if it does, under what conditions) is mainly responsible for variation in the derived surface constituent structures and the "size" of remnant constituents. Filters are sensitive to derived structural complexity in certain targeted positions at Spell-Out and thus act upon the representations that the derivations generate. The work in this book should be seen as a starting point toward a theory of parametric variation within a theory based on antisymmetry and on movement of overt material only.

Appendix A
Reference Guide

A.1 General Assumptions

(1) *Principle of Projection Activation* ((8), chap. 1)
A projection is interpretable iff it contains phonologically realized material at some point in the derivation.

(2) *Corollaries of the modified Linear Correspondence Axiom* ((20) and (22), chap. 4)
No projection may have both an overt specifier and an overt head at the end of the derivation (Generalized Doubly Filled Comp Filter). If a head adjoins to another head, they cannot both be overt.

(3) Movement is driven either by properties of the category that moves ("Move") or by properties of a category into whose vicinity it moves ("Attract"). These properties may include lexical features or a projection's need to be activated.

(4) Pied-piping (feature inheritance) is effected either by specifier-head agreement or by head adjunction. ((23) and (24), chap. 4)

(5) All movement is overt and affects phonologically realized material. ((16), chap. 4)

(6) Remnant movement is allowed. ((2), chap. 4; p. 39)

(7) What moves and where? The *complement of X, or the specifier of the *complement of X, may move to [Spec, XP]. Head movement is left-adjunction to the head of the selecting category. ((17), chap. 4)

(8) The locality of XP-movement is ensured by minimality and the fact that each feature can be used only once. Head movement is strictly local in the sense of Koopman 1994. ((14), chap. 1; p. 32)

(9) Derivations obey the strict cycle (i.e., Chomsky's (1993) Extension Condition): as soon as a head is merged, movement into its specifier must take place. (p. 42)

(10) *Mechanics of movement* ((27) and (28), chap. 4)
   a. By default, move only one category at a time.
   b. Sequences of categories that may move together include (i) ⟨YP+, YP⟩, where YP+ is a projection motivated by the modified LCA, (ii) sequences involving operator projections like RefP, DistP, FP, and the projection hosting the verb, (iii) possibly others, not discussed in this book.

(11) To facilitate observance of the strict cycle, categories can be moved to stacking positions LP(xp). The positions LP(xp)* are ordered by the convention that movement into them must replicate the already existing linear order of the pertinent XPs. Specifier movement into an LP(xp) is allowed only if LP(xp) is also a licensing position for XP or XP is on its way to some position where a feature is checked. (p. 44)

(12) An XP from which all phonetically overt material has been removed does not need to be licensed. ((39), chap. 4)

(13) To avoid complex structure where it is irrelevant, (a) will sometimes be written as (b). ((40), chap. 4)

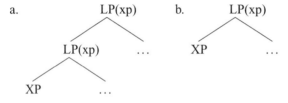

(14) *Morphology* ((21), chap. 4)

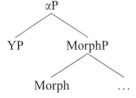

where αP is either MorphP+ or any category not separated from MorphP by overt material.

A.2   Assumptions Pertaining to Verbs and Verbal Complexes

(15) The invariant sequence of categories includes at least the following, plus LP(xp) that include Case positions, adverbial licensing positions, and plain stacking positions:

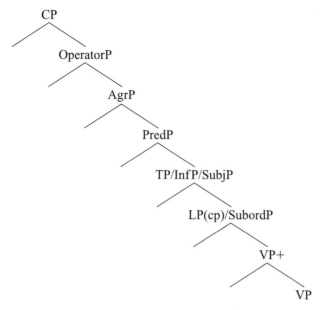

(16) a. VM moves to [Spec, VP+] above the selecting V. ((3a), chap. 4)
   b. "Auxiliaries" require a VP+ in their [Spec, VP+]. ((3b), chap. 4)

(17) If a verb has no VM, VP+ is activated by VP. (sec. 4.7)

(18) VP+ or VP picks up inflectional suffixes in TP/InfP/SubjP and in AgrP.

(19) VP+ is licensed in PredP. ((66), chap. 4)

(20) The infinitival status of the clause selected by the auxiliary is checked in CP. ((9), chap. 4)

(21) Infinitival CP is licensed in LP(cp) (p. 34; n. 3, chap. 4)

(22) Tensed complement CP is licensed in SubordP. (p. 114)

(23) *Hungarian* ((66), chap. 4)

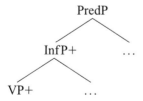

When [Spec, VP+] is a small VM or InfP+ (i.e., an inverted sequence), InfP+ optionally extracts from PredP. Otherwise, InfP+ cannot extract from PredP.

(24) *Hungarian Complexity Filter* (first version) ((69), chap. 4)
VP+ may pied-pipe any βP to the auxiliary in the next clause, but βP must move on if it is more complex than InfP+.

(25) *Hungarian Complexity Filter* (revised) ((70), chap. 5)
At the end of the derivation VP+ may not contain both a category more complex than InfP+ in its specifier and overt material in its complement VP.

(26) *VP+/VP splitting* ((7), chap. 4)
VP may either stay inside VP+ or split out of VP+ (before VP+ undergoes its first move).

(27) In Hungarian VP+/VP splitting occurs in tensed clauses and in the domain of NeutP. (p. 69; (25), chap. 5)

(28) *Nonvacuous VP+/VP splitting* ((94), chap. 4)
VP+/VP splitting applies only when [Spec, VP+] is filled (with material distinct from VP) at the relevant stage of the derivation. Otherwise, VP stays inside VP+ and VP+ moves.

(29) In addition to the well-known focusable categories (DP, PP, etc.), PredP can be focused (but CP, LP(cp), InfP+, etc., cannot). ((8), chap. 5)

(30) In Hungarian NeutP is licensed by a VP+ that has overt material in its specifier. ((19), chap. 5)

(31) In Hungarian NeutP must have TP in its specifier. (p. 95)

(32) VP+/VP splitting occurs only if it does not prevent the satisfaction of some absolute requirement (e.g., that TP occur in [Spec, NeutP]). ((37), chap. 5)

(33) In Hungarian VP$_{nonaux}$ in [Spec, VP+] blocks specifier extraction from PredP. ((65), chap. 5)

A.3   Assumptions Pertaining to Dutch and German

(34) The finite verb is (at least) in Agr$_S$P+. ((2), chap. 7)

(35) The structure obligatorily splits below Agr$_S$P. (p. 128)

(36) A V1 V2 order (in a nonroot environment) signals that V2 is inside the CP complement. ((25), chap. 7)

(37) *Hierarchical structure* ((26), chap. 7)
C (FP) RefP* DistP NegP FP NegP Agr$_S$P+ PredP TP+ LP(xp)* . . .

(38) PredP/TP+ do not split, except in root environments. ((27), chap. 7)

(39) *No-Complex-InfP+-in-PredP Filter* (Dutch) ((26), chap. 8)
At the end of the derivation [Spec, PredP] may contain at most a light InfP+
in a structure no more complex than (i) this:

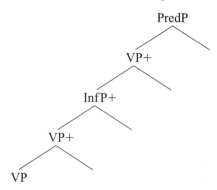

(40) *VP+/VP-splitting parameter* (Dutch) ((30), chap. 8)
In infinitives VP splits out of VP+ only if [Spec, VP+] is filled with material
distinct from VP. VP+/VP splitting is (a) optional if VP+ contains a small
VM, (b) obligatory if VP+ contains a big VM.

(41) [Spec, te/zu] attracts InfP+. ((59), chap. 8)

(42) *Complexity Filter on [Spec, te/zu]* (Dutch *te* and German *zu*) ((60), chap. 8)
InfP+ in [Spec, te/zu] may not be more complex than this:

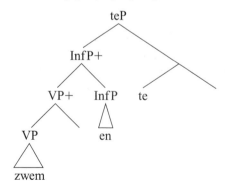

(43) *Complexity Filter on [Spec, geP]* (Dutch and German) ((80), chap. 8)
[Spec, geP] may not be more complex than this:

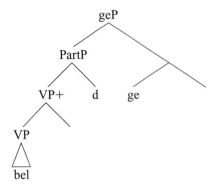

(44) *Complexity Filter on [Spec, CP]* ((89), chap. 8)
      At the end of the derivation, [Spec, CP] may not contain a PartP more
      complex than this, where VM is a small VM:

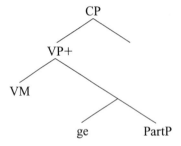

(45) *Scale of complexity of VP+* ((106), chap. 8)
              a. VP+ containing a VM-less infinitive (*zwemmen* 'swim-inf')
              b. VP+ with a small VM (*opbellen* 'call up (lit. up-call-inf)')
      c. and d. VP+ with a big VM (*aardig vinden* 'nice find-inf'); VP+ with a trace
              of a clausal complement in [Spec, VP+] (*intermediate restructuring
              Vs*)

Appendix B
Hungarian Database

This appendix summarizes the Hungarian data discussed in the book and supplements them with further details when appropriate. The presentation is intended to be by and large theory neutral, although we do make several analytical points.

The material in the appendix is taken, almost without modification, from Szabolcsi 1996. Where no source is mentioned, the pertinent facts were first observed in that manuscript.

In section B.1 we introduce those operator projections of the Hungarian preverbal field whose existence is independent of how verbal complexes are analyzed. We also discuss facts pertaining to the assumption that the verb moves to the agreement projection to check its own morphological properties, but not to any of the operator projections related to focus and negation. (The main text, which recasts the process as VP-to-AgrP movement, presupposes this analytical result.) More space is devoted to those facts that have not been systematically described in the literature.

The data in section B.2 pertain to the core phenomena discussed in the book. They are intended to enable readers to develop their own grasp of the data.

B.1 Functional Projections in the Hungarian Preverbal Field

B.1.1 The Operator Positions RefP, DistP, and FP
Hungarian has come to be known as a language that "wears its LF on its sleeve." This is so in at least two important respects: (1) the relative scopes of quantifiers and negation are almost entirely disambiguated by linear order, and (2) focused phrases occur in a designated preverbal position. See É. Kiss 1987, 1991, and Horvath 1986.

When quantifiers occur in the preverbal field, they occupy one of three syntactically distinct positions. In É. Kiss's classical terminology, these are the Topic, Quantifier, and Focus positions. Brody (1990) has argued that the Focus position is best analyzed as [Spec, F(ocus)P]. Szabolcsi (1997) has argued that the Topic and Quantifier positions are best analyzed as [Spec, Ref(erential)P] and [Spec, Dist(ributive)P], respectively. Using these labels, we can illustrate the correspondence between order and scope as follows:

(1) [$_{RefP}$ Két fiúval   [$_{DistP}$ minden problémáról   [$_{FP}$ egy lány [beszélt ...]]]].
     two boy-with   every   problem-about   a   girl   talked
     'There are two boys x such that for every problem y, it was a girl who talked about y with x.'

For a detailed description of the distribution and interpretation of quantifiers in RefP, DistP, and two subtypes of FP, see Szabolcsi 1997.

One reason why the preverbal operator positions are relevant for the syntax of verbs is that they raise the question: how high must the verb move?

B.1.2   Does V Move to F?

Whereas material in RefP and DistP can be separated from the verb stem by lexical XPs, the focused phrase is generally adjacent to it. Specifically, no lexical XP may intervene between [Spec, FP] and the verb stem, and if the verb has a prefix (e.g., *haza* 'home'), it occurs in postverbal rather than preverbal position.

(2) a. Mari haza ment.   (*Mari* in RefP)
         Mari home went
         'Mari went home.'

    b. Mari tegnap   haza ment.   (*Mari* in RefP)
         Mari yesterday home went
         'Mari went home yesterday.'

(3) a. MARI ment haza.   (*Mari* in FP)
         Mari went home
         'It was Mari who went home.'

    b. *MARI haza ment.   (*Mari* in FP)
         Mari home went
         'It was Mari who went home.'

    c. *MARI tegnap   ment haza / haza ment.   (*Mari* in FP)
         Mari yesterday went home / home went
         'It was Mari who went home yesterday.'

(We will show that functional material may intervene between focus and V.)

Following Horvath (1986), Brody (1990) assumes that the [+focus] feature is assigned to focused XPs by the verb in the preverbal position; this explains adjacency. Specifically, on Brody's analysis V moves to F and assigns [+focus] to [Spec, FP].

Kenesei (1994) presents arguments that the [+focus] feature cannot be so assigned. The most important one is as follows. Kenesei observes that Selkirk's (1986) Focus Percolation Rule is operative in Hungarian just as it is in English.

(4) *Focus Rule*

The feature [+focus] percolates onto the lexical head (and/or the lexical head of an argument) of the XP it is assigned to.

The critical examples are these. Small capital letters indicate (the possibility of) contrastive focus interpretation, " indicates focus accent, and square brackets embrace the material moved to [Spec, FP].

(5) a. Mari [A TEGNAPI "CIKKEKET] olvasta.
    Mari the yesterday articles-acc read
    'It's YESTERDAY'S ARTICLES that Mari read.'

  b. Mari [a "TEGNAPI cikkeket] olvasta.
    Mari the yesterday articles-acc read
    'It's YESTERDAY's articles that Mari read.'

(6) a. Mari [a "CIKKEKET OLVASÓ fiút]   látta.
    Mari the articles-acc reading boy-acc saw
    'It's the boy READING THE ARTICLES that Mari saw.'

  b. Mari [a "KÖNYVTÁRBAN olvasó fiút]   látta.
    Mari the library-in   reading boy-acc saw
    'It's the boy reading IN THE LIBRARY that Mari saw.'

The crucial point is that when the adjuncts *tegnapi* 'yesterday's' and *könyvtárban* 'library-in' have focus accent, they, but not the dominating XPs, can have a contrastive focus interpretation, although FP contains such a dominating XP or XPs. In (5b) and (6a,b) there is a dramatic divergence between what is in FP and what is interpreted as contrastive focus. Kenesei observes that any rule that assigns [+focus] to the whole XP in FP and tries to percolate it down to the heads, arguments, or adjuncts in accordance with Selkirk's generalization is bound to face empirical and conceptual difficulties. [+focus] must be assigned in the lexicon or randomly in syntax. Movement to FP additionally involves some pied-piping mechanism, which accounts for the fact that often it is not the whole moved phrase that is interpreted as focus.

If this argument is correct, V-to-F movement is unmotivated.

The fact that the focused phrase is not always adjacent to V likewise suggests that V does not move to F. There are at least two operator particles that may intervene between the focused phrase and the verb stem: *nem* 'not' and emphatic *is* 'too'. If head movement is strictly local, this intervention at least suggests that V is not located in F.

In the next two sections we discuss the behavior of *nem* and *is* in some detail.

B.1.3 Two NegPs

The negative particle *nem* can intervene between the focused phrase and the verb stem. (Note that negation, like focus, triggers "prefix inversion.")

(7) a.   Nem mentem haza.
         not   went-1sg home
         'I didn't go home.'
    b. *Nem haza mentem.   (* unless *haza* is contrastively focused)
         not   home went-1sg
         'I didn't go home.'

(8) a.   TEGNAP   mentem haza.
         yesterday went-1sg home
         'It was yesterday that I went home.'
    b.   TEGNAP   nem mentem haza.
         yesterday not   went-1sg home
         'It was yesterday that I didn't go home.'

In fact, the focused phrase can be independently negated. Note that in (9b) the two negations do not cancel each other out.

(9) a. Nem TEGNAP   mentem haza.
         not   yesterday went-1sg home
         'It was not yesterday that I went home.'
    b. Nem TEGNAP   nem mentem haza.
         not   yesterday not   went-1sg home
         'It was not yesterday that I didn't go home.'

Are both *nem*s instances of the same category? Semantically, they may well be. For example, (8b) is interpreted as presupposing that there is a unique period when I didn't go home and as asserting that this is identical to yesterday. In (9b) *nem*, as always, negates the asserted part and leaves the presupposed part intact.

The two negations behave alike in a number of distributional respects. Both can be paired with *igen* 'yes = do so' (cf. Laka 1990). For example:

(10) a. Mari nem ment haza, de Kati igen.
          Mari not went home but Kati yes
          'Mari didn't go home but Kati did.'
     b. Mari nem MOST ment haza, de Kati igen.
          Mari not now went home but Kati yes
          'For Mari, it is not now that she went home, but for Kati, it is.'

Both can also be immediately followed by emphatic *is*.

(11) a. Azt   mondta, hogy nem megy haza, és   nem is   ment.
          it-acc said   that not goes home and not too went
          'He said that he would not go home, and indeed, he did not.'

  b. Azt   mondta, hogy nem KATI megy haza, és   nem is   KATI ment.
     it-acc said   that not Kati goes home and not too Kati went
     'He said that it is not Kati who would go home, and indeed, it was not Kati.'

We thus assume that Hungarian has two NegPs that flank, at least, FP.

  Are there cases where no FP intervenes between the two negations? B's answer in
the following exchange looks like a relevant case:

(12) A: Nem mentél   haza tegnap.
         not   went-2sg home yesterday
         'You didn't go home yesterday.'
      B: Nem nem mentem "haza, hanem "letartóztattak.
         not   not went-1sg home but   down-arrested-3pl
         'It is not that I didn't go home; I was arrested.'

In the first clause of (12B), postverbal *haza* bears focus accent. In this respect, (12B) is
reminiscent of a case discussed by Szabolcsi (1981), Kenesei (1989), and Zsámboki
(1995).

(13) Nem a   vendég aludt a   "padlón, hanem a   házigazda ment "hotelba.
      not   the guest slept the floor-on but   the host   went hotel-to
      'What happened was not that the guest slept on the floor; rather, the host
      moved to a hotel.'

In both (12B) and (13), a whole proposition is contrastively negated, and the way to
do this in Hungarian is to negate a pair-focus construction. (It appears that the
postverbal focus must be clause final; that is, it marks the right edge of the contrastive
material.)

  Although at first sight there is no FP in (12B), a plausible analysis is that *nem
mentem haza* 'not went-1sg home' is in [Spec, FP], as shown in (14).

(14)   NegP

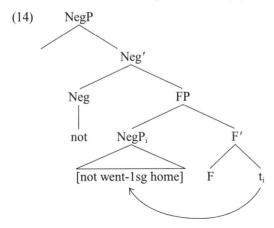

A parallel analysis of (13) might be possible if we assume FP recursion. *A vendég – a padlón* 'the guest – the floor' is pair-focused in the specifier of the lower, traditional FP, and the whole of the lower FP is moved to the specifier of the higher FP. The result is shown in (15).

(15)

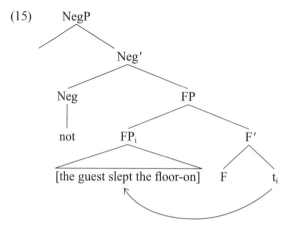

The problem with FP recursion is that we must not predict multiple focus fronting in Hungarian: the higher [Spec, FP] can only be allowed to be filled by movement of its whole FP complement, as in (15). We suggest that the movement of two independent XPs to FP1 and FP2 would violate some form of minimality.[1]

We are not aware of cases where the two NegPs are genuinely adjacent. This may be encoded by stipulating that the higher NegP subcategorizes for FP.

To conclude this discussion of negation and focusing, we note that we have no account of Horvath's (1995) observation that preverbal negation can license a second focus (*ki* 'who' in (16)).

(16) a. *KI   TEGNAP   ment haza?
         who yesterday went home
         'For which person *x*, it was yesterday that *x* went home.'
     b. KI   nem TEGNAP   ment haza?
         who not yesterday went home
         'For which person *x*, it was not yesterday that *x* went home.'

In the interest of further research, we note that Horvath judges that (16b) can be replicated with a non-*wh* expression in the linearly first focus; however, (17) seems to contrast starkly with (16b).

(17) *(Csak) MARI nem TEGNAP   ment haza.
        only Mari not yesterday went home
        'For only *x* = Mari, it was not yesterday that *x* went home.'

B.1.4 Emphatic IsP

Another particle that may intervene between focus and the verb stem is emphatic *is* 'too, indeed'. In fact, as (20c) below shows, even *is nem* may intervene fairly acceptably.

Emphatic *is* needs to be distinguished from quantificational *is* 'too, also' both in its position and in its semantic contribution. Quantificational *is* follows a phrase located in DistP (as is shown by the fact that the prefix precedes the verb stem); Brody (1990) argues that it heads its own IsP.

(18) Mari is   haza ment.
      Mari too home went
      'Mari, too, went home. = In addition to someone else, Mari went home.'

Emphatic *is* 'too, indeed' follows a phrase located in FP (as is shown by the fact that the prefix follows the verb stem).

(19) (Azt   mondtam, hogy MARI megy haza, és)   MARI is   ment haza.
      (it-acc said-1sg   that Mari go-3sg home and) Mari too went home
      '(I said that it will be Mari who goes home, and) it is Mari who did, too.'

The first to analyze emphatic *is* was Piñón (1992b); Szalai (1996) looked at what we believe to be the full range of data.

(20) a.   Azt   mondtam, hogy haza megyek, és *haza is   mentem.*
            it-acc said-1sg   that home go-1sg   and home too went-1sg
            'I said that I would go home and I did so, too.'
      b.   Azt mondtam, hogy KEDDEN megyek haza, és *KEDDEN is mentem.*
            'I said that I would go home on TUESDAY, and on TUESDAY did I go, too.'
      c.   ?Azt mondtam, hogy KEDDEN nem megyek haza, és *KEDDEN is nem mentem.*
            'I said that I would not go home on TUESDAY, and on TUESDAY did I not go home, too.'
      d.   Azt mondtam, hogy alszom, és aludtam *is.*
            'I said that I was asleep, and I was asleep, too.'
      e.   Azt mondtam, hogy nem megyek haza, és *nem is mentem.*
            'I said that I would not go home, and I did not go, either.'
      f.   Azt mondtam, hogy nem alszom, és *nem is aludtam.*
            'I said that I was not asleep, and I was not asleep, either.'
      g.   Azt mondtam, hogy nem KEDDEN megyek haza, és *nem is KEDDEN mentem.*
            'I said that it was not on TUESDAY that I would go home, and it was not on TUESDAY that I did, either.'

The descriptive generalization seems to be that emphatic *is* can follow any of the main "polarity projections" of the sentence. Szalai assumes that emphatic *is* heads its own projection, IsP, distinct from Brody's "quantificational" IsP.

B.1.5 Infinitival Clauses: NegP/FP and the Issue of V-to-F Movement

The functional projection sequence RefP-DistP-NegP-FP-NegP is attested in infinitival clauses as well (IsP is not, perhaps because infinitivals have no independent polarity in the relevant sense). In (21) and (22) the word order constraints and the emergent interpretations exactly match those in (2) and (9b).

(21) PÉTER akart   két fiúval   minden problémáról   EGY LÁNY jelenlétében   beszélni.
      Peter wanted-3sg two boy-with every problem-about a   girl presence-poss.3sg-in talk-inf
      'It was Peter who wanted, for two boys x, for every problem y, for it to be in the presence of
      a girl that he talks with x about y.'

(22) PÉTER akart   nem MARIVAL   nem beszélni.
      Peter wanted-3sg not Mari-with not talk-inf
      'It was Peter who wanted for it to be not Mari that he does not talk with.'

One important difference between finite and infinitival clauses is that whereas in finite clauses focus and negation cannot be separated from the verb by its prefix (see (3a,b)), in infinitival clauses they can be.

(23) a. Jobb lenne   nem haza menni.
          better would-be not home go-inf
          'It would be better not to go home.'
      b. Jobb lenne   nem menni haza.
          better would-be not go-inf home
          (same)

(24) a. Jobb lenne   csak KEDDEN   haza menni.
          better would-be only Tuesday-on home go-inf
          'It would be better to go home only on TUESDAY.'
      b. Jobb lenne   csak KEDDEN   menni haza.
          better would be only Tuesday-on go-inf home
          (same)

Proof that *nem* 'not' in (23) and *csak kedden* 'only Tuesday' in (24) are in the same position as in finite clauses comes from the fact that in neither case can anything simply intervene between them and *hazamenni/menni haza* 'home-go-inf/go-inf home'. (That is, in (23) an XP can intervene, but it is then interpreted as a constituent-negated focus.)

Brody (1995) assumes that V-to-F movement takes place in both finite and infinitival clauses. He attributes the variation in (23a,b) and (24a,b) to the varying strength of the [−tense] feature (optionally strong in the presence of [+focus]).

It appears, however, that "V-to-F movement" in infinitival clauses is not simply optional: in the judgment of the second author, the stranding of monosyllabic prefixes is significantly worse than that of heavier prefixes. Whereas (23b) and (24b) with prefix *haza* 'home' are rather good, the stranding of the monosyllabic prefix *el* 'away' in (25b) is nearly unacceptable.

(25) a. ÉN fogok [csak később] el   menni.
       I will-1sg only later   away go-inf
       'It is me who will leave only later.'
    b. *ÉN fogok [csak később] menni el.
       I will-1sg only later   go-inf away
       (same)

In addition to prefixes, other VMs and infinitival complements can participate in inversion. For example, in (26) *akarni* 'want-inf' is the infinitive in whose clause *csak később* 'only later' is focused; the material that may or may not separate them is *hazamenni* 'home-go-inf'.

In this domain, too, we see that "V-to-F movement" is conditioned by the weight of the material that potentially separates focus/negation from the infinitival verb. This material is highlighted in italics.

(26) a. ÉN fogok [csak később] akarni *haza menni.*
       I will-1sg only later   want-inf home go-inf
       'I am the one who will want to go home only later.'
    b. ?ÉN fogok [csak később] *haza menni* akarni.
       I will-1sg only later   home go-inf want-inf

(27) a. ÉN fogok [csak később] kezdeni *akarni haza menni.*
       I will-1sg only later   begin-inf want-inf home go-inf
       'I am the one who will begin to want to go home only later.'
    b. ÉN fogok [csak később] kezdeni *haza menni akarni.*
       I will-1sg only later   begin-inf home go-inf want-inf
    c. *ÉN fogok [csak később] *haza menni akarni*   kezdeni.
       I will-1sg only later   home go-inf want-inf begin-inf
    d. *ÉN fogok [csak később] *haza menni* kezdeni *akarni.*
       I will-1sg only later   home go-inf begin-inf want-inf

Whereas in (25) "V-to-F movement" is dispreferred over monosyllabic *el* 'away', in (26) it is preferred over *hazamenni* 'home-go-inf' and in (27) it is mandatory over *hazamenni kezdeni* 'home-go-inf begin-inf'. These observations suggest that the process in infinitives may be a PF phenomenon.

B.2 Verbal Complexes

B.2.1 Terminology and Basic Facts Concerning Verbal Complexes

The units that form complexes with the verb, which we survey in section B.2.2, will be called *verbal modifiers (VM)*. Hungarian has two kinds of verbal complex formation. In section B.2.3.1 we discuss verbal complex formation in sentences without focus or negation, called *neutral sentences*; this kind we will label *VM-climbing*. When a neutral sentence contains a sequence of infinitives, their surface order is reminiscent of the order found in English—hence the mnemonic name *English order*. In section B.2.3.2 we discuss verbal complex formation in sentences that do contain negation or focus, called *nonneutral sentences*. Infinitival sequences in nonneutral sentences may occur in the English order or in what we will call the *inverted order*. The same verbs participate in complexes in both the neutral and the nonneutral sentence types; among these verbs, those that select for infinitival complements will be called *auxiliaries*. In section B.2.3.3 we discuss auxiliaries with subjunctive complements. In section B.2.3.4 we discuss the differing behavior of VMs in inversion. In section B.2.3.5 we demonstrate that nonauxiliary infinitival complement takers block both climbing and inversion. In section B.2.3.6 we observe that Ā-projections block inversion (somewhat differently in the two types). In section B.2.4 we discuss the focusability of the infinitives themselves. In section B.2.5 we examine how infinitival material can *scramble* with higher, tensed clause material. Section B.2.6 contains a brief note on *object agreement climbing*.

B.2.2   Verbal Modifiers

B.2.2.1   Classes of Verbal Modifiers   Like Dutch and German, Hungarian has separable prefixes and other expressions that form complexes with the verb. In the literature on Hungarian the cover term *verbal modifier (VM)* is often applied to the whole class; we will retain this term for descriptive purposes.

Since VMs are in complementary distribution with contrastively focused XPs in front of the finite verb stem, the question arises whether they are also in focus. É. Kiss (1981, 1987) assumes that indeed, they are moved to the same position by the same operator movement process; Horvath (1981, 1986) assumes that they are base-generated in the same position into which movement places contrastive foci. The position taken by Szabolcsi (1980, 1987), Komlósy (1985, 1994), and Ackerman (1984) is more similar, though not identical, to Horvath's: they argue that VMs, unless contrastively stressed, are not in focus. Szabolcsi (1980) offers the following "natural negation" test for telling VMs and foci apart:

(28) a. Moziba   mentem.
         movies-to went-1sg
         'I went to the movies.'
      b. Nem mentem moziba.
         not   went-1sg movies-to
         'I didn't go to the movies.'

(29) a. A   moziból   jövök.
the movie-from come-1sg
'I'm coming from the movies.'

   b. Nem a   moziból   jövök.
not   the movies-from come-1sg
'I'm not coming from the movies (I'm coming from somewhere else).'

When the preverbal item is a VM, on the natural negation of the sentence it switches to postverbal position. When it is a focused expression (whether a contrastive VM or another expression that can never be a VM), on the natural negation of the sentence it stays in preverbal position (see section B.1.3). The judgments are straightforward, and all the expressions below qualify as VMs according to this test. (Komlósy and Horvath recognize essentially the same classes of VMs.)

The class of VMs includes prefixes (30a), interpreted compositionally or non-compositionally, directional and locative PPs (30bi), resultative and depictive adjectives and nouns (30bii), determinerless nouns (30biii), and infinitival complements of many subject control verbs (30c). The formation of VM + V complexes is extremely pervasive in the language.

(30) a.   haza + megy 'home + go'
el + megy 'away + go'
szét + szed 'apart + take'
meg + nő 'perf + grow'
be + rúg 'in + kick (= get drunk)'

   b. i.   a szobá-ba + megy 'the room-into + go'
a szobá-ban + van 'the room-in + be'

     ii.   ostobá-nak + bizonyul 'stupid-dat + prove'
elnök-ké + választ 'president-translative + elect'

     iii.   újság-ot + olvas 'newspaper-acc + read'

   c.   úsz-ni + akar 'swim-inf + want'

It will be useful to distinguish three subgroups among VMs. The members of subgroup (30a) are mere prefixes. The members of subgroup (30b) are bigger. First, the members of this subgroup typically bear suffixes.[2] Second, the VMs in subgroup (30bi) are full DPs with overt determiners. They can even be modified to some extent: for example, *a szomszéd szobában van* 'the next room-in is', *nagyon ostobának bizonyul* 'very stupid-dat proves', *a legjobb barátjának tart* 'the best friend-poss.3sg-dat consider', and *magyar nyelvű újságot olvas* 'Hungarian language newspaper-acc read' clearly qualify as VMs, although most other modifiers will require the unit to bear focus accent, in which case we assume the VM occurs in FP and not as part of a complex. Finally, the members of subgroup (30c) are infinitives that themselves do not have a VM.

VM + V complexes undergo word formation processes (see Szabolcsi 1994, 261–265, for data concerning the nominalization of complex predicates). Given this, and the fact that the semantics of some complexes is not transparent, it has been suggested that complexes are formed in the lexicon. The pros and cons of this suggestion are discussed in (among other works) Komlósy 1994 and Ackerman and LeSourd 1997. We follow É. Kiss (1987, 1994) in not assuming a lexical analysis.

B.2.2.2   The Trigger of Complex Verb Formation   The formation of VM + V complexes can be thought to satisfy a property of the VM, or of the verb, or of both.

Consider first the behavior of the expressions that function as VMs. Prefixes (30a) occur only with verbs that can form complexes with them, and they always enter into complexes. This is clear from the fact that there can be only one prefix per clause (it is impossible for one prefix to form a complex with V and for another to roam free). In sentences where a prefix is not procliticized to a host, there is good reason to assume that some process undid the complex. Namely, either the VM itself is contrastively topicalized or focused, or the verb left the complex for a reason of its own.

All the other expressions that can occur as VMs are freer in this respect, though to different degrees. Predicative nominals and adjectives (30bii) can function as adjunct secondary predicates, in which case they do not enter a complex. When they are selected, however, they are almost always selected by a verb that forms a complex with them, and they are incompatible with the presence of a prefix; see (31).[3] (Again, the complex can be undone by contrastive topicalization or focusing and by removal of the verb.)

(31)   PÉTER mutatkozott   (*meg/be) ostobának.
       Peter showed-himself-to-be (*prefix)   stupid-dat
       'It was Peter who seemed stupid.'

Bare nouns (30biii), singular or plural, typically occur with verbs that form complexes with them. However, when either the bare noun or another XP is contrastively focused, the sentence is acceptable even if the bare noun cannot have been a member of a complex at any stage. Compare (32), where *újságot* 'newspaper-acc' is the complement of a prefixed verb, with (31).

(32)   PÉTER vett fel újságot   a   földről.
       Peter took up newspaper-acc the floor-from
       'It was Peter who picked (a) newspaper(s) up from the floor.'

Finally, locative PPs (30bi) and infinitives (30c) can be either arguments or adjuncts, and in both capacities they happily co-occur with many verbs that either form a complex with something else or never form a complex at all.

Thus, we may safely say that entering into a complex is a lexical requirement associated with prefixes, but probably not with the other expressions that can function as VMs.

Let us now turn to the verbs that can host VMs.

There are quite a few verbs that never occur without a VM. They may have various distinct subcategorization frames, but each will include a VM. Such a verb is *bizonyul* 'prove'. Note that *bizonyul* is unaccusative (unlike *bizonyít* 'prove'), as a result of which (33c) cannot have the interpretation 'Peter proved [something]'.

(33) a. Ha ez   be bizonyul, . . .
          if   this in proves
          'If this turns out to be true, . . .'
     b. Péter ostobának bizonyult.
          Peter stupid-dat proved
          'Peter turned out to be stupid.'
     c. *Ez/Péter bizonyult.
          this/Peter proved

It is certainly a lexical requirement associated with these verbs that they enter into complexes.

Most other verbs that may form complexes with prefixes, locatives, or bare nouns typically have alternative subcategorization frames that do not involve any VM. However, the subcategorization switch often corresponds to a change in meaning. Thus, at least on the relevant meaning, it seems to be a lexical requirement for the verb to form a complex with a particular kind of VM.

Pending a detailed investigation of these matters, in this book we make the following, somewhat simplified assumption:

(34) It is a lexical requirement of those verbs that select a VM that they form a complex with that VM.

We leave it open why this lexical requirement holds. For one approach in terms of "bleached" predicates in need of specific lexical content, see Szabolcsi 1986, 1987.

B.2.3   The Formation of Two Kinds of Verbal Complexes

Hungarian has two kinds of verbal complex formation that are at least superficially distinct. One, which we informally label *VM-climbing*, occurs in so-called neutral sentences: those that have no FP or NegP and are "unmarked" with respect to tense and aspect.[4] The other, which we informally label *inversion*, occurs in nonneutral sentences: those that do have FP and/or NegP.

As we will show, the two processes produce quite different linear orders. However, they are similar in that (1) the same VMs participate in both (although VM-climbing affects only "nonrecursive" VMs) and (2) the same verbs participate in both.

B.2.3.1   VM-Climbing: Complex Verb Formation in Neutral Sentences   The first type of complex verb formation involves the procliticization of a (minimal) VM to the finite verb in neutral sentences—those that lack NegP or FP and are "unmarked" with respect to tense and aspect. Neutral sentences may contain DistP or RefP.

(35)   a.   *Haza* mentem.
             home went-1sg
             'I went home.'
       b.   [RefP Mari] *haza* ment.
                  Mari home went-3sg
             'Mari went home.'
       c.   [DistP Mindenki] *haza* ment.
                  everyone   home went-3sg
             'Everyone went home.'

(36)   a.   *Mentem *haza*.   (qua neutral sentence)
       b.   *[RefP Mari] ment *haza*.   (qua neutral sentence)
       c.   *[DistP Mindenki] ment *haza*.   (qua neutral sentence)

All VMs behave alike with respect to complex verb formation in neutral sentences; in fact, this is the defining feature of the class of VMs. All verbs that have a VM require it to be procliticized in neutral sentences.

There is a set of control verbs that require the VM of the lowest infinitival complement to precede the finite verb in neutral sentences, a phenomenon we may call *VM-climbing*.

(37)   a.   *Haza* akarok   menni.
             home want-1sg go-inf
             'I want to go home.'
       b.   *Akarok menni *haza*.   (qua neutral sentence)
       c.   *Akarok *haza* menni.   (qua neutral sentence)

(38)   *Haza* fogok   akarni   menni.
        home will-1sg want-inf go-inf
        'I will want to go home.'

The climber must land in the tensed clause (Kenesei 1989).

(39)   *Nem fogok   *haza* akarni   menni.
         not will-1sg home want-inf go-inf

VM-climbing is compatible with only one order of the infinitival complements, the one shown in (38) (mnemonically called the *English order*). For instance, the following variation on (38) is ungrammatical:

(40) *Haza fogok   menni akarni.
      home will-1sg go-inf want-inf

Kálmán et al. (1989), who offered the first comprehensive description of the data, termed the class of verbs that exhibit VM-climbing *auxiliaries*. Phonologically, auxiliaries are characterized by the fact that in neutral sentences they do not carry main accent; their VM does.

(41) *Auxiliaries* (a closed class of subject control verbs, do not carry main accent, exhibit VM-climbing)
      akar 'want', fog 'will', kell 'must', szokott 'tend', tetszik 'lit. please', tud 'be able to/know how to', kezd 'begin', kíván 'wish', mer 'dare', óhajt 'desire', szeretne 'would like', próbál 'try', szándékozik 'plan', and so on

According to Kálmán et al.'s description, verbs that do not exhibit VM-climbing fall into two classes. The members of the first nonauxiliary infinitival complement taker class, exemplified in (42), carry the main accent in neutral sentences (i.e., they are stressed even if they do not bear emphasis or contrast). The members of the second class, exemplified in (43), are like auxiliaries in that they do not carry the main accent. In this book we are concerned only with the first class. The verbs in the second class exhibit a mixed behavior: they do not support VM-climbing in neutral sentences, but in nonneutral sentences they participate in complexes somewhat the way auxiliaries do.

(42) *Nonauxiliaries 1* (an open class of subject control verbs, carry main accent, do not exhibit VM-climbing)
      elfelejt 'away-forget = forget', elkezd 'away-begin = begin', megpróbál 'perf-try = try', fél 'is afraid', habozik 'hesitate', szégyell 'is ashamed', utál 'hate', szeret 'like', imád 'love', siet 'hasten', and so on

(43) *Nonauxiliaries 2* (subject control and raising verbs, do not carry carry main accent, do not exhibit VM-climbing)
      látszik 'seem', kényszerül 'is forced', tanul 'learn', megy 'go', and so on

B.2.3.2 Inversion of VMs in Nonneutral Sentences Nonneutral sentences are ones that contain FP and/or NegP in their finite clause. Inversion is a phenomenon that occurs visibly in the infinitival complement.

The infinitival-complement-taking verbs that participate in inversion are the same auxiliaries that are transparent to VM-climbing (see (41)). Nonauxiliaries 1 (see (42)) that do not allow VM-climbing do not participate in inversion, either. The two phenomena diverge in the class nonauxiliaries 2 (see (43)): these do not allow VM-climbing but participate in inversion. We have not studied the behavior of the latter class in detail and will therefore make no finer claims about it.

The basic phenomenon of inversion can be demonstrated using a verb with a so-called separable prefix, embedded under a sequence of auxiliaries.

Let us assume that the underlying order of the auxiliary sequence in Hungarian is essentially the same as the English surface order. To focus on the patterns, we will use the following notation:

(44) fogok   (kezdeni) (akarni) menni be
      will-1sg begin-inf want-inf go-inf in
      1   2   3   4   5

We are interested in the surface orders emerging from (44) in sentences in which the matrix is nonneutral but the infinitival clauses themselves do not contain operators with a potential blocking effect.

The only acceptable surface orders are the ones in (45) through (47).

(45) [Nem] fogok   be menni.   1 5 4
      [not] will-1sg in go-inf
      'I will [not] go in.'

(46) a. [Nem] fogok   akarni   be menni.   1 3 5 4
         [not] will-1sg want-inf in go-inf
         'I will [not] want to go in.'
      b. [Nem] fogok   be menni akarni.   1 5 4 3
         [not] will-1sg in go-inf want-inf
         'I will [not] want to go in.'

(47) a. [Nem] fogok   kezdeni   akarni   be menni.   1 2 3 5 4
         [not] will-1sg begin-inf want-inf in go-inf
         'I will [not] begin to want to go in.'
      b. [Nem] fogok   kezdeni   be menni akarni.   1 2 5 4 3
         [not] will-1sg begin-inf in go-inf want-inf
         'I will [not] begin to want to go in.'
      c. [Nem] fogok   be menni akarni   kezdeni.   1 5 4 3 2
         [not] will-1sg in go-inf want-inf begin-inf
         'I will [not] begin to want to go in.'

All these orders are equally acceptable. The length of the string does not affect its acceptability in terms of grammaticality, although a longer sequence of auxiliaries may be more difficult to contextualize.

The insightful observation that the surface orders are partial mirror images of the one in (44) is due to Kenesei (1989). He assumes that the underlying order is something like (47c), and orders like (47a), which comes closest to (44), are formed by a series of rightward movements.

On the assumption that movement always takes place to the left, the informal algorithm shown in (48) can be said to produce the above patterns. *Be* inverts with *menni*, *bemenni* with *akarni*, *bemenni akarni* with *kezdeni*, and *bemenni akarni kezdeni* with *fogok*. The last step is invisible, because finite *fogok* moves on to Case, T, and Agr. The first inversion step (*be* with *menni*) is obligatory; the rest are optional, as (47a,b) show.

(48)   __ fogok __ kezdeni __ akarni __ menni be

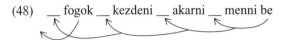

We will mnemonically call the orders involving inversion *inverted orders* and the others *English orders*.

As mentioned earlier, all the remaining orders are unacceptable. They fall into four types. First, a noninfinitival VM fails to invert.

(49) *Nem fogok   menni *be*.   *V_{inf} VM
      not   will-1sg go-inf in

Second, a VM inverts with a verb that is not its governing verb.

(50) *Nem fogok   kezdeni *be*$_i$ akarni   menni t$_i$.   *1 2 5 3 4
      not   will-1sg begin-inf in want-inf go-inf

Third, a segment with an internal English order inverts.

(51) *Nem fogok [*akarni   be menni*]$_i$ kezdeni   t$_i$.   *1 3 5 4 2
      not   will-1sg want-inf in go-inf   begin-inf

Fourth, a verb inverts without taking its VM along.

(52) *Nem fogok *akarni*$_i$ kezdeni   t$_i$ be menni.   *1 3 2 5 4
      not   will-1sg want-inf begin-inf   in go-inf

These are the core facts that a theory of inversion needs to account for.

B.2.3.3 Subjunctive Complements of Auxiliaries VMs climb out of subjunctives with an overt complementizer as well as out of infinitives. The construction in (53) was observed by É. Kiss (1994).

(53) Szét kell, hogy szedjem   a rádiót.
      apart must that take-subj-1sg the radio-acc
      'I must take apart the radio.'

Such examples are both impeccably grammatical and fully acceptable according to the norms of the written language. Climbing involving *szabad* 'permitted' is not quite so good.

(54) Szét szabad, hogy szedjem   a   rádiót?
     apart permitted that take-subj-1sg the radio-acc
     'May I take apart the radio?'

Further examples may be slightly questionable and are in any case colloquial.

(55) ?Szét akarod, hogy szedjem   a   rádiót?
      apart want-2sg that take-subj-1sg the radio-acc
     'Do you want me to take apart the radio?'

On the other hand, subjunctives do not participate in overt inversion, either by dragging the complementizer *hogy* along (56a) or by stranding it (56b). Only the English order is possible (56c).

(56) a. *Nem fog [hogy el   menjél]   kelleni.
          not will that away go-subj-2sg must-inf
     b. *Nem fog el   menjél   kelleni hogy.
          not will away go-subj-2sg must-inf that
     c. Nem fog kelleni, hogy el   menjél.
          not will must-inf that away go-subj-2sg
         'You will not need to leave.'

B.2.3.4 The Differing Behavior of VMs in Nonneutral Sentences VMs do not behave uniformly with respect to inversion. A three-way distinction needs to be made.

Prefixes (i.e., the members of class (30a)) exhibit exactly the pattern described above: the first inversion step, involving just the prefix, is obligatory, and later steps, involving a constituent containing the prefix, are optional.

VMs that are themselves infinitives (30c) differ from these in that even the first inversion step is optional.

(57) a. Nem fogok   kezdeni akarni *úszni*.
         not will-1sg begin-inf want-inf swim-inf
         'I will not begin to want to swim.'
     b. Nem fogok kezdeni *úszni akarni*.
     c. Nem fogok *úszni akarni kezdeni*.

For the remaining VMs (30b) the first inversion step is obligatory but the later ones are disallowed.

(58) a.   Nem fogok   akarni   *a szobában maradni/ostobának bizonyulni.*
           not   will-1sg want-inf the room-in remain-inf/stupid-dat prove-inf
           'I will not want to remain in the room/to prove stupid.'
   b. i.   *Nem fogok akarni maradni *a szobában.*
     ii.   *Nem fogok akarni bizonyulni *ostobának.*
   c. i.   *Nem fogok *a szobában maradni* akarni.
     ii.   *Nem fogok *ostobának bizonyulni* akarni.
   d.   *Nem fogok *maradni akarni* a szobában.

(58c) may be acceptable if *a szobában (maradni)* or *ostobának (bizonyulni)* is contrastively focused; recall that focusing and inversion are entirely distinct processes, although both target a preverbal position.

B.2.3.5 Nonauxiliaries 1 Block Both Types of Complex Verb Formation Complex verb formation in both neutral and nonneutral sentences (VM-climbing and inversion, respectively) is blocked if a nonauxiliary occurs in the sequence between VM and the finite verb. By a "nonauxiliary" we mean a verb that takes infinitival complements but is not an auxiliary.

In (59)–(60) a nonauxiliary (*elkezdeni* 'away-begin-inf = begin-perf' or *utálni* 'hate-inf') intervenes between the auxiliaries *fogok* 'will-1sg' and *menni* 'go-inf'. The prefix of the latter, *haza* 'home', cannot climb (59). To produce a neutral sentence, the highest eligible VM climbs instead: the prefix *el* of *elkezdeni* (60a) or prefixless *utálni* itself (60b). This effect is reminiscent of superiority.

(59) a.   *Haza* fogok   el   kezdeni menni.
          home will-1sg away begin-inf go-inf
          'I will begin to go home.'
   b. *Haza* fogok   utálni   menni.
          home will-1sg hate-inf go-inf
          'I will hate to go home.'

(60) a.   *El*   fogok   kezdeni haza menni.
          away will-1sg begin-inf home go-inf
          'I will begin to go home.'
   b. *Utálni* fogok   haza menni.
          hate-inf will-1sg home go-inf
          'I will hate to go home.'

The same items block inversion with infinitives, in the following sense. As is obvious from the preceding description, nonauxiliaries like *elkezd* 'away-begin' or *utál* 'hate' do not invert with VMs and do not invert as VMs.

(61) a. Nem fogok   akarni el   kezdeni haza menni.
         not   will-1sg want-inf away begin-inf home go-inf
         'I will not want to begin to go home.'
     b. *Nem fogok akarni *haza menni el kezdeni.*
     c. *Nem fogok akarni *haza menni el kezdeni akarni.*
     d. *Nem fogok *el kezdeni akarni* haza menni. (in the sense 'want to begin')

(62) a. Nem fogok   akarni utálni   haza menni.
         not   will-1sg want-inf hate-inf home go-inf
         'I will not want to hate to go home.'
     b. *Nem fogok akarni *haza menni utálni.*
     c. *Nem fogok *haza menni utálni akarni.*
     d. *Nem fogok *utálni akarni* haza menni. (in the sense 'want to hate')

Naturally, inversion below the nonauxiliary is perfectly possible, as attested by *hazamenni.*

B.2.3.6 Ā-Projections Block Complex Verb Formation   As noted in section B.1.5, infinitival clauses may contain FP and/or NegP. (63) demonstrates that these block VM-climbing.[5]

(63) a. **Haza* fogok   akarni   nem menni.
         home will-1sg want-inf not go-inf
     b. **Haza* fogok   akarni   (csak) MOST menni.
         home will-1sg want-inf (only) now go-inf

These particular sentences do not have grammatical neutral orders, because there is no eligible VM between the offending negation/focus and the finite verb. They can only be saved by making the finite clause nonneutral; for example:

(64) a. ÉN/Nem fogok   akarni   nem haza menni.
         I/not   will-1sg want-inf not home go-inf
         'It is me who will want to not go home. /I will not want to not go home.'
     b. ÉN/Nem fogok   akarni   (csak) MOST haza menni.
         I/not   will-1sg want-inf (only) now home go-inf
         'It is me who will want to go home only NOW. /I will not want to go home NOW.'

It is interesting to note that an intervening DistP (e.g., a universal quantifier) or RefP does not block VM-climbing. For example:

(65) *Haza* fogok   akarni   mindent   vinni.
     home will-1sg want-inf everything-acc take-inf
     'I will want to take everything home.'

That is to say, VM must travel through a sequence of neutral infinitives to the neutral finite clause.

Similarly, if an infinitival clause contains FP or NegP, it cannot invert with the governing verb in nonneutral sentences. Consider the following data:

(66) a. Nem fogok   haza menni akarni   most.
         not   will-1sg home go-inf want-inf now
         'I will not want to go home now.'
     b. Nem fogok akarni haza menni most.

(67) a. Nem fogok akarni [MOST haza menni].
     b. Nem fogok akarni [MOST menni haza].

(68) a. *Nem fogok [MOST menni haza] akarni.
     b. Nem fogok [MOST [haza menni akarni]].

In (66) the infinitival clause 'to go home now' contains no focus. *Hazamenni* 'home-go-inf' can be inverted overtly (66a) or remain in situ (66b). (The position of *most* 'now' is not particularly important here.) This establishes that the given lexical items participate in inversion.

In (67) *most* is focused inside the infinitival clause. Focusing inside an infinitive may, but need not, trigger a step of verb movement that results in the separation of the prefix *haza* from the verb *menni*. Recall that such separation is obligatory in finite clauses with focus. At this point we are not trying to explain how (67b) comes about (i.e., to what functional projection the verb moves). We are using the order in (67b) as an unambiguous indicator that *most* is focused inside a clause whose main verb is *menni*.[6]

Observe now that in (67a,b) the infinitival clause containing focused *most* is not inverted. Moreover, the ungrammaticality of (68a) shows that such an infinitival clause cannot be inverted at all. (68b), in which the prefix is procliticized, is grammatical. We argue, however, that (68b) has a crucially different constituent structure: *most* is focused in the *akarni*-clause into which *hazamenni* had been inverted on its own. This is not problematic, since Hungarian focus movement, like *wh*-movement, is unbounded.

To summarize the analytical point, it appears that when an infinitival clause contains a filled [Spec, FP], it cannot overtly invert. Precisely the same effects can be demonstrated using NegP in the place of FP.

B.2.4 The Focusing of Infinitives

As Kenesei (1989) observes, all the infinitival complexes (which we assume to be formed by movement, but which he takes to be base-generated) can be contrastively focused. We assume that (70c) is also grammatical, merely difficult to process. Note that when the lowest infinitive is focused, the higher ones occur in the English order. (69b) is ungrammatical on the intended 'want to begin' interpretation. As (70d) illustrates, no string with the English order can be focused.

(69) a. ÚSZNI   fogok akarni   kezdeni.
        swim-inf will-1sg want-inf begin-inf
        'It is to swim (and not, say, to read) that I will want to begin.'

    b. *ÚSZNI   fogok kezdeni akarni.
        swim-inf will-1sg begin-inf want-inf
        'It is to swim (and not, say, to read) that I will want to begin.'

(70) a. HAZA MENNI fogok   kezdeni akarni.
        home go-inf will-1sg begin-inf want-inf
        'It is to go home that I will begin to want.'

    b. HAZA MENNI AKARNI fogok   kezdeni.
        home go-inf want-inf will-1sg begin-inf
        'It is to want to go home that I will begin.'

    c. ?HAZA MENNI AKARNI KEZDENI fogok.
        home go-inf want-inf begin-inf will-1sg
        'It is to begin to want to go home that I will [do].'

    d. *AKARNI HAZA MENNI fogok   kezdeni.
        want-inf home go-inf will-1sg begin-inf

Focusing is not blocked by FP or negation.[7]

Some interesting pieces of data can be added to Kenesei's list. The finite verb can always be contrastively focused on its own. But the same holds for individual infinitives, at least in the top layers of the sequence.

(71) a. KEZDENI$_i$ fogok   t$_i$ akarni   haza menni.
        begin-inf will-1sg   want-inf home go-inf
        'I will BEGIN to want to go home.'

    b. KEZDENI$_i$ fogok t$_i$ haza menni akarni.

(72)   ?AKARNI$_i$ fogok   kezdeni   t$_i$ haza menni.
        want-inf will-1sg begin-inf   home go-inf
        'I will begin to WANT to go home.'

(73)   *MENNI$_i$ fogok   kezdeni akarni   t$_i$ haza.
        go-inf will-1sg begin-inf want-inf   home
        'I will begin to want to GO home.'

More precisely, the highest infinitive can certainly be focused either in an emphatic ('indeed') sense or contrastively, and the result sounds entirely natural. A lower infinitive can only be focused contrastively. We believe that the reason why this is a more restricted option in the examples we are considering has to do with the auxiliary character of these verbs: most of them do not have enough "content" to allow for a contrast. But some more "contentive" auxiliaries do. For example, the string in (74) seems ambiguous. (74a) represents the reading where *próbálni* 'try-inf' is the highest infinitive, and (74b) the reading where it is the second highest.

(74) Csak PRÓBÁLNI fogok   akarni   haza menni.
    only try-inf   will-1sg want-inf home go-inf
    a. 'I will only TRY to want to go home (but will not manage to want to go
        home).'
    b. 'I will want to only TRY to go home (but will not want to succeed in going
        home).'

B.2.5 Scrambling of Infinitival and Matrix Material

By "scrambling," in this context we mean specifically the mingling of matrix material with infinitival material. Scrambling is possible, although in systematically restricted ways. To ensure that the scrambled item cannot come from anywhere but the matrix, we will use a nominative subject (*Mari*). Note that in the examples above the matrix subject was pro-dropped.

Let us begin with nonneutral sentences. In (75) we try to insert the nominative subject *Mari* between the postverbal phrases. The pattern is clear: *Mari* can intervene between parts of the verbal complex if and only if no inversion took place. The inverted parts are italicized.

(75) a. MOST fog   (Mari) kezdeni (Mari) akarni   (Mari) *haza (*Mari) menni.*
        now will-3sg (Mari) begin-inf (Mari) want-inf (Mari) home (*Mari) go-inf
        'It is now that Mari will begin to want to go home.'
    b. MOST fog   (Mari) kezdeni (Mari) *haza (*Mari) menni (*Mari) akarni.*
        now will-3sg (Mari) begin-inf (Mari) home (*Mari) go-inf (*Mari) want-inf
        (same)
    c. MOST fog   (Mari) *haza (*Mari) menni (*Mari) akarni   (*Mari) kezdeni.*
        now will-3sg (Mari) home (*Mari) go-inf (*Mari) want-inf (*Mari) begin-inf
        (same)

In neutral sentences, which have an English order, insertion of *Mari* is accepted by all speakers, though it is felt to be less perfect than in the English orders in (75).

(76) (Mari) haza fog   (?Mari) akarni   (?Mari) kezdeni (?Mari) menni (?Mari).
    (Mari) home will-3sg (?Mari) want-inf (?Mari) begin-inf (?Mari) go-inf (?Mari)
    'Mari will want to begin to go home.'

We believe that the somewhat degraded character of the scrambled orders is due to the fact that neutral sentences generally have a more rigid word order and observe stricter requirements of "communicative dynamism." For instance, *Mari* ideally occurs in [Spec, RefP] (the neutral topic position). Thus, the ?s are probably irrelevant in connection with the structural properties of the infinitival sequence and we will ignore them.

B.2.6   A Probable Nonconnection: Object Agreement Climbing

Hungarian has overt object agreement: finite verbs have two distinct conjugations, one used, roughly, when the direct object is definite, and the other used when the direct object is indefinite or there is no direct object. (Szabolcsi (1994) and Bartos (2000) argue explicitly that the definite/indefinite distinction is only an approximation and that the relevant factor cannot be purely semantic; this is immaterial here.)

Infinitival verbs assign accusative case (to definite and indefinite direct objects alike) but themselves do not carry object agreement morphology. In the subject control construction, the finite verb agrees with the direct object of (the infinitival complement of . . .) its infinitival complement. For example:

(77) a. Mari látta   ezt.
        Mari saw-3sg+def.obj this-acc
        'Mari saw this.'
     b. Mari látni   akarta   ezt.
        Mari see-inf wanted-3sg+def.obj this-acc
        'Mari wanted to see this.'
     c. Mari látni   fogja   akarni ezt.
        Mari see-inf will-3sg+def.obj want-inf this-acc
        'Mari will want to see this.'

Object agreement climbing is functionally reminiscent of pronominal clitic climbing in Italian, for instance. The two phenomena differ in that object agreement climbing (1) is not restricted to a particular subset of verbs but occurs with all subject control verbs and (2) is obligatory, not optional. Thus, object agreement does not correlate with auxiliary status; that is, it does not depend on inversion. We therefore leave object agreement out of consideration.

Notes

Chapter 1

1. See Sportiche 1993, 1995, Koopman 1993, 1996, Kayne 1994, Rizzi 1995, and Cinque 1999. Ultimately, we want to argue that every feature projects (Koopman 1996) and that structures are universally invariant (Sportiche 1993, Koopman 1996, 2000, Cinque 1999). This assumption is not crucial for the analysis developed in this book.

2. See Rizzi 1990, 1996 and in particular Sportiche 1993, where a research program is proposed that reduces all licensing conditions to specifier-head licensing.

3. Whether one should account for the distribution of different types of CPs by movement or not is an old issue that receives different answers depending on the underlying theories (Koster 1978, Emonds 1976, Stowell 1981, and others vs. Zwart 1993, 1994).

4. The assumption that Dutch is underlyingly head initial forces one to move the predicate of small clauses into preverbal position (Koster 1994, Zwart 1993, 1994, 1997).

5. We will additionally employ movement to "stacking positions." However, we regard these as temporary measures to facilitate observance of the strict cycle. See section 4.2.

Chapter 3

1. The class of auxiliaries is reminiscent of Dutch "verb raisers," and the class of nonauxiliary infinitival complement takers is reminiscent of "extraposition triggers." Kálmán et al. (1989) also establish a second class of nonauxiliary infinitival complement takers, not included in (2), that exhibit a dual behavior reminiscent of verbs participating in the "third construction." For instance, *tanul* 'learn how to' and *készül* 'prepare' participate in inversion, but are not quite transparent for VM-climbing (the climbing examples are somewhat marginal or are only accepted in substandard register). We do not discuss this third class here; nor do we consider why the class of verbs participating in inversion is slightly broader than the class of verbs participating in climbing.

2. É. Kiss (1987) assumes that Hungarian infinitives have a dual, biclausal and monoclausal structure, and she subsumes the placement of prefixes under focusing (i.e., phrasal movement). Szabolcsi (1996) develops a comprehensive account of the data addressed here. She considers two analyses of inversion—a head movement analysis and an XP-movement analysis—and analyzes VM-climbing as phrasal movement (but not as remnant movement, as here). Brody (1997, 2000) and É. Kiss (1998a,b) revisit Szabolcsi's (1996) account and propose alternative analyses for significant subsets of the data. Despite their differences, they both rely on head movement(-like elements).

Within the framework of Mirror Theory, Brody proposes that inverted sequences form morphological words, which involve strictly local, head chain–type relations, while he maintains movement into a syntactic specifier for VM-climbing. É. Kiss (1998a,b) subsumes all the data under incorporation. Incorporation can be endocentric, with a theta-relation between the head and the subordinate, resulting in a right-headed compound, or exocentric, resulting in a head chain of an extended projection (adapting a proposal in Roberts 1997).

We will not compare these proposals with ours in detail. We believe that the arguments to be presented against a head movement analysis of inversion essentially carry over to the relevant elements of Brody's and É. Kiss's proposals. However, we do address two specific analytical issues that, according to Brody and É. Kiss, favor their respective theories: the emphatic versus contrastive focusing of infinitives (in section 5.2) and the failure of across-the-board VM-climbing (in section 5.3).

3. The standard analysis of verb raising in terms of head movement dates back to Evers 1975. Certain dialects or languages are assumed to allow for verb projection raising (= phrasal movement) in the same context (e.g., Haegeman and Van Riemsdijk 1986, Haegeman 1992, 1998, Den Besten and Edmondson 1983). Particular proposals about verb raising and verb projection raising vary widely with regard to assumptions about the underlying order of Dutch and German (head final/head initial). For a recent XP movement analysis of West Germanic, see Hinterhölzl 1997a,b.

4. For the pros and cons of a lexical treatment, see Ackerman and LeSourd 1997.

5. Verbal complexes (i.e., VM+V units) turn out to be relevant in various other connections as well. For instance, in nominalizations only VMs occur, optionally or obligatorily, without the formative *való*.

(i) a   tányéroknak az asztalra   (való) tétele
     the plates-dat   the table-onto being placement-poss.3sg
     'the placement of the plates on the table'

(ii) a   tányéroknak az asztalról   *(való) leszedése
     the plates-dat   the table-from being removal-poss.3sg
     'the removal of the plates from the table'

But *való*-less nominalization is subject to further constraints: "[a]s observed in Laczkó (1985, 1990) and Szabolcsi and Laczkó (1992), the pertinent cases correspond to a subset of those when a complex predicate of some sort has been postulated at the sentence level ..." (Szabolcsi 1994, 261). These works, to which the reader is referred for detailed discussion, suggest that the properties of word formation explain the added strictures on *való*-less nominalization.

6. We take it that the defining property of VMs is that they immediately precede the finite verb in neutral sentences, but when the neutral sentence is negated, they switch to postverbal position (see Szabolcsi 1980, 79–80). Thus, (i)–(ii) show *az asztalra* to be a VM.

(i) Mari az asztalra   tette a   tányérokat.
     Mari the table-onto put   the plates-acc
     'Mari put the plates on the table.'

(ii) Mari nem tette az asztalra   a   tányérokat.
     Mari not put   the table-onto the plates-acc
     'Mari didn't put the plates on the table.'

The phrasal type (i) was first noted by Horvath (1981); in her terms, *az asztalra* is generated in, not moved to, the preverbal position.

If preverbal *az asztalra* were focused, it would retain its preverbal position under negation.

(iii) Mari AZ ASZTALRA tette a   tányérokat.
　　　Mari the table-onto put   the plates-acc
　　　'It was on the table that Mari put the plates.'

(iv) Mari nem AZ ASZTALRA tette a   tányérokat, hanem A   FÖLDRE.
　　　Mari not the table-onto put   the plates-acc but   the floor-onto
　　　'It was not on the table but on the floor that Mari put the plates.'

In the written version of her CLITE paper (1998a), É. Kiss makes the interesting observation that sentences like (i) participate in an inference pattern characteristic of exhaustive focus: (i) is not entailed by (v).

(v) Mari a   polcra   és   az asztalra   tette a   tányérokat.
　　Mari the shelf-onto and the table-onto put   the plates-acc
　　'Mari put the plates on the shelf and on the table.'

She interprets this fact as indicating that an XP in the relevant preverbal position is invariably focused and is not a VM. Although we agree with her judgment of the inference, on the strength of the negation test in (i)–(ii) we would like to attribute the datum to independent semantic factors (resultativity and definiteness, among others). We note that there are other examples in which the unit we assume to be a VM is clearly phrasal and the distributive inference goes through. (vi) entails (vii).

(vi) Csalónak és   a   világ   legnagyobb gazemberének neveztem.
　　　fraud-dat and the world's biggest   rascal-dat   called-I-him
　　　'I called him a fraud and the biggest rascal in the world.'

(vii) A világ   legnagyobb gazemberének neveztem.
　　　 the world's biggest   rascal-dat   called-I-him
　　　 'I called him the biggest rascal in the world.'

In other words, we believe that the mere fact that the alleged VM is phrasal does not guarantee an exhaustive interpretation.

7. This does not imply that the VM is an XP immediately dominated by the designated specifier position. It could be within another category that only contains the VM as a remnant.

8. The intervention data in (26) certainly indicate that this sequence of verbs cannot form a complex head in Koopman's (1994) terms (irrespective of whether we allow right-adjunction, which Farkas and Sadock's proposal would require). The significance of these data for Farkas and Sadock's own theory is not so clear. The autolexical analysis assigns discrepant morphological and syntactic structures. The predictions concerning word order are not straightforward, since they depend on which structures particular orderings are sensitive to. The only prediction made is that in the presence of climbing, the relevant verbs form a (morphologically) tighter unit than in its absence, and therefore that there will be items that can separate the relevant verbs in the absence of climbing, but not in its presence. The fact that the intervention of focus or negation causes ungrammaticality (see section 6.2) supports this general prediction. We thank Donka Farkas for discussion on these matters. Likewise, as Marcel den Dikken (personal communication) points out, an "Attract" perspective on movement would enable head movement to skip intervening heads.

9. Although similar configurations in other languages are routinely analyzed as involving long head movement (Rivero 1994, Roberts 1994), Hungarian does not provide evidence that Universal Grammar allows long head movement.

10. See Roberts 1991 and Koopman 1994 on excorporation.

11. Brody (1995) assumes that in (37) [+focus] makes [−tense] strong.

12. (36b,c) might perhaps be excluded with reference to economy or optimality considerations, by declaring excorporation to be very costly. (36a) and (37), which involve excorporation, would be allowed, because that is the only way to check certain strong features. (36b,c) are disallowed, because the strong feature they would help to check can be checked without excorporation, proceeding as in (36d). (38) is allowed because it does not involve excorporation. We will not pursue this line, because in the sections below we will show that a consistent analysis of the inversion and climbing data is possible within a theory that does not generally invoke economy.

13. In Koopman 1995b this explains the distributional properties of particle verbs, aspectual prefixes (e.g., *her-*), and finite morphology in Dutch. Prefixed-particle verbs (e.g, *heruitgeven* 're-outgive = republish') can carry finite morphology but cannot undergo verb-second.

14. Likewise, in (39) the [−tense] feature of *úszni* can be checked as outlined, but the [−tense] feature of *akarni* can be checked only if *akarni* excorporates, destroying the complex.

Chapter 4

1. The XP analysis we develop is a clausal splitting analysis. Hinterhölzl (1997a,b) was the first to propose that verbal complex formation in West Germanic involves a clausal constituent (an infinitival CP) that is split into two parts, the (infinitival) VP and TP, which undergo licensing movement to specifier positions higher in the structure: [Spec, CP] of the infinitival clause for the VP and [Spec, PredP] of the selecting verb for the TP.

2. Szabolcsi (1986, 1987) argued that natural language predicates that are "bleached" (i.e., have only logical or grammatical content) need to form a complex with something that provides specific lexical content. The process was dubbed *substantiation*, and its locus was identified as the category that we now call VP+. The definiteness effect, exhibited by a rather large set of verbs in Hungarian, was argued to be a special case, with the indefinite substantiating the "bleached" existential predicate.

3. If we assumed that the verb does not pick up its infinitival suffix in syntax, instead only checking an infinitival feature against the Inf head, C might be equated with Inf. This alternative is not available to us, however, because we crucially rely on the infinitival verb's ability to extract from CP, and the verb cannot be separated from its suffix.

4. We might adopt Kayne's (1998a) suggestion that this position is where the complementizer merges with the propositional part of the sentence, but for the purposes of this book we remain noncommittal about the nature of LP(cp) when CP is infinitival. In section 6.1 we will argue that the position of the overt subordinator morpheme *hogy* is analogous or identical to LP(cp).

5. In discussing why unbound traces are tolerable at all, Müller (1998) observes that the real task is to exclude lowering movement, which is essentially achieved by adherence to the strict cycle. To explain how unbound traces in upwardly moved remnants are interpreted, he appeals to either reconstruction or the presence of copies. Although we do not specifically rely on the copy theory of movement in this book, this choice seems innocuous. An alternative is to

assume, as is standardly done in Categorial Grammar, that traces are not free but locally lambda-bound variables (see, e.g., Szabolcsi 1992). For example, in (19) the remnant XP *mutogatni* is interpreted as the function $\lambda x \lambda y \lambda z[\text{show}'(x)(y)(z)]$. In this case no binding problem can arise when the remnant VP moves up, since all its variables are bound. This assumption is fully compatible with our proposal, and it will be specifically useful in section 5.2.3, when we discuss across-the-board climbing.

To explain certain asymmetries in remnant movement, Müller appeals to the principle of Unambiguous Domination (an A-over-A minded principle largely derivable from Last Resort). In chapter 5 he states the derivational version as follows: "In a structure ...[$_A$ ... B...]..., A and B may not undergo the same kind of movement." Our derivations conform to this requirement.

6. How does extraction of XP out of an argument YP proceed? Together with the theory of extraction assumed above, the fact that arguments are moved to specifier positions early on entails that XP must be removed from YP before YP lands in LP(yp).

7. Koopman (1996) argues that the LCA holds only of elements that need to be ordered—that is, of overt material (see also Chomsky 1995). Whereas Kayne (1994) excludes segments from participating in c-command so as to achieve asymmetric c-command of the head by the specifier, Koopman argues that allowing segments to participate in c-command (the null hypothesis) derives the Generalized Doubly Filled Comp Filter and makes it absolute. (See Koopman 1996 for additional discussion.) Thus, a specifier position and a head position cannot both contain overt lexical material at Spell-Out, because asymmetric c-command fails to hold. Given this view, which we adopt here, the modified LCA does not derive the properties of X-bar theory; these are handled by the theory of projection. The LCA concerns itself only with the distribution of overt lexical material over the syntactic space.

8. We are not assuming that the material that counts as a word for the purposes of phonology is dominated by any particular kind of syntactic label. Anything goes, as long as no alien body intervenes. Once the syntactically relevant but phonologically irrelevant structure is trimmed, the resulting structures are no more difficult for phonology (e.g., vowel harmony) to handle than more traditional word structures created by a series of head adjunctions. We thank Dominique Sportiche and Diamandis Gafos for discussion on these issues.

9. The assumption that not only categories but also segments count for the definition of c-command entails that head adjunction cannot be linearized; the same reasoning as in note 7 applies.

10. In fact, Koopman (1993) argues for a more complex PP structure on independent grounds, but this does not affect the essence of the argument. For concreteness, the P is argued to be in a remnant PP in the specifier of the projection to which the [wh] feature raises.

11. Descriptively, this proposal entails that although XP can always inherit a feature from a *specifier arbitrarily far down, it can inherit a feature from a *complement only if the *complement's head can reach X without violating locality and the modified LCA. One case in our domain where this is relevant is as follows. In Hungarian, infinitival CPs may contain the same operator projections as tensed clauses: RefP, DistP, FP, and so on. If so, the RefP-DistP-FP-InfP+ sequence does not split. The infinitival VP+ does not move to [Spec, CP]: it stays below the operator projections, and the RefP-DistP-FP-InfP+ sequence as a whole moves to CP to type the infinitival and satisfies the selecting auxiliary, for instance. As we will show, extrac-

tion of the RefP-DistP-FP-InfP+ sequence does not yield an inverted order, because of the Hungarian Complexity Filter.

(i) akarni [CP[RefP Marival [DistP mindenről   [FP csak titokban [InfP+ beszélni]]]]]
     want-inf   Mari-with   everything-about   only secret-in   talk-inf
     'to want to only talk in secret with Mari about everything'

(ii)

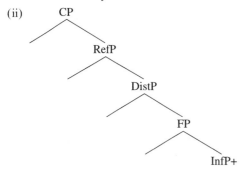

Assuming that this is indeed the constituent structure, how does CP inherit the relevant features of InfP+, across the intervening projections? The only possibility is for the head Inf+ to adjoin to the head F, then for the complex (Inf+)-F to adjoin to the head Dist, and so on, eventually forming (Inf+)-F-Dist-Ref-C. The modified LCA says that this is possible only if at most one of the heads involved is overt, and the fact is that all of them are empty (no head coming from below precedes or intervenes between the specifiers of the operator projections). In this particular case the requirement is satisfied. In this book we do not examine whether this requirement is satisfied in the general case, and we assume that infinitival CPs with operator projections inherit the relevant features as sketched above.

12. In the 1998 version of this book we chose to violate the cycle.

13. A third (not important to the case below) is to move an overt head.

14. We are assuming that 'radio' and 'apart' do not form a single constituent and can thus move independently.

15. It may not be immediately obvious why big VMs are separated from their verbs in Dutch but not in Hungarian. This has to do with an independent difference related to the VP+/VP-splitting parameter, and use of the Dutch data in the text to motivate PredP is fully consistent with our analyses of the pertinent constructions.

16. Below we will argue that with respect to inversion, VM-less verbs that do not take sentential complements pattern with small VMs (sections 4.7 and 5.3), whereas VM-less non-auxiliary infinitival complement takers pattern with big VMs (section 5.3).

17. In particular, Koopman proposes that tense, aspect, and modals are (phonologically silent) restructuring predicates. A simple tensed clause is made up of multiple restructuring predicates: differences arise from morphological selectional requirements. The presence or absence of PredP would correlate with the possible absence of a particular predicate, like Tense. This in turn would fit with the generalization that (most) restructuring complements cannot have an independent tense specification (see, among many others, Guéron and Hoekstra 1988, Wurmbrand 1998) and lack independent Tense.

Chapter 5

1. The contrast between (6a) and (6c) is especially striking if the infinitive has a postverbal VM (here *moziba* 'movie-to').

(6) a'. Nem fogom   akarni   [CP mindig csak Marit   vinni   moziba].
       not will-1sg want-inf   always only Mari-acc take-inf movie-to
       'I will not want to always take only Mari to the movies.'

versus

(6) c'. *Nem fogom   [CP (mindig) csak Marit   vinni   moziba] akarni.
         not will-1sg   always   only Mari-acc take-inf movie-to want-inf

Likewise:

(7') *[FP[CP (Mindig) csak Marit   vinni   moziba] fogom   akarni].
          always   only Mari-acc take-inf movie-to will-1sg want-inf

These structures make it unambiguous that the operators are inside the lowest infinitival clause. See the discussion in section 6.2.

2. In all her works on Hungarian published up to 1997, Katalin É. Kiss assumed that in neutral sentences VMs occur in FP. Thus, our assumption is similar to hers in that VMs move to a preverbal Ā-position, but it differs from hers in distinguishing this position from FP. The reason is obvious: superficially, there are enormous differences between infinitival clauses embedded in finite clauses with a contrastive focus and those embedded in ones with a climbing VM. There is another, even more important difference that we return to shortly: we are not assuming that VM climbs qua VM.

3. Terminologically, one consequence is that the labels *neutral* and *nonneutral* apply only to tensed sentences, possibly including infinitival complements, and not to arbitrary infinitival clauses. Notice that an infinitival clause that does not contain NegP or FP is, by itself, not neutral in any relevant sense. Its fate is determined by whether it is embedded in a neutral or a nonneutral finite clause.

4. As we will show in section 5.3, the assumption that a nonauxiliary delimits the scope of NeutP is not involved in predicting that nonauxiliaries block climbing; it only serves to allow the complements of nonauxiliaries to have their normal internal order.

5. For some reason that we do not understand, some speakers of Hungarian find examples where the VM climbs across three auxiliaries rather marginal. For them, *Be fogok akarni menni* 'I will want to go in' is perfect but longer structures like (21a) are not. Nevertheless, the contrast between (21a) and (21b,c) is sharp for every speaker: the latter sequences, which do not have an English order, are word salads.

6. If traces of movement are locally lambda-bound variables (as is standardly assumed in Categorial Grammar, for instance), then the "multiplicity of antecedents" is not a problem. (i) yields an acceptable interpretation for (31), along the lines of Dowty's (1988) treatment of "nonconstituent" coordination. In (i) x and y are variables of the same logical type as PPs, Q is a variable of the same logical type as 'talk-inf', and the interpretation of (31) is obtained by applying 'will-1sg ...' to 'talk-inf'. Corresponding to the fact that 'talk-inf' binds two traces, after lambda-conversion the function translating 'talk-inf' replaces two occurrences of the variable Q and each occurrence applies to its own arguments unproblematically.

(i) *talk-inf*: $\lambda x \lambda y[\text{talk}(x)(y)]$

will-1sg Mari-with the book-about and Kati-with the film-about: $\lambda Q[\text{will}(Q(\text{Mari-with})(\text{the-book-about})(I) \wedge Q(\text{Kati-with})(\text{the-film-about})(I))]$

7. In this connection, note that the fact that in the VP Condition in Neutral Clauses the non-auxiliary sets a lower bound on the domain of NeutP does not play a role in blocking climbing across the nonauxiliary, that is, in predicting the pattern in (60). Its purpose is to prevent a higher NeutP from triggering VP+/VP splitting below the nonauxiliary. Consider the example in (i). The tensed clause has NeutP, which needs VP+ and also triggers VP+/VP splitting; consequently, the particle *el* 'perf' of the nonauxiliary climbs to NeutP. Since NeutP is satisfied, the particle *haza* 'home' in the complement of the nonauxiliary has no reason to climb to the tensed level. However, if the domain of NeutP is not delimited by the nonauxiliary, VP+/VP splitting will occur (twice) inside CP, giving (ia) and excluding (ib,c).

(i) a. *[$_\text{NeutP}$ El   fogok   kezdeni [$_\text{CP}$ haza$_i$ akarni   t$_i$ menni]].

           perf will-1sg begin-inf   home want-inf   go-inf

        'I will begin to want to go home.'

    b. [$_\text{NeutP}$ El fogok kezdeni [$_\text{CP}$ akarni haza menni]].

    c. [$_\text{NeutP}$ El fogok kezdeni [$_\text{CP}$ haza menni akarni]].

8. This statement is somewhat reminiscent of the Generalized Doubly Filled Comp Filter, with two differences: (1) instead of involving the head and the specifier of the same projection, it involves the head of a projection and the specifier of its "ancillary layer," and (2) it refers not simply to phonetically null versus overt material in that specifier but to simple versus complex structure. Therefore, it is not clear whether (70) can be made to follow from linearization, similarly to the way Koopman (1996) derives the Generalized Doubly Filled Comp Filter from a modification of Kayne's (1994) LCA.

Chapter 6

1. Comparable spoken language data have always been used in the generative literature on Hungarian. For example, focus and *wh*-movement out of indicative complements, with the help of which Katalin É. Kiss established the unbounded nature of these movements some twenty years ago, are likewise restricted to the spoken language.

2. Terzi (1986) argues that it is not the infinitival status of the complement that is crucial for clitic climbing. Rather, clitic climbing across finite and infinitival restructuring contexts requires that the subject positions of matrix and embedded clause be coindexed. The Hungarian data are not consistent with this generalization: not only do *kell* 'must' and *szabad* 'permitted' lack a thematic subject, but the subjects of *akarod* 'want-2sg' and *elmenjek* 'away-go-subj-1sg' are different.

3. The relevant fact is that *hogy*-clauses in Hungarian are generally associated with a pronominal ("correlative") head, which surfaces in neutral sentences. This holds for the complement of *akar* 'want' but, unusually, not of the complement of *kell* 'must' and *szabad* 'permitted'. In other words, the examples in (6) with *akar* have a rival that is normatively preferred, but the examples with *kell* and *szabad* do not.

4. *Kell* 'must' and *szabad* 'permitted' take various kinds of complements. Infinitival complements with or without person-number inflection and subjunctive complements with overt *hogy* belong to the standard language. Subjunctive complements without overt *hogy* are substandard

or dialectal. All infinitives invert and all subjunctives resist inversion. Therefore, we assume that inflected infinitives lack Subord, but subjunctives always have it.

(i) ?Nem fog aludnod   kelleni.
     not   will sleep-inf-2sg must-inf
     'You will not need to sleep.'

(ii) *Nem fog aludjál   kelleni.
     not   will sleep-subj-2sg must-inf
     'You will not need to sleep.'

5. The fact that we use stacking positions has the side effect that the direct object of the infinitival complement gets close to the tensed Agr_OP, which holds out the hope for a structural account of OAC.

Chapter 7

1. See Baltazani 1998 for an analysis of focused constituents in Greek along these lines.

2. There is additional evidence for yet another low sigma-type focus position in the dialect of the first-named author. Tensed auxiliaries and a single participle or infinitive can occur in either V1 V2 or V2 V1 order. Besides using the emphatic particle *wel*, a speaker may render positive emphatic focus by focal stress on the auxiliary. In this case only V1 V2 order is available, suggesting that the inflected verb is associated with some FP. This FP is lower than the surface position of big VMs.

(i) omdat ik al   naar die film   BEN gegaan/*?gegaan BEN
     because I already to   that movie am gone/*?gone am
     'because I DID go to that movie already'

(ii) omdat ik al   met Jan HEB gepraat/*gepraat HEB
     because I already with Jan have spoken/*spoken have
     'because I DID speak with Jan already'

3. Van Riemsdijk (1995) shows that the distribution of adverbs is also sensitive to specificity. Specific adverbs appear in the same stretch of structure as specific DPs, and nonspecific/ quantified adverbs occur lower. This fits with our proposal: specific adverbs move to RefPs, quantified ones to DistP.

4. Scrambled DPs can be focused as well.

(i) dat ik JAN gisteren   niet gezien heb
     that I Jan yesterday not seen   have
     'that I didn't see JAN yesterday'

This can be taken either as having the bracketing in (13) or as a case where FP has moved to RefP.

5. On the basis of the syntax of imperatives, Koopman (1997c) has argued that CPs raise extremely high in the structure and invert with a RefP constituent. For our purposes here it is sufficient that the CP is outside the YP constituent that must move leftward, as well as outside the remnant constituent containing the verb that moves in verb-second constructions. Further distributional differences between various types of CPs, established for West Flemish by Haegeman (1998), are not taken into account in this book but will eventually have to be incorporated into the puzzle as well.

Chapter 8

1. Starting with the influential work of Evers (1975) for Dutch. Also see, among others, Haegeman and Van Riemsdijk 1986, Bennis and Hoekstra 1989, Den Besten and Rutten 1989, Broekhuis 1992, and Rutten 1991. For German, see, among others, Bech 1955, Fanselow 1989, Hinterhölzl 1997a,b, 1998, Haider 1993, and Wurmbrand 1998. For variation within West Germanic, see in particular Den Besten and Edmondson 1983.

2. *Zijn* 'be' co-occurs with infinitives as well: *Jan is zwemmen* 'Jan is swim-inf'.

3. Den Besten and Broekhuis (1989) and Broekhuis (1992), who first established patterns like (29c), develop a basically prosodic account for its ungrammaticality. Both inverted infinitives and small clause predicates must carry primary stress. If two primary stresses precede the finite verb in Dutch, a prosodic problem arises and ungrammaticality results.

For empirical and theoretical reasons, we do not adopt this account. First, the account does not extend to either the failure of inversion in infinitival complements (**zwemmen te moeten* 'swim-inf to must-inf') or the failure of remnant VP+ climbing (**zwemmen zal kunnen* 'swim-inf will can-inf'). In these cases main sentence stress falls on the infinitive, and no other element competes with the infinitive for that stress. Broekhuis (1992) and Den Besten and Broekhuis (1989) exclude these ungrammatical strings on independent grounds, but use rather unconvincing or ad hoc principles to do so. Surely, a unified account is preferable.

Second, we hope to maintain, following Cinque (1993), that main sentence stress is determined purely on the basis of the syntactic configuration. The representations that our derivations generate form an excellent starting point for such a theory: main stress is assigned to the most deeply embedded element in the clause (i.e., material that occurs in VP+). Dutch inverted infinitives end up carrying main stress, because they are in the appropriate environment. Even when Dutch infinitives are not inverted, they still attract main sentence stress because they are in the most deeply embedded VP+.

(i) zal willen   kunnen [$_{\text{InfP+}}$[$_{\text{VP+}}$ zwémmen]]
    will want-inf can-inf   swim-inf

4. West Flemish appears to have no inverted infinitives (Haegeman 1998). This might indicate a generalized ban on InfP+s in PredP. West Flemish otherwise appears to allow climbing of remnant VP+s: participles climb obligatorily and big VMs optionally.

5. Quite generally, this seems correct. Besides big and small VMs, Dutch has tiny VMs—that is, VP+s that do not split (i.e., inseparable prefixes like *onder* in *ondergaan* 'undergo').

6. Infinitives can appear in the first position under a "topicalized" interpretation (i) or a contrastive focus interpretation (ii).

(i) Zwemmen KAN hij niet.
    swim-inf   can he not
    'He CANNOT swim.'

(ii) ZWEMMEN kan hij niet.
     swim-inf can he not

We are interested only in the contrastive focus interpretation. On the basis of Hungarian we established that only constituents in PredP can be focused. Therefore, focusing of infinitives serves as a diagnostic criterion for PredP.

7. This generalization is quite solid in the dialect of the first author. Marcel den Dikken (personal communication), however, finds (47d) fairly acceptable. If variation indeed exists, the situation might be less straightforward.

8. Harkema (1998) shows that the *aan het V_{inf}* progressive construction in Dutch behaves like a big VM. Although this construction contains a deeply embedded InfP+, it behaves like a PP/DP and does not result in a violation of the Complexity Filter on PredP; that is, this sequence can climb as a remnant.

(i) ... aan het zwemmen zal zijn
       at   the swim-inf   will be-inf

'will be swimming'

9. Whether VMs can be stranded in intermediate infinitives becomes an important issue, since our theory predicts that such strings should be ungrammatical. Koopman (1995b) argues that this is indeed the case. She argues, pretheoretically, that there are only three possible positions for small VMs within the verbal complex in Dutch: either immediately preceding the verb it forms a complex predicate with, or immediately preceding or following a finite auxiliary or modal.

(i) (V_f) VM (V_f) ... VM V

   This reduces to two possible positions for VMs, if optional movement of the finite auxiliary or modal is assumed. It is telling that the distribution of Hungarian VMs basically reduces to the same pattern: crucially, VMs cannot be stranded in intermediate positions in this language either. The literature on Dutch is divided on this point, however. Bennis (1992) assumes that small VMs can be stranded between two intermediate restructuring infinitives. We cite Bennis's discussion of the following string (Bennis 1992, 35):

(i) dat hij dat probleem

a.	*op* moet hebben	willen	kunnen	lossen	
b.	moet *op* hebben	willen	kunnen	lossen	
c.	moet hebben *op*	willen	kunnen	lossen	
d.	moet hebben	willen *op*	kunnen	lossen	
e.	moet hebben	willen	kunnen *op*	lossen	

   that he that problem (up must (*up*) have-inf (*up*) want-inf (*up*) can-inf (*up*) solve-inf)

It is indeed true that the acceptability judgments on the very complex sentences in [(i)] are somewhat unclear and inconsistent. However, I have met met no native speaker that provides a clear-cut distinction between acceptable sentences in [(ia)] and [(ie)] and unacceptable ones [(ib–d)]. (Bennis 1992, 35)

The latter part of Bennis's statement is important. Given Koopman's description, we do not expect to find a clear-cut distinction between (ia,e) and (ib–d). We do expect to find a clear-cut distinction between (ia,b,e) and (ic,d). In a judgment task Helmantel (1998) found that 6 out of 7 speakers consistently assigned the same judgments as reported in Koopman 1995b. Since these are not easy judgments, we take these results as strong confirmation of Koopman's description of the data and conclude that particles may not appear between intermediate restructuring infinitives in Dutch.

   On the basis of contrastive judgments Bennis (1992) also argues in favor of the grammaticality of particle stranding between intermediate infinitives. Particle stranding between infinitivals is judged less ungrammatical than having the particle in the wrong linear position with respect to the infinitive (*bellen op* 'call-inf up'). We believe that this is not a sufficient argument. The "wrong" order simply seems to involve many more violations against the system of Dutch.

10. Unlike in Hungarian and Dutch, a simple inverted order is excluded in German.

(i) *... will   lachen
        want laugh-inf

We have no account for this fact. We suspect that it is related to the position of infinitival CPs in general: infinitival complements of nonrestructuring predicates precede the finite verb as well.

11. Although this pattern is excluded in Hungarian, it should not be excluded in principle. It is possible, for example, in past perfect constructions in Serbo-Croatian (Bošković 1997, chap. 5, (28a,b)).

(i) a. Bili$_i$ ste t$_i$ čekali Marijinu prijateljicu.
        been are   waited Maria's   friend
        'You had been waiting for Maria's friend.'
    b. Čekali$_i$ ste bili$_i$ t$_i$ Marijinu prijateljicu.
        waited are been   Maria's friend
        (same)

Serbo-Croatian also allows the Hungarian pattern, as (ib) shows.

12. This does not seem to be an isolated property of Hungarian. Øystein Nilsen (personal communication) informs us that the following types of examples are relatively acceptable in Norwegian with participles or infinitives:

(i) ?Villet$_i$ hadde han nok   ikke t$_i$ gidd opp.
        wanted has   he probably not   given up
        'lit. wanted he has probably not to give up'

(ii) ?Begynne$_i$ vil han nok   ikke t$_i$ a jobbe.
        begin   will he probably not   to work
        'lit. begin he will probably not to work'

These examples contrast with double-participle passives.

(iii)   Huset   ble forsøkt bygd.
        the-house was tried   built
        'lit. the house was tried to be built'

(iv) *Bygd$_i$ ble (ikke) huset   forsøkt t$_i$.
        built   was not   the-house tried

(v) *Forsøkt$_i$ ble (ikke) huset   t$_i$ bygt.
        tried   was not   the-house   built

13. For completeness, we include the orders with full participles.

(i) ⟨gezwommen⟩ zal ⟨% gezwommen⟩ hebben ⟨gezwommen⟩
        ge-swim-part will   ge-swim-part have-inf ge-swim-part

The V1 V3$_{Part}$ V2 order is ungrammatical for the first author, but is reportedly acceptable in some standard dialects (Zwart 1996). The first author's dialect follows straightforwardly from obligatory splitting with big VMs inside the infinitival CP (participles are big VMs and involve at least two VP+s). It is unclear whether variation on the conditions for splitting is involved in the dialect that accepts the order V1 V3$_{Part}$ V2. We ignore the complete paradigm in this dialect. (Is this order restricted to bare participle VP+s? Is it possible with small and big VMs?)

14. In verb projection languages like West Flemish, the participle must appear in the inverted order V2 V1, and the order V1 V2 is excluded. This means, in our terms, that participles may never remain in [Spec, CP]. West Flemish might have an even more general version of the filter, excluding the participial CP from [Spec, CP] completely.

15. As is well known, not all West Germanic dialects have the IPP effect. The absence or presence of the effect does not seem directly related to the presence of *ge*. Although Frisian does not use the prefix *ge* with participial morphology and does not display the IPP effect (Den Besten and Edmondson 1983), some southern German dialects lack the IPP effect with full participles. German dialects that do not have the IPP effect should invert their participles and should not allow participles in English orders.

16. Unlike in Dutch, in German the effect also arises with shorter sequences (see Den Besten and Edmondson 1983 for discussion).

17. Why these CPs may not precede the finite verb in German, as CP infinitivals generally can, remains unclear (see note 10).

18. Thanks to Marie Christine Erb for providing us with judgments on her "own private" dialect.

19. We have been informed that the particle may climb in some northern German dialects, but we have been unable to find an actual reference. If we are correct, it must be the case either that the particle is in VP2 (*an wird rufen* 'up will call-inf', *an hat rufen* 'up has call-inf') or that the other infinitives line up in the English order (*an hat wollen rufen* 'up has want-inf call-inf'). Our system predicts that *an hat rufen wollen* should be excluded.

Appendix B

1. Following this reasoning, when the same type of position (RefP or DistP) is multiply filled from independent sources, absorption must be involved. By *absorption* we mean the syntactic counterpart of creating a polyadic quantifier. The polyadic quantifiers created in this case will be semantically "inessential" (i.e., reducible to a sequence of unary quantifications), and they may well encode an asymmetrical scope relation.

2. A tiny subset of the complexes in (30bi,bii) include suffixless adjectives or nouns: the ones whose verb is *marad* 'remain' and the ones whose verb is *lesz* 'be, become' or the copula, when the latter are complements of tense or of an auxiliary. Compare:

(i)   a. Nem vagyok/maradok   katona.
          not   be-1sg/remain-1sg soldier
          'I am not/will not remain a soldier.'
      b. Nem akarok   katona lenni/maradni.
          not   want-1sg soldier be-inf/remain-inf
          'I do not want to be/remain a soldier.'

(ii) Katonának lenni/maradni   nem volt jó.
      soldier-dat be-inf/remain-inf not was good
      'To be/To remain a soldier was not good.'

3. We are aware of a few exceptions. In *ostobának tűnik fel* 'strikes [one] as stupid' (a somewhat old-fashioned expression), *ostobának* 'stupid-dat' is selected and occurs in the canonical VM position; however, the verb has a perfective prefix (*fel* 'up' in this case is not directional).

Likewise, in *megmarad elnöknek* 'remains president' *elnöknek* 'president-dat' is selected, but the verb has a prefix—in this case it is the prefix that must form a complex with the verb.

4. Hungarian marks progressive aspect and existential tense by word order and intonation, instead of morphology. For instance:

(i) "Mentem "haza (amikor . . .)
    went-1sg home when
    'I was going home (when . . .)'

(ii) "Mentem haza.
    went-1sg home
    'There has been an event of my going home.'

We will not discuss such sentences in this book. See Horvath 1986, É. Kiss 1987, Piñón 1992a,b, 1995.

5. The negation fact comes from Farkas and Sadock 1989. An alternative generalization that a neutral matrix clause cannot have NegP or FP anywhere in its complement would not be correct. The following sentence has a neutral matrix clause and a negated infinitival complement:

(i) A gyerek el   kezdett nem tanulni.
   the child away began not study-inf
   'The child began to not study (properly).'

The reason why (i) is grammatical is that *kezd* 'begin' has a prefixal VM, *el* 'away', whose climbing NegP does not block, since it is lower, in a nonintervening position.

6. In fact, the type exemplified in (67b) is the only case in which assuming V-to-F movement can derive an order that cannot (or cannot easily) be obtained without it in syntax. Above we suggested that this is a PF phenomenon.

7. Contrastive focusing of PredP can generally cross NegP or FP. For example:

(i) a. Csak ÚSZNI   nem fogok akarni.   (focusing across 'not')
     only swim-inf not will-1sg want-inf
     'It is only to swim that I will not want.'

   b. Csak ÚSZNI   fogok csak HOLNAP akarni.   (focusing across focus)
     only swim-inf will-1sg only tomorrow want-inf
     'It is only to swim that I will want only tomorrow.'

References

Ackerman, F. 1984. Verbal modifiers as argument taking predicates. In *Groninger Arbeiten zur germanistichen Linguistik 25*, 23–71. Rijksuniversiteit Groningen.

Ackerman, F., and P. LeSourd. 1997. Toward a lexical representation of phrasal predicates. In A. Alsina, J. Bresnan, and P. Sells, eds., *Complex predicates*, 67–106. Stanford, Calif.: CSLI Publications. [Distributed by Cambridge University Press.]

Androutsopoulou, A. 1994. The distribution of the definite determiner and the syntax of Greek DPs. In K. Beals et al., eds., *CLS 30*. Vol. 1, *The Main Session*, 16–29. Chicago Linguistic Society, University of Chicago.

Androutsopoulou, A. 1995. The licensing of adjectival modification. In J. Camacho, L. Choueiri, and M. Watanabe, eds., *Proceedings of the 14th West Coast Conference on Formal Linguistics*, 17–31. Stanford, Calif.: CSLI Publications. [Distributed by Cambridge University Press.]

Baker, M. 1988. *Incorporation: A theory of grammatical function changing*. Chicago: University of Chicago Press.

Baltazani, M. 1998. Focus in Greek. Master's thesis, UCLA.

Bartos, H. 2000. Object agreement in Hungarian: A case for minimalism. In G. M. Alexandrova and O. Arnaudova, eds., *The minimalist parameter: Selected papers from the Ottawa Linguistics Forum, 21–23 March, 1997*, 327–340. Philadelphia: John Benjamins.

Bech, G. 1955. *Studien zum Deutschen Verbum infinitivum*. Tübingen: Niemeyer.

Beghelli, F., and T. Stowell. 1997. Distributivity and negation: The syntax of *each* and *every*. In A. Szabolcsi, ed., *Ways of scope taking*, 71–109. Dordrecht: Kluwer.

Bennis, H. 1992. Long head movement: The position of particles in the verbal cluster in Dutch. In R. Bok-Bennema and R. van Hout, eds., *Linguistics in the Netherlands 1992*, 37–47. Amsterdam: John Benjamins.

Bennis, H., and T. Hoekstra. 1989. *Generatieve grammatica*. Dordrecht: Foris.

Besten, H. den, and H. Broekhuis. 1989. Woordvolgorde in de werkwoordelijke eindreeks. *Glot* 12, 79–137.

Besten, H. den, and J. Edmondson. 1983. The verbal complex in Continental West Germanic. In W. Abraham, ed., *On the formal syntax of the westgermania*. Amsterdam: John Benjamins.

Besten, H. den, and J. Rutten. 1989. On verb raising, extraposition and word order in Dutch. In D. Jaspers, ed., *Sentential complementation and the lexicon: Studies in honor of Wim de Geest*, 41–56. Dordrecht: Foris.

Besten, H. den, and G. Webelhuth. 1987. Remnant topicalization and the constituent structure of VP in the Germanic SOV languages. *GLOW Newsletter* 18, 15–16.

Besten, H. den, and G. Webelhuth. 1990. Stranding. In G. Grewendorf and W. Sternefeld, eds., *Scrambling and barriers*, 77–92. Amsterdam: John Benjamins.

Bhatt, R., and J. Yoon. 1992. On the composition of COMP and parameters of V2. In R. Bates, ed., *Proceedings of the Tenth West Coast Conference on Formal Linguistics*, 41–53. Stanford, Calif.: CSLI Publications. [Distributed by Cambridge University Press.]

Blom, A., and S. Daalder. 1977. *Syntaktische theorie en taalbeschrijving*. Muiderberg.

Bošković, Ž. 1997. *The syntax of nonfinite complementation: An economy approach.* Cambridge, Mass.: MIT Press.

Brody, M. 1990. Remarks on the order of elements in the Hungarian focus field. In I. Kenesei, ed., *Approaches to Hungarian*. Vol. 3, *Structures and arguments*, 95–121. Szeged: JATE.

Brody, M. 1995. Focus and checking theory. In I. Kenesei, ed., *Approaches to Hungarian*. Vol. 5, *Levels and structures*, 29–43. Szeged: JATE.

Brody, M. 1997. Mirror theory. Ms., University College London. [Available at http://www.phon.ucl.ac.uk/home/misi/index.html]

Brody, M. 2000. Word order, restructuring and Mirror theory. In P. Svenonius, ed., *Derivations of VO and OV*, 27–43. Amsterdam: John Benjamins. [Available at http://www.phon.ucl.ac.uk/home/misi/index.html]

Broekhuis, H. 1992. *Chain government: Issues in Dutch syntax*. Leiden: HIL.

Broekhuis, H., H. den Besten, K. Hoekstra, and J. Rutten. 1995. Infinitival complementation in Dutch: On remnant extraposition. *The Linguistic Review* 12, 93–122.

Burzio, L. 1986. *Italian syntax*. Dordrecht: Reidel.

Chomsky, N. 1981. *Lectures on government and binding*. Dordrecht: Foris.

Chomsky, N. 1993. A minimalist program for linguistic theory. In K. Hale and S. J. Keyser, eds., *The view from Building 20*, 1–52. Cambridge, Mass.: MIT Press.

Chomsky, N. 1995. Categories and transformations. In *The Minimalist Program*, 219–394. Cambridge, Mass.: MIT Press.

Cinque, G. 1993. A null theory of phrase and compound stress. *Linguistic Inquiry* 24, 239–297.

Cinque, G. 1998a. The interaction of passive, causative, and "restructuring" in Romance. Talk given at UCLA, May 1998.

Cinque, G. 1998b. On clitic climbing and other transparency effects. Talk given at UCLA, May 1998.

Cinque, G. 1999. *Adverbs and functional projections: A cross-linguistic perspective.* New York: Oxford University Press.

Dikken, M. den. 1996. The minimal links of verb (projection) raising. In W. Abraham, S. Epstein, H. Thráinsson, and J.-W. Zwart, eds., *Minimal ideas*, 67–96. New York: John Benjamins.

Dowty, D. 1988. Type raising, functional composition, and non-constituent coordination. In R. T. Oehrle, E. Bach, and D. Wheeler, eds., *Categorial grammars and natural language structures*, 153–198. Dordrecht: Reidel.

Emonds, J. E. 1976. *A transformational approach to English syntax: Root, structure-preserving, and local transformations*. New York: Academic Press.

Evers, A. 1975. The transformational cycle in Dutch and German. Doctoral dissertation, University of Utrecht.

Fanselow, G. 1989. Coherent infinitives in German. In R. Bhatt, E. Loebel, and C. Schmidt, eds., *Syntactic phrase structure phenomena in noun phrases and sentences*, 217–238. Amsterdam: John Benjamins.

Farkas, D. F., and J. M. Sadock. 1989. Preverb climbing in Hungarian. *Language* 65, 318–338.

Guéron, J., and T. Hoekstra. 1988. T-chains and the constituent structure of auxiliaries. In A. Cardinaletti, G. Giusti, and G. Cinque, eds., *Constituent structure*, 35–100. Dordrecht: Foris.

Haegeman, L. 1992. *Theory and description in generative syntax: A case study in West Flemish*. Cambridge: Cambridge University Press.

Haegeman, L. 1998. Verb movement in embedded clauses in West Flemish. *Linguistic Inquiry* 29, 631–656.

Haegeman, L. 2000. Remnant movement and OV order. In P. Svenonius, ed., *The derivation of OV and VO*, 69–96. Amsterdam: John Benjamins.

Haegeman, L., and H. van Riemsdijk. 1986. Verb projection raising, scope, and the typology of rules affecting verbs. *Linguistic Inquiry* 17, 417–466.

Haider, H. 1993. *Deutsche Syntax–Generativ*. Tübingen: Gunter Narr Verlag.

Hallman, P. 1997. Reiterative syntax. In J. Black and V. Motapanyane, eds., *Clitics, pronouns and movement*, 87–131. Amsterdam: John Benjamins.

Hallman, P. 1998. No autonomous morphology. Dissertation proposal, UCLA.

Hallman, P. 1999. Verb final as a subcase of verb second. Poster, North Eastern Linguistics Society Annual Meeting (NELS 30), Rutgers University, October 22–24.

Harkema, H. 1998. The *aan het* construction in Dutch. Master's thesis, UCLA.

Helmantel, M. 1998. On the distribution of postpositions and particles in the verbal complex. *Groninger Arbeiten zur germanistischen Linguistik* 42, 169–191.

Hinterhölzl, R. 1997a. Infinitival tense, verb-raising and verb projection raising. In K. Kusumoto, ed., *NELS 27*, 187–201. GLSA, University of Massachusetts, Amherst.

Hinterhölzl, R. 1997b. An XP-movement account of restructuring. Ms., University of Southern California.

Hinterhölzl, R. 1998. Restructuring as XP-movement. Doctoral dissertation, University of Southern California.

Hoeksema, J. 1993. Suppression of a word order pattern in Western Germanic. In J. van Marle, ed., *Historical linguistics*. Amsterdam: John Benjamins.

Höhle, T. N. 1986. Der Begriff ''Mittelfeld'': Anmerkungen über die Theorie der topologischen Felder. In *Akten des VII. Internationalen germanistischen Kongresses* Göttingen 1985. Band 3, 329–340. Tübingen: Max Niemeyer Verlag.

Holmberg, A. 1986. Word order and syntactic features in Scandinavian languages and English. Doctoral dissertation, University of Stockholm.

Hoop, H. de. 1992. Case configuration and noun phrase interpretation. Doctoral dissertation, University of Groningen.

Horvath, J. 1981. Aspects of Hungarian syntax and the theory of grammar. Doctoral dissertation, UCLA.

Horvath, J. 1986. *Focus in the theory of grammar and the syntax of Hungarian.* Dordrecht: Foris.

Horvath, J. 1995. Structural focus, structural Case, and the theory of feature-assignment. In K. É. Kiss, ed., *Discourse configurational languages*, 28–64. New York: Oxford University Press.

Kálmán, C. G., L. Kálmán, Á. Nádasdy, and G. Prószéky. 1989. A magyar segédigék rendszere. *Általános Nyelvészeti Tanulmányok* 17, 49–103.

Kálmán, L., G. Prószéky, Á. Nádasdy, and C. G. Kálmán. 1986. Hocus, focus, and verb types in Hungarian infinitive constructions. In W. Abraham and S. de Meij, eds., *Topic, focus, and configurationality: Papers from the 6th Groningen Grammar Talks, Groningen 1984*, 129–142. Amsterdam: John Benjamins.

Kayne, R. S. 1983. Connectedness. *Linguistic Inquiry* 14, 223–249.

Kayne, R. S. 1989. Null subjects and clitic climbing. In O. Jaeggli and K. Safir, eds., *The null subject parameter*, 239–261. Dordrecht: Kluwer.

Kayne, R. S. 1994. *The antisymmetry of syntax.* Cambridge, Mass.: MIT Press.

Kayne, R. S. 1998a. A note on prepositions and complementizers. http://mitpress.mit.edu/celebration.

Kayne, R. S. 1998b. Overt vs. covert movement. *Syntax* 1, 128–191.

Kayne, R. S. 1999. Lectures at the Universities of Venice and Padua, May.

Kenesei, I. 1989. Logikus-e a magyar szórend? *Általános Nyelvészeti Tanulmányok* 17, 105–152.

Kenesei, I. 1994. The syntax of focus. Ms., József Attila University, Szeged.

É. Kiss, K. 1981. Structural relations in Hungarian, a "free" word order language. *Linguistic Inquiry* 12, 185–213.

É. Kiss, K. 1987. *Configurationality in Hungarian.* Dordrecht: Reidel.

É. Kiss, K. 1991. Logical structure in syntactic structure: The case of Hungarian. In C.-T. J. Huang and R. May, eds., *Logical structure and linguistic structure: Cross-linguistic perspectives*, 111–147. Dordrecht: Kluwer.

É. Kiss, K. 1994. Sentence structure and word order. In F. Kiefer and K. É. Kiss, eds., *The syntactic structure of Hungarian*, 1–90. San Diego, Calif.: Academic Press.

É. Kiss, K. 1998a. The Hungarian verbal complex revisited. Paper presented at the First Conference on Linguistic Theory in Eastern European Languages, April 1998, Szeged.

É. Kiss, K. 1998b. Mondattan. In K. É. Kiss, F. Kiefer, and P. Siptár, eds., *Új magyar nyelvtan*, 17–184. Budapest: Osiris Kiadó.

Komlósy, A. 1985. Predicate complementation. In I. Kenesei, ed., *Approaches to Hungarian.* Vol. 1, *Data and descriptions*, 53–79. Szeged: JATE.

Komlósy, A. 1994. Complements and adjuncts. In F. Kiefer and K. É. Kiss, eds., *The syntactic structure of Hungarian*, 91–178. San Diego, Calif.: Academic Press.

Koopman, H. 1993. The structure of PPs. Ms., UCLA. [Published as "Prepositions, post-positions, circumpositions and particles: The structure of Dutch PPs" in Koopman 2000, 204–263.]

Koopman, H. 1994. Licensing heads. In D. Lightfoot and N. Hornstein, eds., *Verb movement*, 261–304. Cambridge: Cambridge University Press. [Also published in Koopman 2000, 263–300.]

Koopman, H. 1995a. De plaats van geïnkorporeerde hoofden in de werkwoordskluster. *Tabu* 25, 174–179. [Published in English as "The position of incorporated heads within the verbal cluster." In E. Garrett and F. Lee, eds., *Syntax at Sunset*, 31–36. (UCLA Working Papers in Syntax and Semantics 1.) Department of Linguistics, UCLA, 1996.]

Koopman, H. 1995b. On verbs that fail to undergo V-second. *Linguistic Inquiry* 26, 37–63. [Also published in Koopman 2000, 301–330.]

Koopman, H. 1996. The spec head configuration. In E. Garrett and F. Lee, eds., *Syntax at Sunset*, 37–64. (UCLA Working Papers in Syntax and Semantics 1.) Department of Linguistics, UCLA. [Also published in Koopman 2000, 331–365.]

Koopman, H. 1997a. Heavy pied-piping. Paper presented at the Conference on Pied-Piping in Jena.

Koopman, H. 1997b. Pied-piping and subject extraction. Paper presented at the University of California, Irvine.

Koopman, H. 1997c. Topics in imperatives. Paper presented at the Workshop on Clause Architecture in Ibbs a/d Donau.

Koopman, H. 2000. *The syntax of specifiers and heads.* London: Routledge.

Koopman, H. In progress. Tense, negation, and aspect as restructuring predicates. Ms., UCLA.

Koopman, H., and A. Szabolcsi. 1999. Hungarian complex verbs and XP movement. In I. Kenesei, ed., *Crossing boundaries: Advances in the theory of Eastern European languages*, 115–135. Amsterdam: John Benjamins.

Koster, J. 1978. Why subject sentences don't exist. In S. J. Keyser, ed., *Recent transformational studies in European languages*, 53–64. Cambridge, Mass.: MIT Press.

Koster, J. 1994. Predicate incorporation and the word order of Dutch. In G. Cinque, J. Koster, J.-Y. Pollock, L. Rizzi, and R. Zanuttini, eds., *Paths towards Universal Grammar: Studies in honor of Richard S. Kayne,* 255–276. Washington, D.C.: Georgetown University Press.

Laczkó, T. 1985. Deverbal nominals and their complements in noun phrases. In I. Kenesei, ed., *Approaches to Hungarian.* Vol. 1, *Data and descriptions*, 93–119. Szeged: JATE.

Laczkó, T. 1990. On arguments and adjuncts of derived nominals: A lexical-functional approach. In I. Kenesei, ed., *Approaches to Hungarian.* Vol. 3, *Structures and arguments,* 123–147. Szeged: JATE.

Laka, I. 1990. Negation in syntax: On the nature of functional categories and projections. Doctoral dissertation, MIT.

Lattewitz, K. 1977. Adjacency in Dutch and German. (Groningen Dissertations in Linguistics 19.) Groningen.

Lee, F. 1999. Antisymmetry and the syntax of San Lucas Quiaviní Zapotec. Doctoral dissertation, UCLA.

Mahajan, A. 1990. The A/A' distinction and movement theory. Doctoral dissertation, MIT.

Müller, G. 1998. *Incomplete category fronting: A derivational approach to remnant movement in German.* Dordecht: Kluwer.

Munn, A. 1993. Topics in the syntax and semantics of coordinate structures. Doctoral dissertation, University of Maryland.

Nkemnji, M. 1992. Issues in the syntax of negation in Nweh. Master's thesis, UCLA.

Nkemnji, M. 1995. Heavy pied-piping in Nweh. Doctoral dissertation, UCLA.

Pearson, M. 1997. Pied-piping into the left periphery. In K. Kusumoto, ed., *NELS 27*, 321–335. GLSA, University of Massachusetts, Amherst.

Pearson, M. 2000. Two types of OV languages. In P. Svenonius, ed., *The derivation of OV and VO*, 327–363. Amsterdam: John Benjamins.

Picallo, C. 1991. Modal verbs in Catalan. *Natural Language & Linguistic Theory* 8, 285–312.

Piñón, C. J. 1992a. Heads in the focus field. In I. Kenesei and C. Pléh, eds., *Approaches to Hungarian.* Vol. 4, *The structure of Hungarian*, 99–122. Szeged: JATE.

Piñón, C. J. 1992b. The preverb problem in German and Hungarian. In L. Buszard-Welcher, L. Wee, and W. Weigel, eds., *Proceedings of the 18th Annual Meeting of the Berkeley Linguistics Society*, 395–408. Berkeley Linguistics Society, University of California, Berkeley.

Piñón, C. J. 1993a. Presupposition and the syntax of negation in Hungarian. In L. M. Dobrin, L. Nichols, and R. M. Rodriguez, eds., *CLS 27.* Vol. 2, *The Parasession on Negation*, 246–262. Chicago Linguistic Society, University of Chicago.

Piñón, C. J. 1993b. SigmaP and Hungarian. In J. Mead, ed., *Proceedings of the Eleventh West Coast Conference on Formal Linguistics*, 388–404. Stanford, Calif.: CSLI Publications. [Distributed by Cambridge University Press.]

Piñón, C. J. 1995. Around the progressive in Hungarian. In I. Kenesei, ed., *Approaches to Hungarian.* Vol. 5, *Levels and structures*, 153–191. Szeged: JATE.

Puskás, G. 1997. Verb focusing in Hungarian. In *Geneva Generative Papers 5.2*, 60–67. University of Geneva.

Reinhart, T. 1997. Interface economy and markedness. In C. Wilder, H. Gärtner, and M. Bierwisch, eds., *The role of economy principles in linguistic theory*, 146–170. Berlin: Akademie Verlag.

Riemsdijk, H. van. 1995. Adverbia en bepaaldheid. *Tabu* 25, 191–194.

Rivero, M.-L. 1994. Clause structure and V-movement in the languages of the Balkans. *Natural Language & Linguistic Theory* 12, 63–120.

Rizzi, L. 1978. A restructuring rule in Italian syntax. In S. J. Keyser, ed., *Recent transformational studies in European languages*, 113–158. Cambridge, Mass.: MIT Press.

Rizzi, L. 1990. *Relativized Minimality.* Cambridge, Mass.: MIT Press.

Rizzi, L. 1995. On the fine structure of the left periphery. Ms., University of Geneva.

Rizzi, L. 1996. Residual verb second and the *Wh*-Criterion. In A. Belletti and L. Rizzi, eds., *Parameters and functional heads: Essays in comparative syntax*, 63–90. New York: Oxford University Press.

Roberts, I. 1991. Excorporation and minimality. *Linguistic Inquiry* 22, 209–218.

Roberts, I. 1994. Two types of head movement in Romance. In D. Lightfoot and N. Hornstein, eds., *Verb movement*, 207–260. Cambridge: Cambridge University Press.

Roberts, I. 1997. Restructuring, head movement, and locality. *Linguistic Inquiry* 28, 423–461.

Rosen, S. 1989. Argument structure and complex predicates. Doctoral dissertation, Brandeis University.

Rouveret, A., and J.-R. Vergnaud. 1980. Specifying reference to the subject. *Linguistic Inquiry* 11, 97–202.

Rutten, J. 1991. Infinitival complements and auxiliaries. Doctoral dissertation, University of Amsterdam.

Selkirk, E. O. 1986. *Phonology and syntax: The relation between sound and structure*. Cambridge, Mass.: MIT Press.

Sportiche, D. 1993. Sketch of a reductionist approach to syntactic variation and dependencies. Ms., UCLA. [Published as Sportiche 1995 and reprinted in Sportiche 1998, 379–419.]

Sportiche, D. 1995. Sketch of a reductionist approach to syntactic variation and dependencies. In H. Campos and P. Kempchinsky, eds., *Evolution and revolution in linguistic theory*, 356–398. Washington, D.C.: Georgetown University Press.

Sportiche, D. 1997. Reconstruction and constituent structure. Class lectures given at UCLA and talk given at MIT.

Sportiche, D. 1998. *Atoms and partitions of clause structure*. London: Routledge.

Stabler, E. 1999. Remnant movement and complexity. In G. Bouma, E. Hinrichs, G.-J. Kruijff, and R. Oehrle, eds., *Constraints and resources in natural language syntax and semantics*, 299–326. Stanford, Calif.: CSLI Publications.

Stowell, T. 1981. Origins of phrase structure. Doctoral dissertation, MIT.

Stowell, T. 1993. The syntax of tense. Ms., UCLA.

Stowell, T. 1996. The phrase structure of tense. In J. Rooryck and L. Zaring, eds., *Phrase structure and the lexicon*, 277–291. Dordrecht: Kluwer.

Strozer, J. 1976. Clitics in Spanish. Doctoral dissertation, UCLA.

Strozer, J. 1981. An alternative to restructuring in Romance syntax. *Papers in Romance* 3, supp. 2, 177–184.

Szabolcsi, A. 1980. Az aktuális mondattagolás szemantikájához. *Nyelvtudományi Közlemények* 82, 59–83.

Szabolcsi, A. 1981. Compositionality in focus. *Folia Linguistica* 15, 141–162.

Szabolcsi, A. 1983. PRO and cons: A double dealer's account. Ms., Max Planck Institute for Psycholinguistics, Nijmegen.

Szabolcsi, A. 1986. Indefinites in complex predicates. *Theoretical Linguistic Research* 2, 47–85.

Szabolcsi, A. 1987. From the definiteness effect to lexical integrity. In W. Abraham and S. de Mey, eds., *Topic, focus, configurationality*, 321–348. Amsterdam: John Benjamins.

Szabolcsi, A. 1992. Combinatory grammar and projection from the lexicon. In I. Sag and A. Szabolcsi, eds., *Lexical matters*, 241–269. Stanford, Calif.: CSLI Publications. [Distributed by Cambridge University Press.]

Szabolcsi, A. 1994. The noun phrase. In F. Kiefer and K. É. Kiss, eds., *The syntactic structure of Hungarian*, 179–274. San Diego, Calif.: Academic Press.

Szabolcsi, A. 1996. Verb and particle movement in Hungarian. Ms., UCLA.

Szabolcsi, A. 1997. Strategies for scope taking. In A. Szabolcsi, ed., *Ways of scope taking*, 109–155. Dordrecht: Kluwer.

Szabolcsi, A., and T. Laczkó. 1992. A főnévi csoport szerkezete. In F. Kiefer, ed., *Magyar mondattan*, 179–299. Budapest: Akadémiai.

Szalai, T. A. 1996. Non-quantificational *is*. Ms., UCLA.

Terzi, A. 1986. Clitic climbing from finite clauses and tense raising. *Probus* 8, 273–295.

Verhagen, A. 1979. Fokusbepalingen en grammatikale theory. *Spektator* 8, 372–402.

Webelhuth, G. 1992. *Principles and parameters of syntactic saturation.* New York: Oxford University Press.

Wurmbrand, S. 1998. Infinitives. Doctoral dissertation, MIT.

Zagona, K. 1982. Government and proper government of verbal projections. Doctoral dissertation, University of Washington.

Zsámboki, A. 1995. Contrastive co-ordinations with focussed clauses. (Working Papers in the Theory of Grammar 2.5.) Budapest: ELTE.

Zubizarreta, M.-L. 1982. On the relationship of the lexicon to syntax. Doctoral dissertation, MIT.

Zwart, C. J.-W. 1993. Dutch syntax: A minimalist approach. Doctoral dissertation, University of Groningen.

Zwart, C. J.-W. 1994. Dutch is head-initial. *The Linguistic Review* 11, 377–406.

Zwart, C. J.-W. 1996. Verb clusters in Continental West Germanic dialects. In J. Black and V. Motapanyane, eds., *Microparametric syntax and dialect variation*, 229–258. Amsterdam: John Benjamins.

Zwart, C. J.-W. 1997. *Morphosyntax of verb movement: A minimalist approach to the syntax of Dutch.* Dordrecht: Kluwer.

Index

Current Studies in Linguistics

Samuel Jay Keyser, general editor